DISCARDED

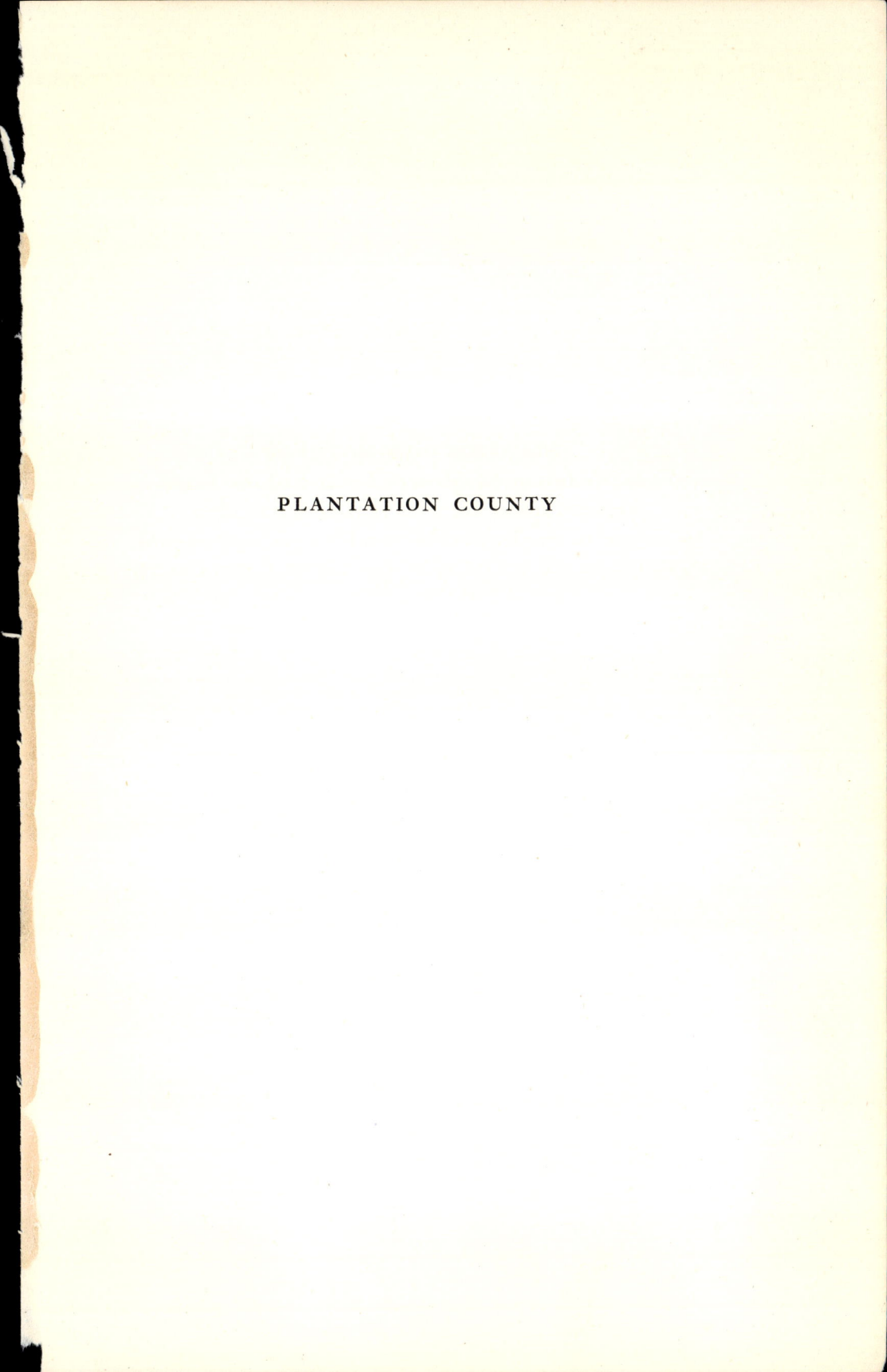

PLANTATION COUNTY

This volume is the first of the
Field Studies in the Modern Culture of the South
prepared under the direction of John Gillin,
sponsored by the INSTITUTE FOR RESEARCH IN SOCIAL
SCIENCE of the UNIVERSITY OF NORTH CAROLINA IN
CHAPEL HILL.

PLANTATION COUNTY / *by*
MORTON RUBIN

1951
THE UNIVERSITY OF NORTH CAROLINA PRESS

COPYRIGHT, 1951, BY

THE UNIVERSITY OF NORTH CAROLINA PRESS

PRINTED IN THE UNITED STATES OF AMERICA
BY THE WILLIAM BYRD PRESS, INCORPORATED
RICHMOND, VIRGINIA

TO
BERTHA
BEN
AND RED

FOREWORD

IT IS DIFFICULT to say anything original about the South, because so many millions of words concerning the region have filled the air and the pages of books. This generous verbalizing has been going on for a long time, since long before the termination, some eighty-six years ago, of that unpleasantness known as The War Between the States. Nevertheless, I believe that Dr. Rubin's book does have something original to say, because it is based on an approach which has been little used by writers and orators. The point of view and the method are those of modern cultural anthropology, and the book deals with real people in the total context of life as they live it. This particular study has to do with what outsiders often think of as the most "typical" aspect of the South—life in the plantation area of the Black Belt.

In saying that the book has something original to say, I do not imply that it says everything there is to be said about the South—or even about its particular exhibit of southern culture in the Black Belt country, as Dr. Rubin, the author, is the first to admit. The approach of social anthropology has nothing magical in it, and it is only one of many useful scientific methods of understanding social realities. Field work in social anthropology, however, does attempt to study live people and to examine their customs and institutions as actual behavior in a functioning whole. This is somewhat different from a purely statistical method, an approach based only on the examination of written documents, or a procedure which analyzes abstract possibilities from a philosophical point of view, useful as each of these and other techniques may be in appropriate cases. Furthermore, the anthropological method has the virtue of being a "nonpartisan" approach. These studies of the South are made neither from the "northern" nor "southern" point of view but are oriented to the purely scientific description and analysis which has proved so illuminating in other anthropological investigations. Dr. Rubin has portrayed the principal patterns of behavior, organization, thought, and feeling of one type of southern community and has shown how they are related together in a configuration which represents one of the extant varieties of southern culture. And he has not lost sight of the fact that a culture is manifested by people and that, in real life, it constitutes their design for living.

The South is a sizeable piece of real estate—863,250 square miles of it, to be exact—on which live a considerable crowd of people —41,728,272 of them, according to the 1950 Census. The real estate occupies that portion of our country portrayed as the thirteen states occupying the lower right-hand part of the map. But this stretch of territory contains quite a variety of natural or environmental regions. To mention only a few of the more obvious, one must recognize the Mountains, the Piedmont, the Coastal Plains or Plantation country, the Piney Woods Belt, and the Coastal Fringe. Climate, soil, terrain, and all other conditions posed by nature present special features and combinations in each of these areas. Thus there is little sense in speaking of the South as if it were an area of relative geographical uniformity, like the Amazon Valley or the Central Sahara Desert.

Since culture is in part a means whereby people adjust to their natural environment, it is not suprising that the respective ways of life of the people who live in these different southern regions should differ among themselves in some significant details. The plantation system is inherently unadapted to the Mountain coves, for example, just as the commercial fishing of the Coastal Fringe would be an absurdity in the Piedmont. So there is no use pretending that southern cultures are in all respects and details homogeneous. Mr. Rubin's book presents only one of these cultural adaptations in the South, and it will be followed by other books delineating the situation in other distinct situations representative of the cultural variations of the region.[1]

Yet, when all this is understood, there remains a good deal which *is* common to the various cultures of the South. First of all, southerners are Americans, and the great majority of their life ways or culture traits are those shared by all Americans. This fact takes some of that exotic appeal out of the study of the southern way of life which

---

[1] The Studies in the Modern Cultures of the South, under the direction of the writer of this Introduction, were financed by the Julius Rosenwald Fund and the University of North Carolina.

romanticists find in certain far-away cultures whose every detail is strikingly different from comparable American customs.

But, even though they are American and even though they differ among themselves to some extent, the various cultures of the South possess certain traits in common which are exclusively theirs—shared among themselves, but not with other American cultures. This fact is sometimes expressed in the phrase that "the South is a state of mind." An anthropologist, using the jargon of his trade, would say that there are certain "mental patterns" common to all southern cultures.

A foreword of this sort is not the place to analyze or even to list these traits, a task which is reserved for a later volume. But a few suggestions may not be amiss by way of orientation to the present and later studies.

A pervading feature of all varieties of southern culture, "from the mountains to the sea," which is not shared by and often not approved of by other Americans, is a basic pattern of thinking and feeling about the relations between white people and Negro people which is summed up in the so-called "doctrine of white supremacy." Some southern white people and some southern colored people, to be sure, do not follow this pattern and its complex of associated traits, but such individuals are "emancipated" or "acculturated." They are deviants, no longer full practitioners and followers of the southern pattern.

The southern pattern of thought and feeling on race relations is a delicate subject, because the mere mention of it often arouses emotions, both in southerners and in "outsiders." But any objective and dispassionate appraisal of southern culture must take it into account. "White supremacy" and its correlates are the basic premises, one might say, of the southern way of life insofar as this differs from North American culture in general. They permeate practically all institutions in the South and control practically all patterns of relations between southerners as well as relationships between southerners and others. The race patterns, as mental customs, are just as firmly believed in those parts of the South, such as the Mountains and the Coastal Fringe, where there are practically no Negroes, as in the areas of high Negro population. Furthermore, it is expected in the system that Negroes themselves will subscribe to these ideas, and in any case it is required that they act as if they did. Evidence seems to show that most lower-class uneducated Negroes do subscribe to the patterns of white supremacy in a way which is reciprocal to the white ideas and practices. Of course, many educated Negroes have rejected these formulations of southern culture and, together with certain similar deviants among the whites, are bending their efforts to change the patterns by one means or another.

This aspect of the southern system is difficult to present dispassionately because it has usually been approached in moralistic terms. Viewed objectively it is, of course, obvious that the racial premises of southern culture are fundamentally inconsistent with certain other premises of American civilization as a whole. But in presenting the facts of southern culture in this series of studies, it is felt that the content and structure of the culture tend to be obscured if judgments are made concerning the "rightness" or "wrongness" of the culture in connection with a factual presentation. Our purpose is to present what exists, not to argue or quarrel about it.

Most completely socialized southerners—that is, those who have fully internalized the patterns of their culture—believe that the racial premise and its corollaries are "right" or "good." And this is the point that must be borne in mind if one attempts to understand behavior and institutions in this region. There is evidence that the culture is changing, but as yet the racial premise has not been removed from the basic controls of the orthodox southern ways of life.

A great war was fought by the South in defense of its premise, and although slavery as one expression of the principle of white supremacy was destroyed, the premise itself remained and new manifestations of its influence developed. A painful period of "reconstruction" followed the war, in which the victors devoted a considerable part of their energies to the extirpation of this feature of the southern system by force, by economic manipulation, and by moral suasion. The members of any society will defend the integrity of their cultural system if they believe it has value for them above that of other systems—and southerners were no exceptions to this generalization. And it would have gone against all comparable experience, if they had not generated and maintained emotion in the process of defense. It can be demonstrated on technical—not moral—grounds that the southerners weakened the structure and consequently the efficacy of their system vis-à-vis other systems by their methods of defense and by their failure to make adequate readjust-

Foreword

ments, and that "outsiders" were not slow to take advantage of such weaknesses. But what happened happened, and our purpose here is not to draw morals but to show what is now happening in terms of human behavior and organization. The defensive posture of the southern cultures, however, needs to be mentioned because it accounts for many "traits" of the South which outsiders often think of as nothing more than pure "orneriness" or "cussedness." The fact is that there is probably more "charm" per unit of population in the South than in any other part of North America, but their cultural position has tended to make southerners "touchy" about "outside" interference and criticism. They have sought security in traditionalism and conservatism and Biblical fundamentalism. They often are ambivalent: some southerners are both ardent church-goers and hard drinkers; some resent "northern domination" yet go to great lengths to attract mills and factories financed by northerners; most whites insist on white supremacy and segregation, but treat individual Negroes in a friendly and human fashion; many are "easy going" most of the time, but give way to violence on occasion; many complain about "conditions" in the South, but resent suggestions for their improvement. Yes, there are inconsistencies in southern culture and contradictions in southern character. But the South did not "plan it that way." Comparable defects can be found in other peoples and other cultures, as southerners do not hesitate to point out. The South is a large aggregation of people on a large piece of land, and if these people were not to some extent "culture-bound" they would not be human beings.

The southern cultures are not standing still. Like all other systems of human adjustment they change in response to new conditions. And in many sections of the South the leaders are purposely planning and accelerating the adoption of such new patterns and new directions. It will probably be surprising to many to read Dr. Rubin's description of what is going on in the Black Belt.

JOHN GILLIN

Chapel Hill
March, 1951

ACKNOWLEDGMENTS

I AM GRATEFUL to the Institute for Research in Social Science of the University of North Carolina for the one year appointment as research assistant during 1947-1948 which enabled me to carry on this investigation in the plantation area of the Southeast.

Dr. John Gillin, Professor of Anthropology at the University of North Carolina and Director of Field Studies in the Modern Culture of the South at the Institute for Research in Social Science, has been patient teacher, constant friend, and chief critic throughout. He is responsible for whatever value this study may have for a scientific understanding of human behavior in this area. He does not share in the errors or limitations that may be found herein.

I have had good counsel from Professors Gordon W. Blackwell, Guy B. Johnson, Rupert B. Vance, and Nicholas J. Demerath. Numerous persons in official and semi-official capacities have aided this research from the early "contact" stages through to final publication. I hope this product will justify their efforts.

When all is said and done, however, the people of Plantation County are the real sponsors of this volume. As good friends and neighbors, both during and since the research period, they have held to their initial promise of cooperation and participation. If individual and place names are disguised in this study, it is to protect the informants from publicity's glare.

I hope my friends in Plantation County will accept the findings of this research as those of an objective and scientific investigator. Such controversies over issues that may be raised here should be laid to differences in cultural background and previous training, not to personal animosity.

This field worker owes much to the people responsible for the exacting work of liaison between field and office, for the typing of manuscripts, and for the ever-ready spirit of cooperation that has existed. Mrs. Wayne Kernodle participated in the coordination of

Acknowledgments

field work and office; she also typed the first draft of a succession of manuscripts of which this is the final one. Thanks to Miss Miriam Blechman this copy has seen the light, and the materials are ready for the public.

MORTON RUBIN

Chapel Hill, N. C.
February 1, 1950

CONTENTS

Foreword	vi
Acknowledgments	xii
Introduction	xix
1. Into the Field	3
2. Operating a Plantation	10
3. The Changing Plantation	32
4. Small Farmers Try to Make Good	52
5. Factories to Balance Farms	73
6. When Whites and Negroes Come Together	88
7. Status in Negro and in White Society	108
8. The Church and the Belief System	133
9. Growing Up in Plantation County	152
10. Adulthood and Old Age	174
11. Plantation Area Culture	191
Appendix: Theoretical Frame of Reference	209
Bibliography	219
Index	227

Figures

1. Plantation County and Environs 6
2. Plantation Town 8
3. Structure of the Sampson Plantation 13
4. One-room Negro Cabin 14
5. Two-room Cabin with "Dog-trot" 15
6. Two-room Cabin with Kitchen 15
7. Farmers Home Administration Unit House 15
8. Traditional Plantation-style House 16

INTRODUCTION

Plantation Town and Plantation County, as we know them in this book, were selected as the most likely sites for research after a careful process of elimination by discussion and first-hand investigation. For a single investigator to spend one year in a community to study its way of life in as comprehensive a manner as possible, it was necessary to secure a community or area which had no more than five thousand people and which would be more or less sympathetic toward the aims of the research project. Plantation Town was a county seat with approximately 150 white families and 150 Negro families in a county populated by twenty thousand Negroes and five thousand whites. There were also many smaller communities scattered throughout the county which would make it possible to sample life outside the county seat. The main occupation of the people was agriculture, with cotton culture and the plantation system predominating. The rural life of the area was quite dynamic, moreover, with beef cattle raising beginning to supplant cotton to an increasing degree. Lumbering was a growing industry also. New social and economic forms were rising from the exploitation of additional resources and the introduction of new techniques.

Three sponsors were approached by agricultural extension officials and other contacts. These included an important politician who also owned a sizeable plantation in the county; a physician, well known throughout the area and also with plantation background; and a local minister, renowned for his liberal stand on controversial issues.

The three sponsors enabled the investigator to make his way among a wide network of contacts, for they were able to answer the first questions of people not only unaccustomed to being studied by social scientists but who were quite curious and suspicious of strangers in the community. The investigator was not able to rely entirely on initial sponsors, however. In order to undertake intensive research, the network of contacts and informants was expanded to include persons of all stations in the community. Here the investigator was required to bring his personality into play. He had to be affable, to remain neutral on local controversial issues, to promote the feeling that he was participating in the life of the community, and yet to remind the public that the requirements of the research necessitated a certain amount of freedom and independence from community mores. The investigator had to remain in control of key people and to analyze important situations and his role in them as they arose. Ofttimes the strain of being forced to remain neutral while certain issues cried out for resolution outraged the investigator's sense of duty as a citizen, yet it was necessary to subdue bias and to make compromises with the situation which would soothe both private conscience and academic conscience to the best degree possible. At the other extreme, the investigator had to avoid "going native" and letting the culture determine what was moral and what was not.

The preparation for field work involves a vast amount of reading in the theory and methods of the social science discipline in addition to gathering information about the locale to be studied. Two seminars spent in studying socio-cultural research in modern communities plus the general academic training I was undertaking for my master's degree at the University of North Carolina proved quite inadequate when it came to gathering field materials in such a manner as to make the best use of the time and resources available. Much of the delay in presenting the materials in manuscript form came about from this investigator's need for more reading and study of socio-cultural theory. While Dr. Gillin's directives to the field men were invaluable and the counsel of other academic advisers helped considerably, only the academic maturity of the investigator could make the research utilize all the potentialities of the situation in both the organization of the research, the actual field work, and the ultimate presentation of the materials. It would be advisable for those who give student research grants to allow the investigator more time to prepare himself in theory and in the background of the locale before he enters the field.

The potentialities of the field research were limited beyond the investigator's interests and the theoretical assumptions. The social components of the situation with respect to race relations made it necessary to choose areas for more intensive investigation and to limit other areas which might have been investigated. Because the investigator was a white man, it was felt that if there had to be a choice between the two racial groups, it would be better for the purposes of the study to concentrate on the whites as chief carriers of the culture and leaders in the power structure. All possible attempts were made, nevertheless, to enter as much as possible into Negro activities and to establish contacts with as many individuals and groups as possible. Although the role of a white man in the plantation area has restricting influences in relations with Negroes, the fact that the investigator was a northerner and had a purpose for being in the community to which the white people had given assent permitted him to participate in Negro activities to a greater degree than might have been possible otherwise. The easiest entries were through church meetings and the gatherings of Negro farm people, veterans, children, and others in formal meetings. Contacts with Negro officials and leaders were secured at these meetings, and this permitted further study of the situation as confidences were built up. The personality of the investigator, especially his ability to convey a sincere interest in the welfare of the Negroes while at the same time not appearing to lose the confidence of the whites, came into special play in this delicate interracial situation. Negro domestics in the hotel and rooming house who watched the daily activities of the investigator were able to assure their friends of his sincerity. In this manner some contacts with a variety of intensity could be established with Negro groups. The trips with white public officials and with other persons who also enjoyed the confidence of certain groups of Negroes likewise provided entrance into a variety of activities.

My rapport with the lower levels of white society was achieved much later than with the leaders and large middle section of the white community. Again it was a matter of personality, choosing contacts who held the confidence of this group and eventually establishing rapport both with the leaders and the masses within the lower middle and the lower classes in white society. The hotel and later the rooming house where I lived proved excellent choices, for they were not identified with either extreme of white society. The kinspeople of my landlady at the rooming house ran the gamut from plantation owners and local officials to small farmers in the woods and hills of Plantation County. Luck also played its role; for example, a wedding in which I was best man, enabled me to participate in the society of a group of small farmers who otherwise would have been relatively inaccessible. My 1931 Model A Ford coupe with its continuous ailments provided entry into the group of "back yard" mechanics who lived and worked on the edge of town. I made further contacts with members of this group by participating in veterans' organizations, the local unit of the National Guard, and by actual overnight stays and visits to isolated communities in the clay hill regions of the county.

The major orientation of this study tends toward the middle and upper classes of whites, since this was the original group with whom rapport was achieved and the group from whom information could most easily be gathered. This is the group that controls the power structure. While I have gathered and presented material on the other groups in plantation area society also, I feel more information is needed here. Additional field personnel, each concentrating on a main social category in the society, would be preferable. It is hoped that allowance will be made for the limitations herein in light of the above statements.

The time that elapses between a field study and the final publication of the materials is often disastrous to hypotheses on trends and events. Moreover, the investigator who becomes busy with other activities after the field research is completed begins to lose interest in the work, and the materials gradually grow cold. Quite fortunately my experiences in Plantation County were such as to provide me with a host of friends who continued to correspond and to entreat me to pay them visits. The county weekly and numerous letters do not give the complete picture of social and cultural change by any means—they only whet the appetite of the investigator for more field research. For both social and scientific reasons, therefore, I was able to spend Christmas week of 1948 in Plantation County at the invitation, especially, of my former landlady. The six months that had elapsed since I left the field for the University of North Carolina closed in fast during that week, and I quickly renewed old acquaintances and gathered information to complete the gaps. I found myself accepted as an old friend, in fact, as a former "citizen." I made a second visit to Plantation County for New Year's week in 1950, a year and a half after the termination of the field research and one month prior to this transcription. This revisit proved to me above

Introduction

all the importance of keeping in touch with current events and persons. In the light of these successive meetings and interviews, the materials presented here are valid for late 1949. Certain hypotheses formulated in 1947 have been borne out in events that have transpired. I have been able to correct many impressions and to complete obvious gaps of information. If I am able to revisit Plantation County *after* the publication of these materials, I shall feel completely rewarded in these efforts.

The plantation system is so clearly the dominant social and economic feature of the plantation area that the first portion of this study has been devoted to a discussion of the plantation as a social system and the changes inherent in its structure.

The small farmer in the plantation area has perhaps undergone as radical a transition as the plantation owner. The influence of federal agriculture agencies and other organizations has created new groups of small farmers in this section, which in turn have affected the social characteristics of the region.

The role of business and industry in the plantation area today remains one of the chief forces for the emergence of new socio-economic and cultural patterns and potentials. The groups associated with nascent business and industry here are playing roles which may well alter all aspects of life in the plantation area as we have known it.

The stratification system in this area, as in other subregions in the Southeast, reveals a biracial society. Social, economic, and psychological factors influence the race-caste culture of the plantation area. All institutions are affected. Yet the situation is dynamic, and there are forces making for change. Within white society and within Negro society we also find a stratification system whose criteria are peculiar to the area and the culture. We can study these groups and subgroups in a culture-structure-function analysis.

Supernatural beliefs give "meaning" to the life of individuals and groups in the plantation area. In studying the role of supernatural beliefs in the structure we shall notice both sacred and secular characteristics. As in other institutions, social and cultural changes are in evidence in the areas of religion, magic, and superstition. There are reciprocal relations among all the institutions to this effect.

In order to understand what makes a person in the plantation area we must study the patterns of socialization or enculturation. Both biological and cultural factors are operative in infant and child care, and these elements exist in the role of age and sex groups in the social structure. Traditional ways vie with forces for change.

In summarizing our findings about culture in the plantation area we can evaluate and measure the patterns in terms of the compatibility of the elements with the components of the situation. We can also evaluate the consistency of the elements with the goals or value-objectives of the culture. Both the major orientations of the culture and the goals of the subgroups within the culture may be considered in measuring integration and the distinguishing characteristics of plantation area society and culture. Finally, we can assay the characteristics of social and cultural change, the influence of both the internal forces and the culture-contact or foreign components of the situation. The role of technological civilization and mass culture in the plantation area is important in order to understand the role of the mass culture in other areas of the United States and world society. It is hoped that this presentation will throw light on the static and dynamic aspects of life in the plantation area of the Southeast for which Plantation County is our example.

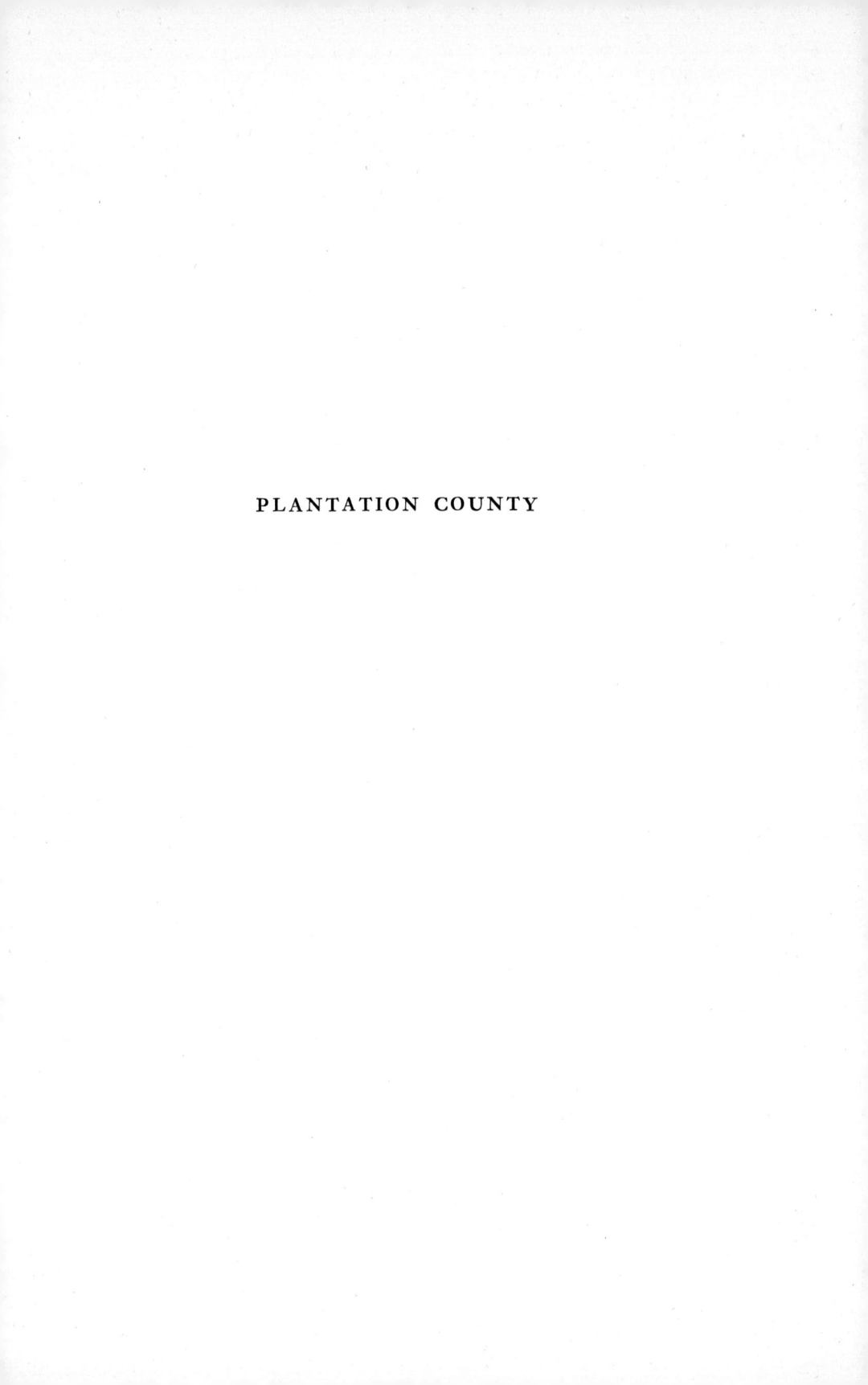

PLANTATION COUNTY

1

INTO THE FIELD

When Professor John Gillin asked me if I should like to spend a year in the plantation area and write a book about it, all sorts of problems and doubts came to my mind. A Yankee, born and reared in Boston, of Jewish religion, a student wedded to textbooks, just does not pack up his clothes and typewriter and take off for a town of three hundred white and Negro families in the heart of the Black Belt without some trepidation.

Professor Gillin did not want me to go to Plantation County merely to write a book about the place. What he had in mind was a study of life in the plantation area which would utilize the theory and methods of social science, principally social anthropology. The field worker could not select just "any" community for such study. He had to make his entrance in a particular manner and cover the material in a specific way. If the study was to be of value to social science, it had to be planned in a scientific manner. (For the theoretical frame of reference, the reader may refer to the Appendix.)

I arrived in the Deep South on a Friday afternoon in June—the twenty-seventh, to be exact—in 1947. The bus station in Black Belt City was hot and humid. When the bus to Plantation Town pulled up and opened its door, the driver motioned the white people in first. They entered and sat in the front. The Negroes went to the rear and there carried on conversation in a world of their own.

In the white group, I soon found myself talking with the people about me. I discovered early that people from these parts liked to chat. They seemed interested in persons above all.

The first stage in the conversation, after remarks about the weather, represented an attempt to identify each person in relation to the local countryside. I found myself the only "stranger" in the group, for bit by bit one passenger after another "claimed kin" with acquaintances of other passengers. It was not until a few months later, after I had established a boarding place in Plantation Town, that I was able to utilize this relationship to claim kin with persons in Plantation County.

First impressions of Plantation Town were mixed. The business section was a hodge-podge of tin-roofed, multi-colored brick structures of one or two stories. A colonial style red brick courthouse with massive white pillars dominated the square. On one side of town the white "plantation style" colonial houses gave an appearance of serenity and good living. At another end of town the wooden shacks of the Negroes and the less ostentatious frame houses of the poorer whites seemed crowded and insecure. These first impressions were never successfully challenged; the research of a year merely revealed further nuances that breathed life into the structure.

That hot Friday afternoon presented a forerunner of Saturday's milling Negro country folk with the "laying-by" time for crops at hand. The watermelons were ripe. Scores of Negro men and women dressed in brightly colored cottons or tans sat on curb benches in front of the groceries and "visited." They spat watermelon seeds onto the sidewalk before them; they shouted at the children who ran hither and yon or dripped chocolate ice cream over their blouse-fronts. The white people, by contrast, either closeted themselves in their automobiles or within the shade of the stores. Here they exchanged the news of the day, shopped, and sipped endless cokes. One group of whites—local farmers and relaxing politicos—sat under the pecan tree near the courthouse and controlled all approaches. Here was Plantation Town on a hot afternoon at the end of the week—the center of the county, a representative of Black Belt life.

The hotel in Plantation Town was an ancient red brick two-storied building where giant rotary fans attempted to cool simple drab hallways. Old cronies from in town or out of town set each other up to cokes, and made conversation not unlike that going on under the pecan tree, in the stores, or on the curb benches downtown. The hotel was my first "home" in Plantation Town. It was here that I made my first contacts and friendships. The hotel was always a familiar base of operations, and it was my dining room at noontime. The first friends remained true; they provided initial contacts through church meetings, picnics, and invitations to dances and to suppers.

Old Miss Erma Erskine gave me my first orientation to Plantation Town and the county. A retired school teacher, member of a once-proud plantation family, she loved to dote on the "good old days" while she held down the hotel desk during that summer. Subsequent days were spent generally in conversation and in making new acquaintances. As contacts multiplied, I was busy collecting names, charting genealogies, and trying to place my new informants in social space. I found that by attending large gatherings, civic club meetings, church schools and services, sports events, and the like, my appearance became known and persons would advance to greet me as a newcomer to the community. Invariably I would have to explain what my purpose was in coming to Plantation County. The theories, methods, and goals of social science research had to be translated into various mediums so that farmers, housewives, storekeepers, and even children could understand and be motivated to cooperate. Another early procedure was to purchase maps of the county and the town and mark the population in physical space. A property map of the county enabled me to outline the holdings, and to note land ownership in its quantitative characteristics.

After a typical day's activities, I sketched rough notes and impressions in a notebook. I typed the permanent notes regularly onto four by six papers and coded them according to the topics in the Yale *Outline of Cultural Materials*.[1] I sent one set of these notes with a weekly résumé of activities and impressions to Professor Gillin at the Institute for Research in Social Science at the University of North Carolina. There his staff collated the notes of all the field personnel and filed them for further use, primarily as background for a summary book on culture in the South. I reviewed my own set of notes constantly, formulating and revising hypotheses. My visits to meetings and to officials invariably netted a collection of printed and mimeographed materials which proved valuable in noting prominent leaders of the community, periodic activities, and the like. I still subscribe to the county weekly newspaper and find it a source of information about current events which may alter some of the conclusions I reached while in the field. On the basis of such new information I have found it desirable to correspond with friends on the scene.

I took field trips into the country almost as soon as I arrived in Plantation County. The county agent, social workers, insurance sales-

---

[1] George P. Murdock and others, *Outline of Cultural Materials* (rev. ed,; New Haven: Yale University Press, 1945).

men, and others, were extremely helpful in my gaining access to isolated places to establish contact with a variety of social groups and individuals. The long rides we took also provided excellent interview situations, the conversations often being more rewarding than the observations in the field. I should say that the automobile represents an ideal place for interviews—it is private, and the hum of the motor relaxes both informant and interviewer.

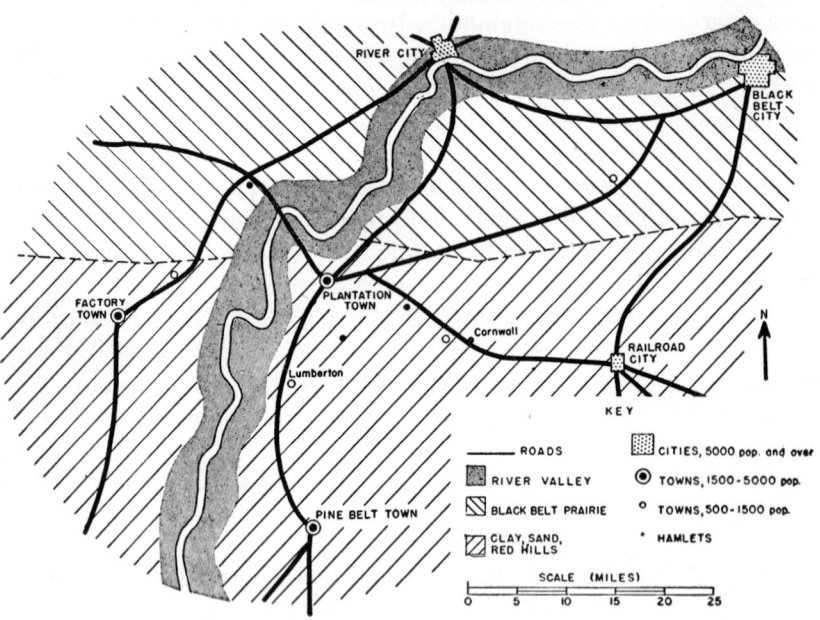

1. PLANTATION COUNTY AND ENVIRONS

I documented my trips with numerous photographs. An Argus C-3 camera established me in a role of photographer which was quite useful for entering into situations where there might otherwise be difficulty in establishing initial rapport. I was careful to present copies of pictures to those informants who requested them. Negroes were quite willing to be photographed when they were "dressed up"; a little coaxing, however, persuaded them to be photographed in their usual activity. White individuals and groups likewise became willing subjects before the camera. It enabled many persons and groups to have their activities recorded for the first time. Church and school groups, clubs, mothers and infants, and numerous other persons looked forward to receiving pictures of themselves. I was able to record one of the rare snow storms in the Black Belt which occurred while I was in Plantation County. The photographs have been useful for recalling incidents and for a description of the material aspects of the culture.

I utilized a Webster wire recording machine to catch interviews and meetings, especially Negro choral groups. Limitation of time prevented a more extensive use of the machine. It proved its value, however, in marking local accents and events for transcription into longhand. The machine also provided an entree into new interview situations.

I found it valuable to begin writing down questions, notes, and hypotheses at least weekly while in the field. Within three months I began to organize the materials into a brief statement of the research problem as it appeared at that time. I continued this method of writing and revising manuscripts so that by the end of the field study I had a fairly comprehensive report ready. This method made the notes alive; it also enabled me to spot weaknesses in information so that I was able to check them before leaving the field. This present manuscript draft represents the fifth of a series that I began when I had been in the field six months.

Between the documentary baggage, represented by many months' preparatory reading and research, and the reminiscences of Miss Erma, the following sketch of Plantation County and its tradition gradually emerged. This background has been essential to the contemporary field research.

A primary natural feature of Plantation County is the river that meanders through the center of the state and then flows lazily southward to empty into the Gulf. The Black Belt soil region lies on either side of the river in the northern part of the county, and this, together with the alluvial soils of creek and river valleys, provides nourishment for the crops that predominate. The river was the artery for the first settlers who came after the War of 1812.

The first plantations were established on either side of the river, for the soil was good, and the bales of cotton could be shipped downstream to the Gulf port. As the first settlements close to the river soon proved themselves unhealthy, however, the white planters began to move back. But their Negro slaves continued to dwell in the "bottoms," and only recently began to take to the highways in the interior.

At the turn of the century, with the coming of the railroad and subsequently the highway, the river and its settlements began to go into eclipse as factors in the cotton trade. The function of the river today is to divide the county physically and socially and to provide a seasonal flooding of the bottom lands. But the river is also a source of catfish which in summer and spring furnish the main dish for countless fishfries in the area. To this extent it remains a main feature of the scene.

The Black Belt soil region in the north of the county formerly

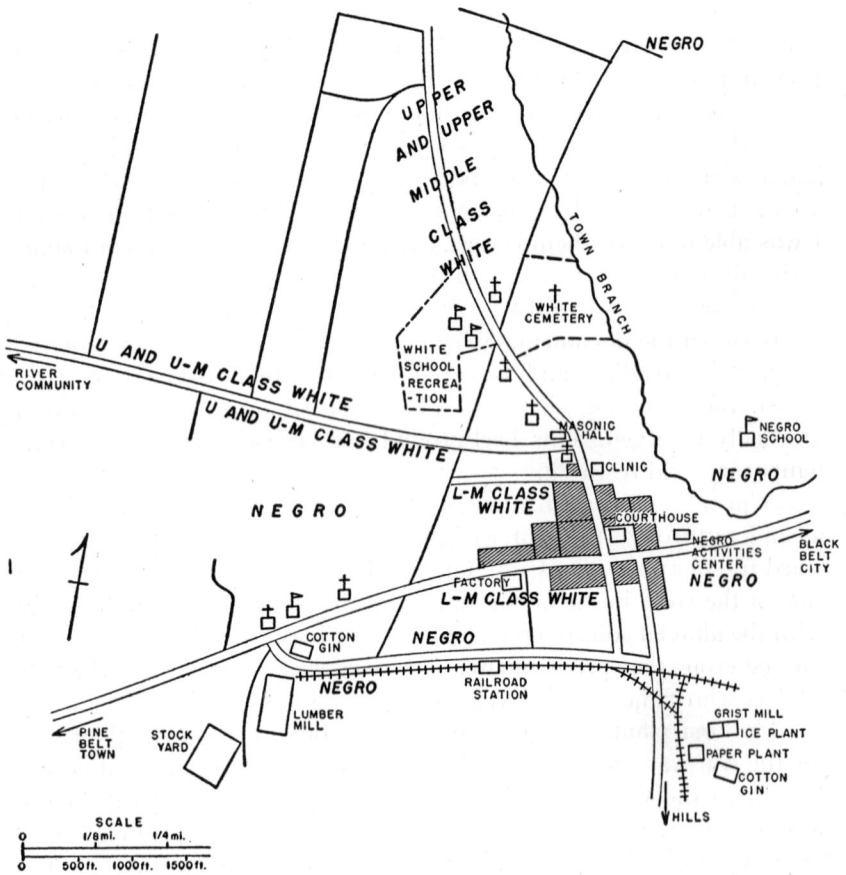

2. PLANTATION TOWN

Into the Field

produced the major proportion of cotton in the area. But the boll weevil struck here during the second decade of the twentieth century. Farmers found it necessary to make new adjustments to the changing conditions of the situation, or fail. They used all sorts of poisons, and they cultivated their lands intensively, but the wild fluctuations of the cotton market again threatened them with ruin. Gradually, herds of brown and white Hereford beef cattle were introduced, and improved methods of growing grass came into practice, so that today the Black Belt is cattle country instead of cotton. Subsequent sections in this writing will be devoted to a discussion of this transition. Suffice it to say that the picture of the Black Belt to a visitor of today is far different from that of thirty years ago. Contented Herefords and other breeds of cattle now chew their cud the year round in the high grass, where stalks of cotton once filled the prairies of the Black Belt.

A clay hilly region lies between the Black Belt and the Gulf Coastal Plain. This is encountered in the southern portion of Plantation County. The soil is less fertile than the Black Belt, but it is fair for cotton and corn. Lumber interests are buying up the poorest and smallest farms in the area because of their large timber reserve. The more progressive of the small farmers in this area are combining traditional corn and cotton culture with cattle and timber. This trend is promoted by such federal and state agencies as the Agricultural Extension Service.

Federal troops on their way to New Orleans during the War of 1812 drove the Creek Indians from the river valley and thus paved the way for European settlement. The planters came from the seaboard states and brought their few Negro slaves with them. Others came as yeomen farmers and purchased slaves as they prospered.

Plantation Town came into being during the 1820's as a collection of planters' homes and a trading center some ten miles from the river. Churches, schools, stores, and the social and economic organizations of typical ante-bellum plantation society eventually developed. When Plantation Town was made the county seat of Plantation County, the new red brick colonial courthouse became the focal point for life in and about the area. It still occupies this position today. A business section lies around the courthouse. The spacious dwellings of the whites are north and west of the center, and the plank Negro shacks are to the south, all within a quarter mile from the hub. Shortly beyond this, one finds himself in open country once more.

2

OPERATING A PLANTATION

THE MOVIE, "Gone with the Wind" has undoubtedly furnished the picture most people have of plantation life. Does the word "plantation" suggest to you a white pillared mansion with magnolia and honeysuckle abounding? Do you visualize fair damsels in pastel-shaded hoop skirts dancing with their suitors from military school to the tune of a "darkey" string band? Does your plantation owner sport a black moustache and relax on his veranda in a white linen suit while his wants are satisfied by the faithful old servant who brings him mint juleps?

If this is your vision of a plantation, your ideal may be somewhat rudely disturbed in the pages that follow. For the plantation today is fundamentally a business enterprise. It is an economic institution in which a large tract of land is subdivided among smaller operators, called tenants. It is operated for profit by an owner and his assistants. As in most economic organizations, the plantation also has a hierarchy of employer-employee relationships and statuses with concomitant roles.

In addition to being a business enterprise, the plantation is a total socio-cultural system located in ecological space. Historically, the plantation has been rather self-contained, having the marks of a community with its own buildings and services. There are even neighborhoods on a plantation. The power structure of the plantation is authoritarian—in the plantation area there is usually a white owner, white and Negro supervisors and taskmasters, and Negro tenants. Other plantations in the Southeast may have Negro owners; some areas are predominately white in tenancy as well as ownership.

Perhaps the structure and functions of the plantation as a socio-cultural system may be best described by taking a trip from Plantation Town into the open country to the largest plantation in the area, the Sampson plantation.

You will recall in "Gone with the Wind" that the dreaded

Yankees allegedly laid waste to the Southland, and the loyal southerners supposedly were either forced from their property by its destruction, or by the high taxes which were fostered by the Republican regime that followed the peace. In Plantation County there was a form of invasion and deprivation, but this was less severe than in areas where there was heavy fighting. Many of the plantations along the river in Plantation County fell heavily in debt after the war. Captain Sampson, a midwestern veteran of the Union Army, liked the South and came with his wife to settle in the rich Black Belt. He came into the possession of some small plantations and eventually built himself a holding of several thousand acres. The cabins of Negro slaves had been organized in neighborhoods about the old plantation houses. Captain Sampson did not disturb these arrangements when he acquired these properties. Today the old neighborhood names are retained, and the tenant cabins are clustered as in former times.

Even though he was a "carpetbagger" and a Republican, Captain Sampson learned to adjust to the way of life of the area. The nature of politics during the Reconstruction period enabled him to be elected probate judge of Plantation County. But Captain Sampson was interested in community activities in Plantation Town—he helped to establish the Presbyterian church, and he contributed to other worthy causes. Captain Sampson planned for the full acceptance of his descendants in plantation area society by marrying his children into the families of native plantation owners who were then in less fortunate circumstances. The children and grandchildren of Captain Sampson can hardly be distinguished from other persons native to the section. Their outlook on life is typical if not in a measure more conservative than the average native whose ancestors came from the seaboard states thirty years before the War Between the States. The Sampson plantation today is managed by the sons and grandsons of the Captain. These people have had scientific agricultural training in colleges; they continue to expand their holdings; they are good businessmen, able to adjust continuously to the changing conditions of the situations.

The eight mile road from Plantation Town to the Sampson plantation is now paved with blacktop. Before the Second World War there were few such paved roads in the county. Legislation for farmer-to-market, or "mailbox" roads is still a political issue high on the agendas at the state capital. The open country is only a quarter of a mile from the courthouse in Plantation Town. From sidewalks, spacious lawns, and the white painted single and two-storied colonial homes of the white people of Plantation Town, it is so near yet so far to the rows of cotton and corn or seas of grass, broken only by the unpainted wooden plank cabins of Negro tenants. At intervals the landscape is darkened by stands of pines, the forest-reserve of the area. Sweetgums mark the presence of low places near streams.

The traffic on the road during the day is heavy and varied. There are white persons and colored persons in passenger cars and trucks of many vintages. Heavy lumber trucks can be seen carrying their precariously chained logs, a sign of the growing lumber industry in the area. The interurban bus comes through Plantation Town occasionally giving those persons without access to cars an opportunity to visit the outside world. On a week day, though more on Saturday, the Negro farmer rides his mule cart between farm and town, carrying a load of hay, a bale of cotton, or his wife and children, according to the season of the year. It is often possible to see young Negroes ride mules or, more rarely, horses, on the highway; town-bred young Negroes are also partial to bicycle travel if they cannot afford a jalopy. The highway is not lacking in foot traffic either. Negro men wear tans and helmets to shield them from the sun. Women sport brightly colored cotton dresses and straw hats with wide brims. Their shoes are generally run down at the heels or open at the toes; Negro farmers wear boots, but their women may go about barefooted, inured to the heat of the pavement or the sandy shoulders of the road. The children, during the school season, walk along the road in clusters, most of them lacking a school bus to take them two or three miles to the consolidated school. In summer time the children play about the cabins or prepare themselves for cotton chopping and picking, a family enterprise.

The cabins of Negro tenants meet the eye long before we arrive at the center of the plantation. Most of the old log cabins have disappeared to be replaced by simple structures of pine board with wood shingles or tin roofing. The log cabins which remain have their chinks filled with cement. The space between the planks of the pine board cabins is less well filled, and at night one can see kerosene lamplight glowing through the cracks into the darkness. The rickety appearance of the cabins is further enhanced by wooden shutters on windows

Operating a Plantation

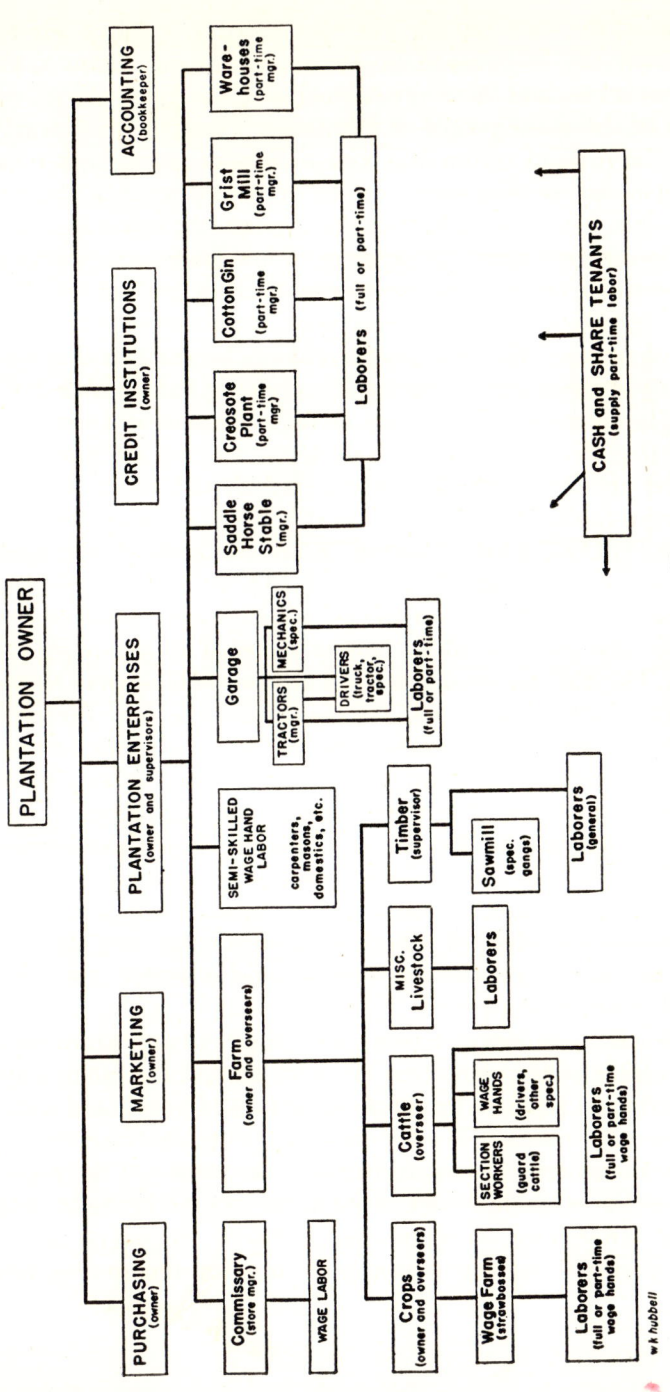

3. Structure of the Sampson Plantation

without glass, tree-trunk supports for the front porch, a few broken steps, and stone or wooden supports beneath the whole to keep it from sinking into the mud. The cabins may have their rooms adjoining, or else there may be a "dog-trot" (open hallway) between two sections that serve as rooms. Cabins of any size or shape are inevitably crowded, however.

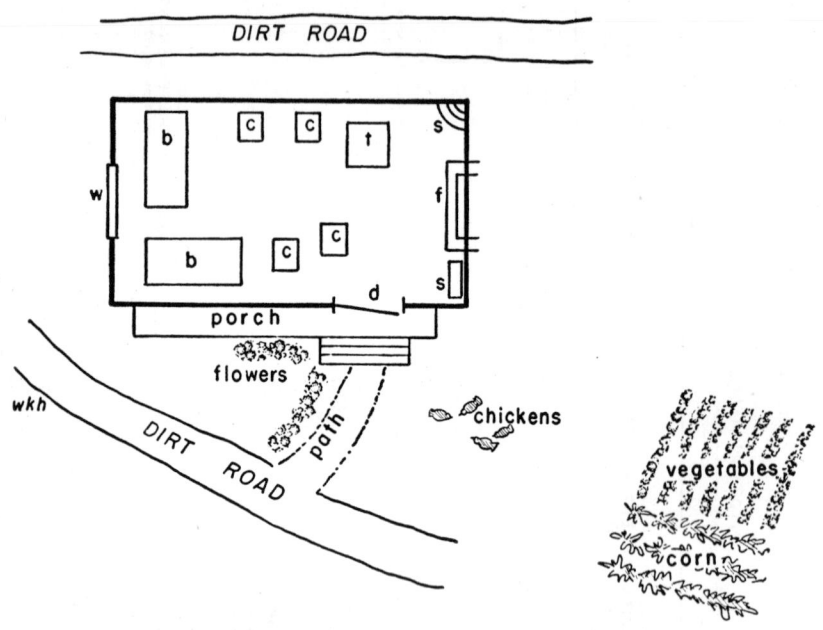

4. ONE-ROOM NEGRO CABIN. *This particular cabin was made of notched logs, with clay filler, wooden floors, wooden supports under the floor, tin roof, and newspaper-covered walls.*

Each room functions as sleeping quarters for adults and innumerable children. Old iron beds may hold as many as four or five persons, both adults and children if need be. Old couches or sleeping pallets of straw serve the lesser members of the household. No cabin is deemed too small to accommodate a stray child or an adult visitor from afar.

The second function of the dwelling is cooking. The fireplace of brick with its permanent chimney (usually outliving flimsy wooden buildings which burn to the ground) may be at one end of a room or in the center, serving two rooms. More fortunate tenants cook

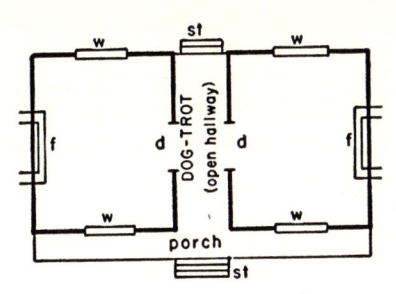

5. Two-room Cabin with "Dog-trot"

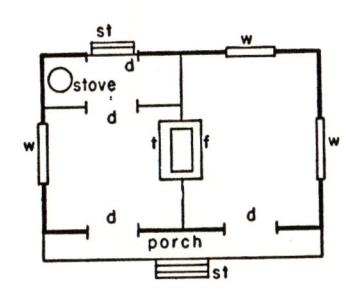

6. Two-room Cabin with Kitchen

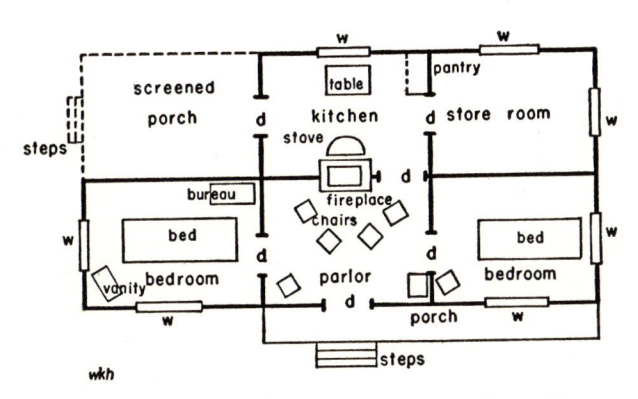

7. Farmers Home Administration Unit House

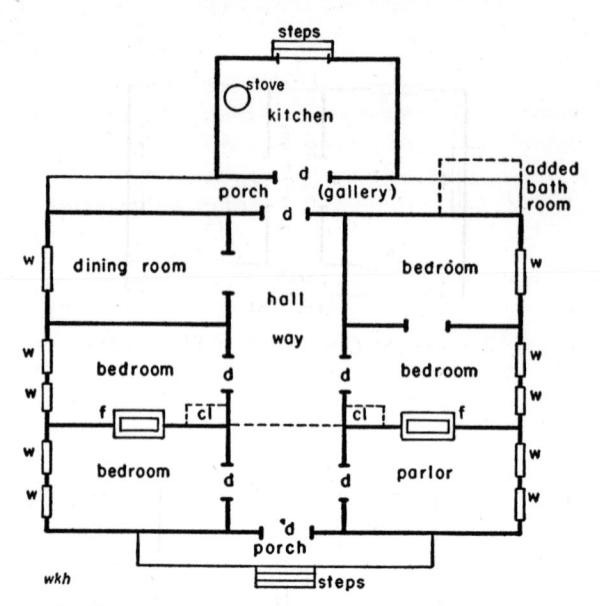

8. TRADITIONAL PLANTATION-STYLE HOUSE

over wood-burning stoves. Fuel-gathering is a privilege that usually goes with the rental of a cabin and garden space. The proximity of woods is a factor in the luxury of the winter fire.

The cabin has furniture of a simple and antiquated type. Some of it is home-made; other furniture is "store-bought," often right from a dealer's mail-order catalogue; still other furniture is the gift of white friends. This is usually the most ornate and Victorian of all. The beds are dominant among the furnishings. Next come straight-backed chairs of white oak with seats which are matted with corn shuck or oak splinters. The chairs are in various stages of repair, as is the wooden table that serves relays of diners. By good fortune the family may have a bureau or chest of drawers. Shelves and nails in the wall serve for hanging clothing and storing medicines. The brightly colored print dresses or dark blue denim overalls contrast with newspaper pages or rotogravure pictures that cover the walls. For luxury and leisure there is a rocker or two, and occasionally an overstuffed chair or sofa. Except in the coldest of weather, life is lived out of doors. Within the cabin, however, it is intimate indeed. Contrast the dwelling and status of these tenants with the landowner's home up the road.

The heart of the plantation is a community of the landowner's house, the homes of the overseers, the commissary, garage, warehouses, gin, sheds, and silos. Of all these necessary components of the plantation as a socio-economic enterprise, it is the plantation house that symbolizes the integrating force, the management.

In answer to our knock, Mrs. Fanny Sampson, the lady of the plantation, appears dressed in a simple cotton print. She invites us in, apologizing for the "upset" condition of the place so early in the morning. This is a familiar note in Plantation County. It means only that the flower cuttings have not been put in place; otherwise everything seems in order.

The living room, like the rest of the house, is furnished in a modern manner, after the taste of the upper middle classes and *Good Housekeeping* magazine. There is a prominent red brick fireplace with brass andirons to complement the color scheme. Drapes hang at the windows to contribute to the colorful arrangement of the room and, of course, to shield the room from the glare of the hot sun. An Oriental rug draws the big room together; the large pieces of furniture—a wing chair, a sofa, a Lawson chair, and a radio-phonograph console—are placed strategically to permit easy group conversation. None of the furniture in the room is older than twenty years. The antiques in the house are on display in the hallway or else in corner areas of the main rooms in the house. The room indicates its function for the business of the housewife and landowner by the secretary in the corner. Miscellaneous furniture—book cases, end tables, lamps, and odd chairs—complete the room which is lighted simply and in good taste by store-bought brass fixtures with large globes of modern design. There is, on the whole, little about the room or the home to distinguish its locale. The other rooms of the house—the dining room, electric kitchen, and bedrooms upstairs—are too much like other American homes of the ten to twenty-thousand-dollar income class to warrant detailed description.

In the next chapter we shall discover that there is a type of plantation house that recalls the ante-bellum period. Here one finds high ceilings, poster beds, antique wood-burning stoves, old oak flooring, and many other evidences of an earlier era. However, the Sampson home, like the Sampson plantation, is as modern an organization as its owners can make it.

Mrs. Sampson is about to drive down to the commissary for the morning groceries, and our coming advises her that there will be additional guests for dinner. The visitor to a plantation or to any farmstead in the county is seldom allowed to escape without a hot noontime meal replete with chicken or ham, garden vegetables, iced tea, and hot buttered biscuits. Marketing is the task of the housewife, after she has supervised the Negro girl's dusting and sweeping. After her return from the store, Mrs. Sampson will give the food to the Negro cook, and together they will plan and work on the dishes that please men's palates. The plantation store and the garden provide most of the food for the table, but special delicacies come from town. In the afternoon Mrs. Sampson will drive there to shop and to visit. All her close friends live in town or on neighboring plantations, and there is a periodic gathering of these women in Plantation Town in the late afternoon. They shop, meet for bridge, or just plain "sit and visit," which means chatting about the world of women and the plantation area.

At the commissary, a single-storied white frame building topped by a tin roof which glistens in the sun and is surrounded by Coca Cola signs, Mr. Sampson is in conference with some experts from the Agricultural Extension Service. All these men are dressed for outdoor work, with their cotton tans, Stetsons, and heavy high boots. Mr. Sampson's face is ruddy from the wind and sun, and his general appearance belies the stereotype of the planter sipping mint juleps in the cool of the veranda. (The Sampson home has no veranda, in fact, and Mr. Sampson is a deacon in the church and a teetotaler.) After handshakes and the offer of a coke, Mr. Sampson invites the group for a tour of inspection of the premises. We use a Ford truck to get about, as far as the terrain will permit. Other plantations still rely on horses, but the Sampsons find the Ford more efficient and useful for hauling at the same time.

We can accomplish our tour by studying the functions of the buildings at the plantation center, for here is the real pulse of the enterprise.

The commissary, like other general stores about the county, contains shelves with yard goods, cans of vegetables, fish, fruits, cases of sticky candy, cokes and other soft drinks, garden tools, mule harnesses, plow points, rubber hip boots, suntan shirts and trousers, calico dresses, and the numerous other items necessary to satisfy the needs and the wants of the tenants and Negro laborers. The commissary is a business enterprise on the plantation as well as a service.

Operating a Plantation

In the old days river barges returned from the Gulf port loaded down with goods to be credited to the plantation owner's account. Today a wholesaler's truck from River City stops by weekly to bring chewing gum, sausages, sacks of flour, and numerous other items to the store. The plantation slaves formerly were assigned rations of food and clothing at stated intervals. Now the Negro tenants make their own purchases with cash or scrip, a substitute for cash at some plantation stores, if they are buying a few items. Large purchases are made on credit terms to be settled in the fall when the crop is in. The storekeeper makes an entry in his big ledger behind the wooden "cage" where the accounts are kept. Tenants pay as much as 10 to 25 percent interest on these purchases, which are sold at retail to them. The average tenant does not keep written accounts of his purchases and debts, so he wonders why he has so little cash left after a good crop year.

The risk of the landlord is great, and he must guard against granting the tenant too large an advance. He may limit their purchases, or preferably, will insist on some member of the family's doing work for wages to pay off the advance. The tenants when confronted with an enormous debt will more than likely feel they can never pay it, so will run off or will wipe it from their minds. Wagework is plentiful on plantations where there is land to clear for pasture, but labor must be motivated in order to do this menial work. Another risk for the landlord is the unpredictability of the cotton market. He justifies the high interest charges in the light of his risks.

The plantation store is meeting competition from stores in town and in the cities. The prices are slightly cheaper there, but then these stores demand cash. Some plantation owners have a credit arrangement with certain stores in Plantation Town whereby their tenants are transported there by truck in order to shop. When the tenants board the truck for a return trip to the plantation their packages are examined, and they are forbidden to carry away items purchased at other stores. The tenants may hide such forbidden articles in their clothing or else wear them. Altogether the plantation store is still the main shopping center for the tenant; it is a flourishing business for the plantation owner, despite his risks. The plantation store also functions as a meeting and gossip center especially for the men. Here is where wage labor can be recruited for various jobs that arise.

Being a large business enterprise, the plantation requires a special bookkeeping section. A combination accountant and bookkeeper holds down an old desk with swivel chair in the rear of the Sampson plantation commissary. Here he records the debits and credits, the profits and losses over the months and years. A few years ago a fire destroyed the old commissary and the records, a loss which was made up only with great pain and racking of memories. Luckily, the bookkeeper knew his accounts fairly well, and the books are once more assuming shape and order so that the business can carry on. The piles of cement blocks and red bricks across the road from this building signify that a new fireproof commissary will soon be built.

Since the modern plantation is above all a mechanized farm, there are garages, tool houses, and tractor sheds at the plantation center. The old buildings are wooden with tin roofs, but newer structures being put up throughout the county are made of concrete block which is cheap, durable, and fireproof. The Sampsons have a white overseer who is in charge of the tractor crew of young Negro operators.

The supervisor informs us that the young Negroes like to drive tractors. "The nigger gals go for a tractor driver. We can't let 'em all drive, though. Most of the work around here calls for strong backs and quick fingers. Cotton picking and chopping takes the most work. Them mechanical cotton pickers out West won't come around here for a long time. We got all the labor we need—it's cheaper for us and the cotton's lots cleaner. Besides, we're raising more cattle every year, and when cotton out West gets too tough for us to match we'll just stay with the cattle. Don't know what'll happen to all the niggers then. Guess they'll have to go North—you Yankees love 'em anyway; you'll learn how to handle them, ha, ha!"

When asked if the Negroes go to school to learn about tractor-driving, the supervisor informs us, "We teach 'em all they need to know here. Some of 'em on the veterans' program go to school. They learn some machine repair, but it don't do them no good around here. School makes 'em want to get somewheres and they quit and go to the city to work in a garage. We don't use enough machines around here to need more than one or two repair men. I'm in charge of the crew, and I see that the machines are ready when we need them."

It seems that the need of the plantation is largely for unskilled labor. The few semiskilled or skilled workers that are needed can be supplied easily. Mechanization of agriculture is progressing, but the chief bottleneck remains in the chopping and picking operations. Here large Negro tenant families supply the requisite labor. Ambitious young people must seek their fortunes elsewhere.

The plantation hereabouts is girding itself for the day when gigantic cotton empires of the Southwest and the Delta, with their flat lands so amenable to mechanical pickers, force the plantation area of the Old South out of the cotton business. Recently California has also begun to present a real threat, and plantation owners from Plantation County who have travelled out West have brought back reports of enormous enterprises. While local farmers do not have a detailed picture of the foreign cotton growing and buying situation, their organization, the Farm Bureau Federation, keeps them informed, and they sense the change that is in the offing. The plantation owners consider beef cattle a safer investment for them—they provide a regular income that does not fluctuate as much as cotton. Beef cattle raising requires much less labor than cotton. The question that is posed next is what will be the effect of an enforced mass exodus of Negro and white tenants from the old cotton country. How much of the emigration will southern industry be able to absorb; what will be the effect on areas like Plantation County where the race ratio is weighted so heavily in favor of the Negroes; what will be the effect on receiving areas in the North and West?

The warehouses and gins at the center of the Sampson plantation are another index of the primacy of cotton for the plantation. These warehouses are constructed of corrugated tin, built upon piles of concrete block. The cotton gin separates the seed from the lint. Only the largest plantations maintain warehouses and gins. Most smaller farmers and planters carry their cotton to the two gins in Plantation Town or the many gins scattered about the county. The other farmers store their bales of cotton in warehouses in town where they are in turn sold to the mills through local cotton buyers and agents.

In the old days the river was the highway from plantation to port. The bales of cotton slid down the steep river banks onto barges. Then they were floated down to the Gulf where they were sold to a commission merchant for a $2\frac{1}{2}$ per cent commission fee. Most credit was centered in the cotton "factor," or commission agent, and he helped purchase the plantation's supplies at the Gulf port. Foreign and northern ships tied up here and took the bales from the commission merchant.

With the improvement in all kinds of transportation, the commission merchants in the interior began to increase their business. River City's creditors and wholesale supply houses began to supplement those at the Gulf port. Local centers now supplant the port entirely. The ante-bellum plantation could order in mass because it outfitted its slaves at periodic intervals and clothed and fed them in the same way. The post-bellum tenant, on the other hand, had to shift for himself, though he could make purchases when and where he found it most convenient. Modern transportation also brought new and better goods more frequently to the plantation commissary.

If we ask Mr. Sampson why he maintains warehouses while most of the other farmers prefer to deal with town he tells us, "The large plantation can afford to pay the insurance on wind and fire. With a large crop it pays us to wait for a good market. The smaller farmer cannot afford the insurance, and he tries to sell as soon as he finishes ginning."

But speculating on the cotton market is a gamble at best. Mr. Sampson recalls one neighbor who was "burned out" (warehouse fire), and another neighbor whose cotton sold at six cents a pound when it could have sold at forty cents. Plantation owners have been accused of profiting on the crops of their tenants when they buy them at the current market price and sell them later at a higher price. The extent of this practice was not indicated during the study of Plantation County, but it is rumored to be small. The Sampsons have direct contacts with cotton brokers throughout the Southeast; they do not have to sell through local cotton merchants. They are given advice when to sell. A few plantation owners in the vicinity are rumored to speculate on the cotton stock exchange. Their success varies—when one planter offered three thousand acres of land for sale recently, it was rumored he had lost heavily on the market.

Ginning is a seasonal operation, absorbing the period from the end of August into October and November. The ginning season finds carts and trucks filled with white cotton lined up before the tin-roofed wooden cotton gin building. The queue is the place for talk of crops and the events of the past season. On the larger plantations, owners usually supervise all the ginning and the sales of their Negro tenants, though the tenants, themselves, carry the product to the gin. The rumble of carts in the wee hours of the morning announces the beginning of the season. The roads are strewn with wisps of white lint, and all talk is about the current market prices.

Operating a Plantation 23

The ritual at the gin begins when the wagon is drawn up under a suction pipe which sucks the cotton into the machinery that separates the seed from the lint. In the meantime the clerk records the farmer's name and assigns a number to the bale. The records serve to check the quantity and quality of the product when it is offered for sale later on.

A wagonload of fifteen hundred pounds of raw cotton from the field tends to yield one bale (five hundred pounds) of lint cotton and one thousand pounds of seed. At thirty cents a pound average for lint cotton and ninety dollars a ton for the seed in 1948, the farmer makes about two hundred dollars gross for the wagonload. In the background are hours and days spent planting and plowing, chopping and picking in the hot sun. Uppermost in the farmer-tenant's mind is "settlement time" with the landowner and creditors, with perhaps a little left over to purchase food, clothing, furnishings, and a few luxury items.

The blowers and the sawteeth beat against the cotton. Then conveyers draw off the lint to a compressor where it is formed into the bale. Sweaty Negro workers place a hemp sacking about the bale and turn it about to receive a metal banding. The bale is lifted by pulley onto an iron hook to be weighed under the supervision of a white clerk. He makes a record, brands the numbers with indelible paint, and cuts out two samples for the federal government's grading agency and the buyer respectively. The ritual at the gin ends when the bale slides down a ramp to join the scores of other bales on the ground. Trailer trucks come here and haul the bales away to warehouses of the railway yards.

"Settlement time" is a period of hopes and disappointment. If the price of cotton is high, the ready cash looks good to the tenant and he does not figure his returns too closely. The year's labor and struggle is forgotten in the flood of greenbacks. The money disappears all too soon in paying off creditors, buying clothing, equipment, and the inevitable Christmas presents and notions. A good year will find Negroes "paying down" on secondhand automobiles, bicycles, and radios, only to have them taken up again when the "time" payments are forced to cease. Soon after Christmas time both the tenant and his landlord are out seeking credit again for next year's "furnishing," the tenant going to the commissary and the landlord to the banks. Debts accrue during bad years. The good years do not allow much savings. No wonder so many tenants and independent farmers quit cotton farming and turn to the cities, or to cattle raising.

There is a story told about a Negro who went to River City to have his cotton ginned and sold. The gin operator told the Negro that prices had fallen so low that the Negro owed the gin money for buying his cotton. The Negro scratched his head and said he would pay off with a chicken. The next week the Negro returned with two chickens. The gin operator asked why he had two chickens with him. The Negro replied that he had brought the extra chicken along because he had another bale of cotton to be ginned and sold.

The function of the gristmill at the center of the Sampson plantation is to grind the corn into meal, which is the mainstay in the diets of white man and Negro alike. Most corn, however, is fed to the stock—mules, hogs, cattle, and chickens. Corn is the second largest crop next to cotton. Negroes often intersperse corn with their cotton, but more often the fields are separate. Corn requires less labor than cotton and the cultivation procedure is more mechanized. The average yield for corn is less than thirty-five bushels an acre, far below that of the Midwest. Negro families in the fall of the year are seen in the tall corn pulling the ears and piling them in baskets to be taken to the cribs where they are shucked by hand and prepared for man and beast. Corn is also sold to large companies who prepare feed mixtures for animals.

Concrete silos and numerous wooden sheds and barns attest to the increasing importance of beef cattle, grasses, and home-grown feeds in Plantation County and the Black Belt. The process of raising hay and baling it is one of the most mechanized of all the operations on the plantation. The climate of the plantation area is suitable for year-round cultivation of many varieties of grasses. Stock is allowed to graze on the prairies most of the year; in cold weather they seek protection in surrounding woods or under sheds. The plantation owners and progressive farmers take advantage of the Agricultural Extension Service and the information that comes from their experiment stations. Mr. Sampson is known for his interest in such experimentation; he has several experiments being conducted on his plantation.

The Sampsons also raise some sheep, which graze on the prairies and provide some income for their meat. There is a stable where the Sampsons breed a few choice horses which generally carry away

Operating a Plantation

prizes at the saddle horse shows about the country. An artificial fish pond is used more for recreation, for fishing and swimming and picnics, than for the commercial exploitation of the fish.

The most recent phase of the plantation enterprise is represented by the creosote plant. The farmers in Plantation County are only recently beginning to realize the value of their woods. Many of them have mercilessly cut down their holdings at the beck of quick profit, but larger operators, like the Sampsons, cut their timber more selectively. The Sampsons are able to utilize the smaller hardwoods as well as the large pines. The creosote plant functions to coat fence posts that are manufactured from small hardwoods. The woods of Plantation County, in the less fertile hills and bordering the prairies, are a source of wealth. A new stand of pines grows every fifteen years. The state forestry service, in promoting forest conservation, is fighting generations of waste in the woods.

An examination of the buildings at the Sampson plantation center and their functions gives an idea of the enormity of economic activity that takes place on a large plantation. It is obvious that such an undertaking requires organization. It is here that the plantation meets the demands of the situation by a hierarchy of personnel, offices, duties, and individuals occupying statuses and playing institutionalized roles.

The economic institution is dominant, but the race-caste nature of the plantation area stratification system and its concomitant behavior patterns cannot be ignored. Most of the tenants in Plantation County are Negro, by virtue of historical factors which brought about an unbalanced ratio between the two races and which transformed Negro plantation slaves into tenants. The traditional economic status of the Negroes as tenants has also influenced race-caste behavior and beliefs. Race-caste behavior and beliefs, on the other hand, have influenced the patterns of authority and power we find at present on the plantation. We shall later note how the plantation system of authority is transmitted to other aspects of plantation area society. Added to this, Negro out-migration is changing the race ratio somewhat, and a labor shortage is causing further changes in the structure and functions of the plantation.

Mr. Sampson, as the owner and operator of his plantation, is the absolute ruler of his little empire. He is superior to his underlings by virtue of his economic wealth, social prestige, political power, educational background, and intellectual achievement and know-how. The plantation owner and his family are at the peak of the plantation area social structure. Historically they have constituted its aristocracy by virtue of their hitherto undisputed economic, social, and political power. Only recently, as we shall note further, has there been sign of a challenge from merchants, lumbermen, and cattle raisers. The plantation owner or his relatives formerly operated local stores that sufficed for the goods and credit needed by smaller farmers and townspeople. But the increase in population, especially in the services and trades occupations, has necessitated more specialized and larger stores. The growing national character of merchandising and advertising, and the advent of the chain store has led to a new form of business and commercial enterprise in the cities and towns of the plantation area. A new merchant class has risen.

The ties between town and country, merchant and farmer are close indeed, but most recently the signs of independence among the merchants of Plantation Town have begun to manifest themselves in movements to introduce new industry, a chamber of commerce, and other town-centered enterprises. The economic depression of the thirties made the merchants realize that dependence on the cotton trade alone was too risky. Lumbermen who employ whites and Negroes on a weekly pay roll and cattlemen who sell for cash throughout the year are now regarded as promoters of prosperity for Plantation County. Their prestige and influence consequently have mounted. The plantation owners can maintain their economic and social standing only as they participate in diversified enterprise. Likewise, their custom of turning profits back into the land has retarded the economic growth of the area; the new merchant and industrial group need this capital for the enterprises they are planning, and it is part of their campaign to interest the plantation owners in such economic expansion for the benefit of all groups. The campaign in Plantation County seems to be succeeding, and town and country continue to work together to promote a general prosperity.

Mr. Sampson has profited from the experiences of plantation owners who have failed to adjust to the changing conditions of the situation in agriculture. He utilizes his scientific agricultural knowledge, his farm management training, and his social relations to promote both his plantation enterprise and his personal, social, and economic advancement in the area. His family participates in local civic, religious, and educational organizations. They give to white and

Negro charities; they support political candidates and legislation that are favorable to the farmer. Most important of all, the Sampson plantation is a success because it is quick to adopt new methods of agriculture and to expand the enterprises that prove profitable.

Mr. Sampson, as plantation owner-operator, directs purchasing, marketing, and credit operations. He engages assistants to direct the other plantation enterprises, but he formulates policy. One secret of his success is "knowing his people," whom to trust with certain tasks and how far to extend credit. Mr. Sampson notes that many a plantation owner has failed because he let his tenants "charge" too much, or else he has failed to "follow through" with his supervisors. Mr. Sampson is never too busy to visit a pregnant colored woman, to "judge" a dispute between tenant neighbors, or to encourage a tenant boy to enter a calf in the county Agricultural Extension Service contest. Mr. Sampson's paternalistic relation with his "people," his knowledge of and interest in their problems, is a heritage of old slave-owning days. The motives are social and personal as well as economic. More than eighty-five years after the freeing of the slaves, the plantation owner remains the master of his land and the inhabitants of it. The race-caste rules reinforce a paternalistic employer-employee relationship in all plantation area enterprise. Farm and non-farm alike are influenced by the plantation system.

The power, prestige, and authority of the plantation owner naturally enable him to control the human factor in the situation to a degree far exceeding comparable institutions in a supposedly democratic society. The plantation remains a last vestige of beneficent despotism. The system makes for potential justice or injustice at the whim of the individual owner. It takes a God-fearing and noble person to administer impartially among the tenants and wage-hands on the place. The plantation owner who abuses his power is called to account only by the dissatisfaction of tenants and wage-hands, and even here there are debtor laws which forbid freedom of movement of persons in debt. A plantation owner's popularity can be judged by the labor turnover he experiences. Negroes for miles around know the reputation of a landlord for fairness at "settlement time" or in judging disputes. The semiliterate Negro, by rational or non-rational means, calls his landlord to account by gossip or by quitting. The rules of race-caste behavior prevent more obvious retaliation such as might be had through the courts.

The white employees on the plantation are directly responsible to

Mr. Sampson. They are given directives; at the same time, however, the plantation owner must sustain their prestige in the eyes of the tenants and wage hands. Mr. Sampson cites the case of an overseer who "had it in" for a Negro worker. The plantation grants bonuses for good work during the week, and the Negro was trying his best to earn one. Try as he would, the award went to somebody else. The Negro finally quit the plantation in disgust. Mr. Sampson had to acquiesce in the loss of this good worker, for he could not challenge the decision of his overseer before the Negroes. Only in private did he berate the overseer for his lack of fairness and judgment. Mr. Sampson says, "The worker has to respect the boss, and the chief has to back up the boss all the way." The fact that the immediate lieutenants are all whites makes it easier to control the workers, who are all Negroes. Mr. Sampson previously employed some Negro overseers, but he feels that the workers respect the whites more. Most plantation owners, on the other hand, have little to do with white tenants or laborers. They usually say, "They represent a disgrace to the white race, and you can't control them like you can a nigger." Race-pride and power tend to be the chief reasons for the whites holding positions of authority in the plantation area and Negroes occupying subordinate positions even when they might be quite capable in higher positions.

The white employees on the plantation enjoy the "privileges of their race" in an area where the Negro is subordinate and outnumbers the whites four to one. Among themselves, the white employees are of lower middle or lower class. They are educated through grade school and sometimes high school. They earn wages equivalent to other service personnel in the area. Their living quarters consist of frame cottages of a simple sort, typical of the houses of small white farmers or lower middle class workers in the county. The specialists among the white employees include the accountant and bookkeeper, the mechanic, the cattle foreman, carpenter, and others of the type. There is also need for foremen who know something about farming in general, and can "work" wage hands. These persons are invariably drawn from white farmer or tenant groups.

The Negro overseer is the highest Negro position on the plantation. This group has diminished considerably with the decline in tenant families and as the plantation owner has come to prefer white supervisors. Many Negro overseers have found it more profitable to establish themselves on farms of their own. Others have quit agriculture altogether for life in the town or city. With the passage of time, the Negro overseer is being replaced by the Negro straw boss, who is under the direct supervision of a white overseer.

The Negro straw boss occupies a position on the plantation that is not too stable or secure. He is often called a "white man's nigger" where he has worked for the white man against the best interest of his own race. In the days when all the Negroes were slaves, the straw boss was rewarded with better food and quarters, and he relieved his frustrations by aggression against his underlings. Today, most plantation owners agree, the successful straw boss must maintain the respect of his workers, he must show them how the job is done by actually working with them. The supervisor stands about and gives orders; the straw boss is the pacemaker. His reward is extra credit at the commissary and the prestige of office. Straw bosses are generally selected if they seem to be the natural leaders of the Negro group and if they are good workers. Mr. Sampson notes the necessity for guarding against straw bosses who side with the Negroes and try to "put it over" the landlord. He has found through experience that very reliable pacemakers are to be found among bonded criminals. They are beholden to the landlord and are usually good workers.

The position of the straw boss, who leads the labor gangs in the cotton and corn fields, on construction jobs, and the like, is to serve the white man and at the same time inspire the black man. If he becomes known as a "white man's nigger," he loses prestige in the Negro community. If he sides with the Negroes, the white man can no longer use him. No wonder the white man has been moving into positions of supervision as the Negroes become more independent with the generations. Fewer of them are now willing to be "white man's niggers."

The Negro specialist—the tractor driver, mechanic, cattleman, or carpenter—enjoys a prestige somewhat lower than the straw boss, yet he is in a position much freer from anxiety. He works in a creative manner, his services are in demand, and his prestige rises as his bosses praise his work. The specialists may be under the direction of a white supervisor, as in the case of construction workers or cattlemen, or they may come directly under the tutelage of the plantation owner, as do the servants about the house. The more permanent and necessary the specialty, the higher the prestige attached to it. Yet there is a limitation on the number of specialists needed on the plantation. This has led to considerable dissatisfaction among Negro youth who have had some education. Their recourse is to leave the plantation for town or for the city.

Negro cash tenants enjoy a higher status than share tenants. The ordinary unskilled wage laborer is at the bottom of the hierarchy. The cash renter is most independent. Larger plantations rent land for cash either because a landlord is absent or because the owner-operator cannot supervise and farm all his acres. In all cases of cash or rental by a fixed amount of cotton the landlord furnishes cabin, land, and fuel-gathering privileges. The number of cash tenants is decreasing since mechanization of agriculture, but more especially because of the conversion of cotton acreage to pasture for beef cattle.

Share tenants operate under different arrangements. The half-crop share system is one in which the landlord furnishes the tools, work stock, seed, feed, and one-half the fertilizer. The tenant furnishes his labor and one-half the fertilizer and receives one-half the value of the yield. Where the tenant pays the landlord one-fourth or one-third of the crop, the tenant furnishes his labor, work stock, feed, tools, seed, and three-fourths or two-thirds of the fertilizer. The landlord furnishes one-fourth or one-third of the fertilizer, in addition to the land, house, and fuel-gathering privileges. The greater financial investment the landlord has in the tenant's cotton crop, the closer his supervision, and the more likely he is to market the tenant's crop. During good years the tenants prefer cash rental. In hard times they desire lint or share rental.

Mr. Sampson says he is employing more wage hands now than formerly. "My tenants have taken off for the war industries and the sawmills. I miss their labor, but at the same time I am putting more land into pasture. I can now plant a lot of those tenant farms myself. The cattle don't need as much labor as cotton, and the more machines I use, the less labor I'll need. I can use a few good tractor drivers and mechanics, also a crew of laborers. But I dread the time when those tenants who left come knocking at my door after their city jobs close down. Some of the plantation owners around here have torn down the cabins to make way for pasture. The wages nowadays are $1.50—lots higher than the fifty cents a day we paid before the war. But the price of cotton is higher too. We manage all right."

Operating a Plantation

When asked about the future of such profitable plantation enterprises as the commissary, Mr. Sampson shakes his head. "The store is a service to the people here. It's a fair little business, but town's beginning to compete with me, and the accounting sometimes gets to be more than it's worth." But a seven- to ten-thousand-dollar-a-year net profit enterprise might not be thrown away that fast. Perhaps the total conversion to cattle raising and wage farm hands will not proceed too rapidly.

The plantation area has not yet faced the problem of the "landless" tenant or the migratory laborer. The meanest share tenant feels he has a stake in the land he has rented. He can usually stay on his plot of land as long as he wishes. Yet the trends of the time are forcing a squeeze-out of the tenant class between the specialist and the ordinary wage laborer.

Our description of the Sampson plantation reveals an economic enterprise operating in its fullest capacity in the postwar period. From the heart of the plantation as a base of operations, we have attempted to cover many facets of economic life. Operating a plantation is big business, and like most businesses, the plantation must have adequate organization to enable it to operate with maximum efficiency and profit.

Our analysis of the chain of command and the social structure reveals factors at work which do not seem to encourage maximum efficiency. Race-caste behavior sustains an historical paternalism, with concomitant features of ignorance, dependency, and a lack of initiative on the part of the Negroes. The historical slave-operated plantation lives on today in the authority and prestige of the plantation owner. Likewise the Negro remains at the bottom of the social and economic scale. The two extremes of the scale are complementary.

But we also note that the situation is changing—cotton is being dethroned in favor of beef cattle raising. The Negro is leaving the plantation for town. Mechanization of agriculture is on the upswing. The merchant, the cattleman, and the lumber operator are achieving status coextensive with the plantation owner. Although the plantation as a social and economic system has influenced the plantation area in all of its history, the changing times are forcing the plantation itself to readjust. We now turn to a discussion of these changes which ultimately will influence all phases of life in the plantation area.

3

THE CHANGING PLANTATION

PERHAPS our trip to the Sampson Plantation has dispelled some of the visions of plantation life that have been conjured up by the romanticists. Lest we judge all the plantations in the county to be as well adjusted to changing times as the Sampson plantation, however, we had better make further investigation.

Our culture-structure-function theory holds that human beings behave, not in a vacuum, but in specifiable situations. They are always required to make adjustments to the changing conditions presented by these situations. The way of life, or culture, they practice is the socially-learned, socially-shared, and socially-transmitted patterned activity by which they adjust to changes in the natural, social, or psychological phenomena about them.

People in the plantation area are no exception, and they are required to make continual adjustments to changing conditions. We have seen how these people occupy certain status positions with concomitant duties, obligations, and expectations, both as to behavior and rewards. For example, the plantation owner has a paternalistic relationship with his tenants; he receives prestige and power by this position; both plantation owners and tenants perform expected institutional roles; the reward for the Negro tenant may be only protection and lack of punishment, nevertheless it is sufficient to keep him playing his role. When it becomes insufficiently rewarding, he will quit tenancy or desert the plantation.

We shall demonstrate here how economic roles, fostered by the plantation system, tend to dominate all other roles, whether social, religious, educational, political, or familial in the plantation area. Where there is a conflict among roles, the economic tends to dominate. Many changes occurring in the plantation area which affect all areas of life tend to be successful primarily because they are economically rewarding for the performers.

We shall note how the changing conditions of the situation with respect to the plantation require continuous adjustment on the part of plantation owners, their families, tenants, and other members of the society. The definitions of statuses and roles, their rights, duties, and expectations, are also in a state of change. We shall note the consequences of these changes for the social structure in the plantation area. We are likewise interested in whether these new patterns of activity are compatible with the components of the situation, if there is consistency among the internal levels of behavior (mental, representational, actional). Where there is conflict among roles and goals, we shall note tensions, anxieties, and the attempts of the people to achieve some *modus vivendi* which is more rewarding than other ways of life for them.

A diversified program of agriculture seems to be one of the main necessities for adjustment to the changes in the natural component in the situation. Likewise it is necessitated by changes in the culture-contact or foreign component of the situation—new areas of cotton raising, federal agricultural programs, and the like. The following examples will show how adjustment varies with varying rewards and consequences for the structure.

The Jackson-Dolphin plantation of forty-five hundred acres is perhaps a smaller version of the Sampson plantation. Here are the traditional row crops and the more recently developed pasture and woodlands. The Negro tenants who live in cabins along the roadways rent their farms, for the most part, for a bale of cotton a year. A smaller proportion are share tenants, since Mr. Jackson has not reached the point where he can farm most of his land himself. The Jackson-Dolphin plantation has fewer enterprises than the Sampson place—no cotton gin, silo, cotton warehouses, saddle horse stables, or timber operation. Historically, while the Sampson plantation represents the consolidation of several smaller plantations and farms following the Civil War, the Jacksons have had their plantation for many generations. The Dolphin place is a recent addition.

The histories of the Jackson and Dolphin plantations demonstrate how the need for adjusting to new components of the situation brought the present Mr. Jackson to purchase the Dolphin place.

Although the original Jackson holdings once comprised several thousand acres of good river land, the division of the land among sons and daughters and grandchildren has eventually reduced individual holdings to about fifteen hundred acres each. This applies to heirs who have decided to continue farming the land; others have sold their shares to kinspeople or else they are receiving annual rental. New estates have been formed through marriage and purchase. Some wills forbid the division of property, and such entailed property is thus kept off the market. Those descendants who do not wish to farm usually entrust the care of the property to relatives and receive a rental. Some absentee landownership has resulted from this form of inheritance, with the result that unsupervised tenants soon reduce the soil to low levels of productivity. Entailed properties prevent the spread of scientific farming; they retard the breakup of old plantations or the development of small or large holdings into cattle farms.

In the case of the Jackson plantation, however, the exigencies of the situation demanded more land, so that the present Mr. Jackson and his grown sons might operate a family plantation. The need of the Jacksons was met when the Dolphin plantation came up for sale, and some three thousand acres were added to the family's holdings. The fact that the Dolphin plantation was a typically old-style operation explains first, why it came up for sale, and secondly, what had to be done by the Jacksons to make it adjust to the requirements of the times.

We discussed in the first chapter how plantations in the beginning of white settlement first developed by the river. Here was the best land and a direct route to the Gulf ports. The Dolphin plantation had the disadvantage before the turn of the century of being some three or four miles from the river. This obstacle was overcome only with the change to railway and road transportation. The Mr. Dolphin of Civil War days had nearly failed; only the perseverence of his son saved the place. A son was willed the plantation over the protests of his brothers and sisters who felt cheated out of their property. Friends say, however, that there would have been no plantation at all "if all that hard work hadn't been put into the place."

Unlike the two-storied modified colonial home of the Sampsons, the Dolphin plantation house was single storied, of white plank, with a front porch, high ceiling, central hallway, and a kitchen in the rear, detached from the main house. This is the traditional form of the small plantation house in the area. (See drawing, page 16.)

Mr. Dolphin farmed in the days when cotton reigned supreme and labor was plentiful. He had over one hundred Negro tenants, and most of these on shares. His cotton was carried to the gin in Plantation Town and sold to the warehouse buyer there. He "advanced" to his tenants and supervised their work and rented out the cropland he could not farm himself. Mr. Dolphin had only a few cattle. His interest in the timber that grew there was slight. When cotton prices were high, he and his tenants "prospered." When the boll weevil and the depression hit, they had to tighten their way of living. Mr. Dolphin was paternalistic toward his tenants, granting them credit, judging their disputes, caring for the sick and the aged among them, and helping with the rude school building and churches on the place when the occasion demanded.

The boll weevil epidemic during the second decade of this century and the depression of the thirties hit Mr. Dolphin along with his neighbors. When the federal government during the late thirties offered to purchase some plantation land to set up a Farm Security Administration (F.S.A.) tenant-purchase project, Mr. Dolphin acquiesced in the sale and saw some dozen-odd Negro families try to make a go of renting and purchasing their own small farms. Today this particular settlement project is one of several in the county representing a small-farm trend away from the plantation.

Mr. Dolphin recovered financially during the later thirties. He had moved into Plantation Town some years before, and now he built a beautiful white colonial town house with towering columns and a winding interior staircase in the very center of the hall. Mr. Dolphin rode his horse daily to the plantation, but in his later years he found a truck more convenient. Old age and hard work finally caught up with him, and he died in 1945.

The plantation, as we have seen, is a highly organized business. It requires constant supervision to be a success. The Dolphin widow was in her sixties, and she felt unable to manage such a large enterprise. Unlike the majority of people in Plantation County who regard property in land as the *sine qua non* of security and prestige, Mrs. Dolphin reckoned with the wartime real estate boom and decided to sell her land. Her stipulation, however, was that the property should be sold intact. The townspeople wondered who would purchase such a large piece of property and at inflationary prices. They talked frequently of risks involved in such a venture.

Fifteen hundred acres of the Jackson plantation might very well have supported Mr. Jackson and his family, but they would not have held his children to Plantation County once they were grown and had begun to raise families of their own. Unlike his neighbors who watched their sons and daughters leave for other parts of the South, Mr. Jackson saw a solution to his problem in the purchase of the Dolphin place. One son had already found government work in agriculture and had married. Another was helping his father on the plantation. The third was serving his apprenticeship as a veterinarian in various sections of the state, and he needed more than the Plantation County practice to bring him home. The wartime price of cotton had risen to thirty cents a pound, and it seemed that this price might hold for several years. Mr. Jackson had been following the trends in farming and was introducing more Hereford cattle and timber cutting. He felt that the Dolphin plantation would yield a good income if developed properly. Thus he took the chance and plunged into a purchase that returned him to the debt he had cancelled at the close of the depression. He was gambling on perhaps a half dozen prosperous years from 1946 in order to pay off the mortgage. With his three sons and with a program of more cattle raising, Mr. Jackson felt that he could meet his obligations.

"Mister Ralph," as his Negroes and white friends called him, moved the Jackson plantation store from its old location near the river to the center of the Dolphin plantation near the old Dolphin homestead. "Little Ralph," his son, who manages the cattle and the "outside work," now lives in the "old house" on the Dolphin place with his wife and baby. Martin returned from government work and the war, and he is now in charge of the commissary and the bookkeeping. He has built himself a temporary bungalow near the store, and his wife divides her time between social welfare work in Plantation Town and housekeeping. This arrangement is typical of young married women with professional training who are helping out their struggling husbands and at the same time are meeting a shortage of professional persons in the county. Martin hopes some day to build a large home and to rent the bungalow to a white tenant or overseer. The little house has a bedroom, kitchen, living room, and bathroom. Martin did most of the planning himself, and he and local labor did the building at a cost less than $1500 at 1947 rates. The bungalow is furnished with effects from the Jackson plantation house.

The third son, Tom, lives with his parents on the Jackson plantation and does veterinary medical work from a newly built cement block office headquarters in Plantation Town. He attends his father's cattle sales weekly at the local auction place.

Mister Ralph now supervises the outside work, especially the field crops Little Ralph likes to trade in mules in Plantation Town. He has stalls near the veterinary office of his brother. Mister Ralph says that of his three sons, Little Ralph is a "natural" trader, Martin loves the soil, and Tom is the manager and planner. Mister Ralph is waiting for the day when his three sons will take over the complete operation of the plantation, and he believes things will work out all right.

Comparing the operation of the Jackson-Dolphin plantation to the Sampson place, we note that both owners are operators, and they are dressed for work in the field. The Jackson-Dolphin plantation is a smaller enterprise, and rather than employing white supervisors, the sons divide the managerial aspects of the work. This makes the Jackson-Dolphin place more of a group enterprise, but the Sampson plantation will also develop in this direction as Mr. Sampson's children begin to take over certain aspects of the farm management.

Half of the hundred tenants who were on the old Dolphin plantation have left since the war and postwar period to join urban industry. When asked about this, Mr. Jackson says, "I'm not sorry they're gone. I'm planning in due time to take over those tenant farms near the road and make pasture out of them. It'll take labor to clear the land, but I'll get it from the tenant families or from wage hands. I'm glad a lot of my tenants are working at the sawmills. It gives them some cash; I can't hire them all year around. When I need labor, I only have to pass the word around and they usually send someone. I give them a house and a little land for a garden; they see that I have workers at chopping and picking time. Their women and children can work here even if the daddy works in town."

This symbiotic relationship between part-time sawmill activity and the plantation works well for both. The plantation owner does not have to advance as much credit as he would for farmer Negroes who are idle much of the year; he gets a labor supply when he needs it; and the Negro has a place to live, place for a garden, and work when he wants it. Of course, there is pressure on the tenant to supply labor for the plantation, but rents in town are higher, and conditions more crowded. By living on the plantation, these tenants also sustain the commissary, which Mister Ralph admits is a profitable business. The traditional opposition of the plantation owners to industry in the county is partially alleviated when they see that their labor supply is not threatened.

Although he would like to see most of the plantation converted to cattle raising, Mister Ralph says he would not displace any of the tenants who are now on the place. "They've been with me and my father before me. You get attached to them when you've grown up together." The motives of altruism and profit from labor and the commissary are fused in the changing plantation. Cattle raising means higher profits with less labor; cotton requires more labor, but also profits in the plantation store and a prestige of command. Thus we see forces for change balancing forces for conservatism.

Plantation County farmers have a slogan to the effect that for success in the cattle business, "you have to grow your own feed." Mr. Jackson is expanding his cattle interests only as he is able to keep pace in clearing land for pasture. A December trip to the plantation in 1947 revealed Little Ralph on a tractor, hauling bales of hay to the barn, while a crew of six Negro wage hands operated a baler powered by another tractor. This hay served well during an unusual January snow storm and freeze.

Mister Ralph began his large-scale cattle investments with a ten thousand dollar loan from the Plantation County Cattlemen's Association of which he is a member. He purchased two hundred head of cattle at the local stockyard and put them out to fatten. Two years later, in 1948, he sold ninety-one head to pay back the loan. Some of these cattle were of low quality stock, but Mister Ralph is beginning to concentrate on registered stock. He also plans to increase his hog production by introducing quality stock. Though there will always be cotton, Mister Ralph intends to use most of his labor clearing pasture. He also wants to survey his woods and prepare them for production by selective cutting.

Mister Ralph has definite ideas about manager-tenant relations. "When a tenant makes money he works better. When I make money, I also see to it that my tenants make money."

The plantation owner must be concerned with the welfare of his tenants. "You have to give an old woman a cabin and some garden space, else the others will think you don't care for them and they'd either leave or they'd be unhappy and wouldn't work so well." Security is one of the traditional features of the plantations paternalism. While older operators like Mister Ralph recognize the obligations to tenants in old age, we shall see that an increasing role of government in old-age welfare is displacing much of the traditional cradle-to-grave guardianship of Negro life by the whites. "Everybody" admits that Negroes are becoming more independent of whites. At the same time the whites are replacing *noblesse oblige* with modern personnel methods which are more businesslike and efficient.

On the Jackson plantation the owner still provides a pine coffin for a tenant funeral and pays the burial expense. Negro church members come to the plantation owner for contributions to their small treasury. But the plantation schoolhouse is beginning to undergo a change as state education laws are gradually enforced; the county has taken over most of the little shacks of schools on the plantations; as old buildings burn down or are torn down, consolidation is taking place.

Mister Ralph eyes some of the signs of the times with cynicism and also with fear. "If my tenants saved all they made during these war years they'd soon own Plantation County. It's just as well," he observes, "they spend all they make, and nobody is going to encourage them to do otherwise." Mister Ralph, like his plantation owner neighbors, is constantly worried about the possible organization of labor by unions. Strangers in Plantation County are under suspicion of being "organizers" or "communists" until they can prove otherwise.

The increasing role of government, especially the federal government since New Deal days, is of concern to Mister Ralph. He is not so large an operator that federal loans are not appreciated and used, yet he feels that "government is getting too much power over people." As a member of the board of recommendation for the local Farmers Home Administration office, Mister Ralph feels that the tenant-purchasers are "pampered" by the government. Perhaps this antagonism comes from the fact that these small farm units of the F.H.A. have been carved from plantations that could not survive the depression and were purchased by the federal government; the rise of Negroes as small farmers is also contrary to their traditional status as tenants.

Negro advance is praised especially when tenants put up fences or wallpaper their homes. Mister Ralph gives them credit for this, and major improvements are reckoned in final settlements. The industrious Negroes are employed as pacemakers for the others in a sort of straw boss arrangement.

But Negro advance, to the extent that he seeks further education and economic opportunities, begins to worry Mister Ralph. He may say that when he prospers his tenants should also prosper, but he fears their learning to save. He fears they will aspire to goods and services traditionally reserved for the white man. There is an inconsistency in the whites' giving money to Negro schools (however poorly they compare to white educational contributions) and at the same time expecting the Negro to remain satisfied with his subordinate status. As the Negro laborer quits the plantation, Mister Ralph sees the traditional power of the whites threatened. The desire on the part of plantation owners to have a body of Negroes to control is a force for conservatism; forces for change would convert the cotton plantations to cattle farms. While the whites continue to oppose Negro independence in social, economic, and political spheres, improved Negro educational standards and the influence of national mass culture, through movies, books, newspapers, Civil Rights, and the like, encourage the Negroes to shake off the domination of the whites. The whites are plainly confused and worried. Their programs of action (or reaction) neither halt the trends nor quiet the antagonism of the outside world.

The student of Plantation County history will be impressed with the record of the Carroll family who settled here during the 1830's. The original Carroll settler came from the Atlantic Seaboard where he was a cotton planter in the old tradition. His diaries in Plantation County are replete with advice to his son about such problems as the proper care of slaves, the planting of crops, supervising of overseers, and the marketing of cotton. The Carrolls seem to have had their heyday a decade before the outbreak of the Civil War. This is the date of the five Carroll plantation houses, all grand mansions employing classical and Greek revival motifs in the columns, doorposts, and the friezes. Some of these homes were two-storied, but the single-storied homes were no less impressive.

Two of the houses have succumbed to fire, so that only three are left. Remains of the others are to be seen in the form of lone chimneys standing in vacant fields. The surviving homes are now inhabited by members of the family or outside purchasers who maintain them to varying degrees. The descendants of the original Carroll settlers have had their ups and downs with the years. The fifth generation descendants carry on such diverse occupations as row crop and cattle farming, mail route driving, bank cashiering, home-keeping, and just plain loafing. A great many of the Carrolls have quit Plantation County and rural life for city ways.

When the fortunes of a certain Mr. Carroll at the end of the nineteenth century took a turn for the worse, he sold the most beautiful of all the Carroll plantation homes to Mr. Hughes, a farmer. Rumors about Plantation County suggest that the home was sold to pay off debts incurred at horse races, at the gambling tables of the river boats, or at gamecocking, a sport which flourished during the middle nineteenth century.

The Hughes family has tried its best to retain the original beauty of the home. Some etchings, which were willed to the family by a famous artist relative, highlight the bare walls. Servants are impossible to get these days because of the labor shortage and the relatively high cost (treble the depression wages of fifty cents a day). There are only Victorian pieces of furniture in the house, rather utilitarian and out of place. Mrs. Hughes is being worn down gradually by the burden of keeping up the appearance of the nineteen-room mansion, especially since it is a show place for the countryside.

In the days when the mansion was built, there were numerous Negro slaves to carry in wood and to light early morning fires, to sweep, mop, and wax floors. Today only four or five of the rooms are in use. One of the half dozen chimneys can be seen smoking during the winter months. Life in a high-ceilinged mansion is pleasant enough in summertime, but in the humid cold of winter the plantation family must huddle about a wood or kerosene stove in one or two rooms on the ground floor.

Mr. Hughes seems to have made a better adjustment in working the land than his family has with the plantation house. He has gone in heavily for cattle raising since tenants are scarce and cotton raising has been too risky. He has a sawmill in the woods and sells the boards which he manufactures from his stands of pine. He is a practical farmer and a businessman, while his wife, quite typical of plantation area women, glories in memories of the Old South.

It would seem that the women of the plantation area are more interested than the men in antiquities. In another Carroll mansion, not far from the Hughes', a white haired woman of seventy-five, her son, his wife, and their children, make a living off the land and dwell in this citadel of memories.

The home is not quite so large as the Hughes', but it is in an excellent state of repair. Much of the furniture is antique, and it seems to fit in well with the tradition-laden atmosphere. Old family portraits hang on the walls. The old servant entrances are in use. Each room functions as it was originally planned. The plaster on the walls, though peeling in spots, tends to remain good. The floors have been refinished and glisten in their natural pine. The original appearance of the outside is preserved by a white coat of paint and red composite roofing.

One can understand the responsibility for this outstanding work of preservation and restoration on meeting Mrs. Warner, the old mistress of the house. She is an active member of the Daughters of the American Revolution, the United Daughters of the Confederacy, and other patriotic societies. She participates in her community Home Demonstration Club and in the Plantation Town Culture Club (a unit of the Federation of Women's Clubs). Mrs. Warner is active in Presbyterian church circle meetings, and throughout all her activity she moves with poise and dignity. Her snow-white hair and light clothing become her age and aristocratic nature.

It is outside the plantation home, beyond the flower beds and women's care, that one begins to note the changes and innovations of the present. Artificial fishponds near the house are a feature of the federal government's agriculture program to increase the use of fish in the diet. Mr. Warner, the son, aged forty, is a "born" wild turkey hunter and fisherman. Like the average man of the plantation area, he is an outdoor man, perpetually clothed in cotton tans and a battered felt hat. He sees to his tractors and tools at the rear of the house and is forever opening and closing barbed wire fence-gates to keep in the livestock.

Old Mrs. Warner and her children hold an estate of some four thousand acres of land. But again, as we have noted previously, it is cattle rather than cotton that has become the main investment for the future. Most of the Warner tenants are gone; old cotton fields have been converted to rich pasture land.

Mr. Warner's wife is also a woman of the present and the future. The family has been hard put to keep up the house and to pay off the debts of the depression. A former school teacher—one of many who have come to Plantation County to teach, then marry, and stay— young Mrs. Warner works in the local bank and contributes her share toward keeping the home in the tradition of the past, while the land serves as an investment in the present and for the future.

Although they are related by blood to some of the larger plantation owners in the county, the Warners share their social life with the smaller plantation owners on their own economic level. Permission for their daughter to marry a school teacher in town bespeaks perhaps a need for financial security above that of preserving the romantic state of plantation owner class.

The foregoing comments on the various adjustment problems of the Carrolls of today show that there must be adjustment to life in the home and the community as well as to the land. Four miles out from Plantation Town there is a fallen-in unpainted house that seems like a ghost out of the past. The visitor is told that this was the home of the Oberlins, once a prominent plantation owner family in the county. The visitor does not recall having heard of Oberlins among present-day owner-operators; he is left to deduce, quite correctly, that the family has died out and lost its holdings.

The Oberlin sisters were educated in Europe during the latter days of the nineteenth century. The music from their spinet drifted through the high-ceilinged central hallway and out the doors of the large house. The sisters had Negro servants who drove them on sunny afternoons to visit with other ladies of their circle.

Their father's death committed the sisters to the charge of the plantation and the home. Since they were incapable of farming it themselves, they rented out most of the land to tenants. Ancient notes, bills, receipts, and old letters in the rubbish pile in a corner of the old dilapidated house of today attest to the ravages of erosion, the boll weevil, and the economic depression. Eventually the sisters were reduced to a state where old friends had to superintend provision for their old age.

A visit to the wreck of a once handsome structure finds the high grass in front a hindrance to full view. No vestige remains of once tenderly cared for flowers and shrubs. Where windows were once daintily curtained with lace, the glass is now shattered and shutters swing off rusty hinges. Old whiskey and beer bottles stand on the sills and in corners, the remains of clandestine drinking bouts and parties of today. The interior walls are bare with their natural finish remaining only in spots. The good pine has not yet rotted, but it may if the roof is not repaired. The house is abandoned, and the only life about is that of a poor white family that occupies a trailer in the front yard.

The sisters left their small souvenirs to relatives and friends who had stood by them in the later years of their distressful life. Some feuds developed among these relatives and friends, the latter including some Carrolls who had boarded with the second sister and had attended her at her deathbed. These Carrolls were willed the house and property; it is rumored they will tear down the house because no one will live in it.

One of the most gracious acts of Miss Oberlin was to grant five acres fronting the road to a poor white family who had nursed her. This brought down the wrath of plantation owner neighbors who did not wish these new people in their midst. These people, however, built themselves a frame house and continue to live there unmindful of the others. Miss Oberlin also granted a faithful Negro servant couple their house and garden for the remainder of their lives. This is a common practice among paternalistic white plantation folk.

If the tangible evidences of ruin are present in the old plantation house of the Oberlins, at least the beauty of the past is preserved in those antiques which recline in the corners of many plantation homes in the county. Neither house nor land has been able to readjust to the times; only the spirit of the past survives in antiques.

These cases of partial adjustment contrast sharply with the Jackson-Dolphin and Sampson programs of expansion and diversification. While Mr. Jackson was faced with natural problems like erosion and the boll weevil, by the economic depression and the loss of labor, plus a desire to provide opportunity for his sons, he grappled with the situation realistically by a program of hard work, shrewd investment, and by introducing the latest methods of scientific agriculture, including mechanization and diversification. He utilized capital funds both from the federal government and from local sources. As a leader in his community, he has maintained his status even while undertaking a venture as uncertain of its outcome as the Dolphin plantation. Most of all, Mr. Jackson did not live in the past—he has always been planning for the future.

The Carroll family and their associates represent attempts at adjustment which are only partial. Another case is a complete failure, primarily because the Oberlin sisters had neither the ability nor the will to leave the traditional ways for new patterns of activity. The farmers, in the other instances, seem to adjust adequately to the natural and culture-contact components of the situation by adopting recent diversified scientific agricultural techniques. But the women continue to revere the past, chiefly maintaining houses that are inadequate from the point of view of financing, comfort, or meeting social needs in reduced financial circumstances. The women refuse to compromise social status which is symbolized by the plantation house with the new economic status they actually have because of the nature of their husband's farming operations. They even work outside the home to maintain their traditional positions. The men seem much more rustic than the women; they seem closer to nature and to the demands of the present world of economic competition; the women tend to be aware of social competition and rely on the symbols of the past to retain their status. Outside employment of an approved sort does not compromise the position of these women. The reverence for symbols of the past bolsters their morale as they go through one economic crisis after another. The men have an outlet in hunting and fishing.

The women of the plantation area have long shouldered economic burdens with their husbands—coming in wagons through the frontier, maintaining plantations while their husbands fought for the Confederacy. They are able to continue their tie with the past by working for wages in a world of the present. Yet this very desire to save a remnant of the past may be significant in the struggle going on today in the South to maintain its traditional way of white supremacy for which the plantation has been the greatest symbol, and white womanhood the prize.

The Hartley farm represents a different solution to the problems of the changing conditions in the plantation area. While it shows some plantation survivals, there are few of the old symbols in evidence. Mr. Hartley's farm was worthless chalk land some fifty years ago. Nothing but the determination of a man existed in those days, but today one finds a community of white wooden houses and barns where a cattle and seed business is carried on.

Mr. Hartley first came to these parts at a time when all the land was bound to cotton and tenancy. At first he followed this tradition of farming, but only until new ideas could be adapted. Mr. Hartley decided that his twenty-five hundred acres of chalk land were not meant to produce poor stands of cotton. Besides, he had not been raised in the plantation tradition, and grasses interested him more.

The townspeople shook their heads as Mr. Hartley walked to

town, stopping by the roadside to pick grasses and stuff the seed in his gunny sack. It was not at all in the tradition of the land-owner of Plantation County. The trips netted dividends for Mr. Hartley, however. He graded the high quality seed and began to sell it to the farmers of the Black Belt who were beginning at that time to raise grass-fed cattle.

Mr. Hartley did not stop at grasses. He invested in a few registered Herefords which in time became purebred herds that are known today through the Southeast and beyond. The first cattle to be raised in Plantation County were usually of mediocre stock. Mr. Hartley's purebreds were signs along the way to a major shift in agricultural emphasis to grass and to thoroughbred cattle.

Mrs. Hartley helped her husband in his enterprise. She was an Episcopalian, he a Baptist, but she shared in the work of the Baptist church in Plantation Town and contributed to its development and expansion. At home she supervised the running of the house, reared her sons and daughters to follow the path of their father, and even found time to tend to the post office that was opened in the new community. She did not neglect other community affairs, either. She could be counted upon to lead women's clubs, church groups, and to donate to charitable endeavors around the county.

Mr. Hartley's frugal and experimental ways were followed by his two sons who grew up to the management of the farm. They were educated at the State College of Agriculture and have participated in all community agricultural and civic activities. After their father's death, they divided the work between them, one taking the administrative duties, and the other looking after the outdoor work with cattle and seeds.

Unlike century-old frame dwellings and the survivals of tenant cabins of the plantation, the buildings on the Hartley farm are neat white frame bungalows, freshly painted and screened. These modest homes of white employees appear to be modern and clean. There are flowers in the front yards and vegetable gardens and chickens in the rear. There is running water and electricity, and the employees generally live like other salaried families in the area who make fifteen to twenty-five hundred dollars a year.

The homes of the Hartley brothers are very much like the modern plantation house of the Sampsons. The resemblance to American middle class magazine illustrations is apparent in the organization of

The Changing Plantation

the household and in the furnishings. The Hartley wives and the Hartley children participate in town and country activities very much like the Sampsons. They have connections with other plantation-owning families in and about the plantation area through friendship and marriage.

The children in the Hartley community are closer to each other than the women. The children play together and attend the same consolidated school in town. But the Hartley children also play host quite often to children from Plantation Town, and they visit in town more often than their playmates who are children of white employees. The wives of owners and employees visit each other only in times of distress. The interest of the Mrs. Hartleys is divided largely between farm and town, while the employees' wives are more nearly farm-centered. Also, since most of the employees are not native to this area, there is a trek "home" for week-end and holiday visits. Thus neither a strong community solidarity nor loyalty is developed, and relations between the employees' families and Plantation Town are also impaired. They seem at most to be temporary residents. Such ties as exist with the Hartley farm are largely economic and play-group bonds. The church, movies, school, and shopping facilities not provided by the farm's general store, are found in Plantation Town.

The position of the Negroes on the Hartley farm differs considerably from the whites. The Negroes have lived here for generations, tilling the plantation soil since before the days of cattle and pastures. They have a community school and church, small to be sure, but nevertheless made up of old and established families. The change in Negro life has largely been centered in economics. Many have emigrated, and the twenty or so families who have remained have been put largely on wages.

The Hartley farm differs from the traditional plantation in its emphasis on pasture, its reduced need for labor, and the prevalence of wage hands as against share tenancy. The selection of wage hands from among the tenants is a throwback to the plantation, and is in fact a noticeable trend throughout this area. Negro hands on the Hartley farm are employed throughout the year at an hourly rate. The difference between the Hartley and the Sampson interests is most marked in the symbol of the time punch-card system at the work center on the Hartley farm. Each worker, white and Negro, records his hours of work and receives payment for same. Note how this differs from the traditional plantation where an overseer directs labor with little thought as to hours worked or tasks to be performed, where the payment is either in scrip which is good only at the local commissary or a share in the cotton at the end of the season.

The Hartleys pay wages to the Negroes which vary from fifteen to thirty cents an hour, depending on the job. While this seems low compared to town values or to farm labor wages in other areas, the Negroes are also supplied with housing and garden space. The Hartleys plan to construct a community of cement block permanent dwellings for the Negroes, the first of their kind in the county. The new dwellings will sound the final knell to the old plantation and the tenant system with traditional plank cabins, kerosene light, and fireplace heat. As rural electrification is extended it will reach the new homes of the Negro help as well. The patches of cotton and corn which continue to grow by the wayside are the side work of the Negro wage hands—some little cream for them to skim to raise their subsistence level. This is a last survival of plantation days.

The organization of the Hartley farm encourages a high differentiation in tasks, rates of pay, living standards, and positions of authority and prestige. The office, under Mr. Bert Hartley, has its crew of clerks, stenographers, seed salesmen, agricultural experts, and advertising people. These "inside" people are dressed in the business clothes of an office. Mr. Paul Hartley supervises the "outside" work. He is assisted by white and Negro men who are all dressed in work clothes of cotton tans or blue denims according to the weather, from the "boss-man" to the picker in the fields. Mister Paul knows every operation on the place—seed selection, cattle diets, machine repair, and the numerous other complex enterprises on the farm.

The echelon directly responsible to Mister Paul includes a mechanic-foreman, tractor foreman, truckmen, cattle foreman, and a seed foreman, all white men. Under each of these people, and usually working side by side with them, are whites and Negroes who do machine repairs, driving, hauling and feeding the cattle, carpentry and other repair work, loading, herding, and a multitude of other tasks which characterize a modern farm and business enterprise. The seed is cleaned, separated, and loaded for shipment by young Negroes who are "growing up" on the job under the supervision of a white employee. Mister Paul is always on inspection rounds, so the work progresses at an efficient pace.

Most of the warehouses are of corrugated tin; the silos are of concrete block. The barn which houses the prize Hereford bulls, heifers, and calves, is spacious, white, and immaculate. Some animals are kept here to fatten on grains; a majority are out pasturing on grass. White and Negro cowhands assist the white supervisor here. They clean out the stalls, comb the animals, drive them in and out, load them, and attend them on the trucks which haul them to market in the cities or to numerous cattle shows about the country.

The Hartleys have a store of scientific agricultural know-how which they use for pasture care and development. They have had the experience of their father, a college training, and the services of federal government agencies and personnel. They experiment with new and better grasses, and they have a mutual exchange with the agricultural scientists.

From the Oberlin plantation to the Hartley farm is a long way. Many of the traditional forms of plantation days—Negro-white relations, housing, cotton culture, tenancy—remain as survivals on the Hartley place; otherwise we note vast differences. These are symbolized by the bungalows for white workers, the proposed cement block community for the Negroes, and lastly, the symbol represented by a time clock and the hourly wage.

The Hartley farm is more like an industry, a factory in the field, than a plantation. The prestige and authority of the plantation owner is present with characteristic paternalism and socio-economic-political power. But the worker is guaranteed a wage for the units he works. He has greater opportunity for specialization. His living conditions and socio-economic position are enhanced. Unlike Mr. Jackson who has more tenants than he needs and bemoans the inefficiency of the mass of them, Mr. Paul Hartley can say with vigor, "We have the right man on the right job." Is this a goal for the plantation of the future?

The plantation is changing to meet the needs for adjusting to changing conditions of the situation. The natural component of the situation has included soil erosion and the boll weevil. The demographic component involves an out-migration of Negroes and whites with a resulting labor shortage. The social component includes a desire to retain members of the next generation on the family homestead. The culture-contact component is indicated by the increasing pressure of economic cycles and depressions, scientific agricultural and industrial techniques being developed, the interest of the federal government in the welfare of its citizens, the influence of the mass culture in raising levels of aspiration for material wants, and also the ideal values of democracy—equality of opportunity and individual freedom.

The Jackson-Dolphin and the Sampson plantations are meeting these changing components of the situation by trends toward diversification in agriculture, especially toward cattle raising and a conversion from tenant to wage-hand farming. These plantations are also increasing in size to accomodate the next generation. The Hughes and Warner families have modified their plantation methods considerably, relying more exclusively on cattle raising. The Oberlins were incapable of changing the old patterns at all, and the plantation represents a complete failure. The last example, the Hartley farm, demonstrates a rejection of the old methods of agriculture rather than a compromise. It is the most efficient enterprise of all from the standpoint of operation as an economic and social system.

If we examine the patterns of adjustment of the plantation to the changing conditions of the situation in a socio-psychological context we find far less compatibility. The new diversification and conversion to wage-hand farming has helped the plantation owners, but the Negro tenants have either been transformed into landless wage hands or they face a future threat of complete displacement. The future of the Negro in the plantation area thus becomes a problem and a source of increasing anxiety on their part and eventually on the part of the rest of the nation. The present shortage of labor is only temporary. When plantation owners tear down deserted cabins, Negroes will never be able to claim them again, for the Black Belt will become pasture. The future of displaced tenants has become a real worry in 1950 when federal crop restrictions on cotton, caused by world cotton markets conditions, threatened to close out large acreages of cotton on every plantation. What security will exist for wage hands who are still under race-caste conditions, without land, and working for low wages? The plantation owners more recently are worried about the extension of labor unions among agricultural employees. Race-caste and economics are closely united in the plantation area. The decline in traditional paternalism introduces the further need for federal care for the aged, for children, and other needy persons. The plantation owners regard this as further evidence of state intervention in areas they rightfully consider their own. Large plantations like the Sampson and the Hartley enterprises can afford to build and to experiment. Smaller plantations and farms are forced to consider more certain means of income, and this accelerates their conversion to cattle, their utilization of timber, and a lessened need for Negro tenants.

White women also find it difficult to adjust to the changing conditions of the situation. While their husbands have grappled more or less successfully with the boll weevil and the depression by converting to cattle raising and seeking government loans, the women continue to hold on to the symbols of the past by maintaining the plantation house and membership in patriotic societies. They continue a form of ancestor worship by keeping genealogies and by their tales of the past in Plantation County. Although they are able to work outside the home if necessary to keep up their symbols of the past, their desire to do so suggests that perhaps they do not get as much reward out of the present as the men. The prevalence of frontier characteristics among the men, such as hunting and fishing, clandestine drinking and gambling, and the love for old clothes and the outdoors, may likewise be a conservation of old values. In both cases, then, some survivals from the past remain: historical symbols of glory and power in the plantation home and way of life for the women; the great outdoors, the frontier forms of recreation, and the retention of race-caste prerogatives for the men.

It is interesting to note the emergence of the Hartley farm as the most successful socio-economic enterprise among large operations in the county. This is not a plantation at all, but a sort of industrial enterprise in the field. Before we conclude that this form of enterprise is the most positive form of agricultural life in the plantation area, however, we must turn to the small farms and see how small-farm life is made compatible with the changing components of the situation. While the plantation system gives character to many forms of life in the plantation area, the small farm is no less significant for the present and the future.

4

SMALL FARMERS TRY TO MAKE GOOD

OUR DISCUSSION of the plantation may give the reader the false impression that all farms in Plantation County comprise seven hundred acres or more, or that they all have tenants and systems of organization characteristic of the Sampson plantation.

Numerically, the small farmers outnumber the plantation owners. The aggregate acreage of the plantations, however, is larger than that of the small farmers. Likewise, the plantations are in the more fertile and accessible areas in the county. This is understandable when we review the history of settlement of the county and the nature of the soil regions.

The small farmer settled the land that remained after the plantation owners took the river and creek bottom lands. The small farmer took the clay hill regions in the south of the county and the branch-heads (sources of streams) far from the river or the larger creeks. These disadvantages in soil fertility and distance to port hampered the growth and prosperity of small farmers.

The social and economic influence of the small farmers has always been subordinate to the plantation owners. Small farmers held few or no slaves; they lacked wealth, prestige, manners, and other attributes of a powerful slave-owning class. Even today in Plantation County people reckon their ancestry in terms of the number of slaves their grandparents owned. If one's grandfather struggled hard with poor soil and no extra labor, his descendant finds it more difficult to climb the social ladder.

There are communities in the clay hill regions of Plantation County that reflect the life and struggles of the small farmer as he ekes out a living with corn, cotton, some hogs, a few vegetables, and some scrubby cattle. The piney woods in this sector attest to the poverty of the soil for intensive agriculture. Indeed, with many failures among small farms in this area, the land is being taken over by large lumber companies. In this region of the county, where lumber interests are growing all the time, an industry has developed which employs hundreds of Negroes and whites who otherwise would have to leave the country.

Our interest in the patterns of adjustment to the natural environment, the demographic, social, and culture-contact or foreign components of the situation may be brought to a focus in a visit with some typical small farmer folk who live around Cornwall at the southeast corner of Plantation County. Their position socially in the county is far from uniform; individual characteristics count much in the final analysis. However, there is a definite outlook on life shown by this group, and outsiders characterize them all in similar fashion.

My first contacts with Cornwall came through a squirrel hunting week end with a friend who boarded there. My middle class friends in Plantation Town warned me about "getting mixed up with those wild people." They told me I would be lost in the woods if I went hunting with them, that they were great tricksters, "always up to something."

The houses around Cornwall are either painted or unpainted plank structures with central hallways and four to six rooms on either side. There is the inevitable porch with rocking chairs and a swing where the members of the family while away their time whittling or sewing or just "settin' and visitin' with each other and with the neighbors."

Mrs. Morrell, my hostess for the week end, had been the daughter of a fairly successful cotton farmer, but she had married a backwoods farmer who stayed drunk much of the time and died leaving her with several sons and daughters, some of them much like their father. As her sisters had married men of their own class, poor Annie Morrell became the outcast of her family.

By the time of my visit, Annie had become thoroughly integrated in the life at Cornwall. As a widow woman trying to operate a small farm as best she can, she "rustles up some greens" from the garden, keeps a fryer at hand, and visits with her neighbors up the road. Annie is a fatalistic soul, having even resigned herself to losing some property when one of her brothers-in-law "did her out of her share." Local people say that his conscience has "gotten" him, for he has to make periodic sojourns in a sanitarium. The lumber interests, with which the brother-in-law is associated, gradually hope to take over much of this small farm area. From a standpoint of agricultural economics, perhaps they have the surest program for the future.

Annie's house is the traditional plank home of the area. The rooms have been electrified only during recent months. On lonely winter evenings, Annie sits by her battery radio, listening to the latest "war news," shakes her head, and proceeds to add more squares to the latest patchwork quilt in her collection. Meanwhile the hogs run under the house, occasionally bumping their backs against the plank floor. The storeroom, which is one of the rooms of the house, is open for the chickens to roost on the sills and to leave their droppings. Corn is piled up here for the shucking. Life revolves about the kitchen, with its double fireplace (opening into the neighboring room), eating table, and wood-burning stove. Here Annie works and amuses herself; she entertains here, and thinks upon the world.

The master bedroom is the "nicest" room in the house, there being no parlor. The Sears Roebuck furniture remains in good condition, contrasting strongly with a miscellanea of iron beds and wooden chairs of local manufacture in the other rooms.

The long central hallway is open and bare, except for some bookcases which contain dime novels and a few *Readers' Digests*. Off one end of the hall is a back porch where there is a shelf for shaving articles, a wash basin, and wooden buckets which are brought up from the well in the yard. The other half of the porch is given over to the numerous chickens who make their run between porch and yard and storeroom.

The yard contains an open well on one side and a newly built pine privy some fifty feet away. The ground about the kitchen door is wet and sour from the soapy and greasy water which is thrown here. On one side of the house is a garden of ample size for the family's vegetable supply. There is a large chicken brooder on the other side; the eggs are consumed at home but occasionally there is a surplus which is sold. Chickens and hogs provide most of the family's meat supply, and any surplus meat is also sold.

The view from the rear fence discloses a wire fence and a creek beyond. This is the watering place for several litters of hogs, a mule, and a milk cow. Mrs. Morrell raises only a little cotton, much depending on the availability of Negro labor at a price she can afford to pay. Her main living comes from corn and peanuts.

Life for women like Annie Morrell revolves around the home, the garden, the stock, and corn and peanuts. She visits with the neighbors and gossips with them. She shops at the general store in the village on weekdays and goes to church there on Sundays.

The men around Cornwall have a reputation for pistol-toting and knife fighting. They are veteran hunters and fishermen, independent, and wary of strangers. They drink hard and gamble until the law drives them over into the neighboring county. But these men are also hard working farmers who have netted little from their poor soil. Those who have succeeded are the diligent farmers who have followed scientific agricultural advice to diversify—to concentrate on corn and peanuts, hogs and cattle, and to keep cotton within bounds as a cash crop.

There is much of the frontier in and around Cornwall. People like Annie have made only a minimal adjustment to changing conditions. She is tired and makes the best of her condition. People pity her for the opportunity she lost by moving to Cornwall, but Annie likes her neighbors—they are "good folk." The farm she runs is productive enough for her small needs, but a young man might make it pay well with a diversified crop program.

Around Plantation Town there are some hilly communities where farmers raise their corn and cotton and attempt to introduce some livestock to make a small farm pay. Young men and women with ambition and vision do well enough. Their newly built bungalows of cement block and white painted sealboard are beginning to vie with the older unpainted plank houses of less successful parents and relatives. In town, the small farmer who is a good customer at the store is considered respectable enough. Many of them now own secondhand cars, and they are "getting around more," becoming less "tacky." Their children attend the consolidated school in town, and many of them do quite well despite the competition with the children of college-trained plantation owners and townspeople. The mass culture—its movies, the radio, magazine and newspaper advertising—teach the small farmer's daughter to use lipstick and rouge and to have her hair "done" at the beauty parlor on a Saturday afternoon. These new notions cost money though, and if the farm does not pay off sufficiently in cash, the young people come to town to work, or, more frequently, go off to the city. Local merchants are fostering local industry to keep such young people on the small farms by providing a means of cash income by the women's working. The training of small-farm young people has usually been so poor that they have ended up for the most part in unskilled jobs, or at best in such semiskilled jobs as mechanics' assistants, sales clerks, or in the service occupations. The county and state school system are trying to cope with this vocational problem of out-going young farm people by introducing vocational education into the curriculum.

Drink and the depression of the thirties joined forces to put old Mr. Fellers "over the barrel." One cannot help but admire the old man, especially as he speaks of his younger days when he was strong and could walk behind a mule and could stand up for his rights as well as any man. Mr. Fellers blames much of his present plight on the fact that he had but few years of schooling, and he is determined that his children graduate from the Plantation County high school, so that "they'll have a better chance than I had."

Mr. Fellers and his sons have several small enterprises around the community: small farms which are diversified, a crossroads general store, a blacksmith shop, a Negro insurance agency, clerical work in a store in town, and carpentry. These multifarious activities enable the Fellers to "get along," and they fare well economically. Socially, depending on personality characteristics, they are considered in the lower middle class plantation area society.

The small farmer, like Mr. Fellers, with the help of a hired hand or two and his mules, actually works only part of the time on his crops, his stock, and the garden. His few hundred acres usually consist of enough woods to yield a small annual income. He plants seven or eight acres in cotton (which yield four to six bales), a similar acreage in corn, and has enough pasture for eight or more cattle, depending on his investment potential and interest in cattle raising. Hogs yield meat during the year and consume less feed than cattle. Chickens, his wife's province, likewise provide a meat supply and eggs for home use and sale. His wife also milks the cow and tends the vegetable garden which her husband or the laborer plows for her. White women do not work in the fields in Plantation County except in the "poor white" areas. The plantation system looks down upon white "cotton-picking hands." The presence of Negro labor or a tenant enables the small white farmer to work his land most of the year. He does not spend full time at it, however, for a secondary occupation is necessary both for tenant and owner to bring in additional cash. Fences, outbuildings, and the homestead often are in need of repair, but in the winter months when this might be done the small farmer is working in town to help balance the farm budget.

Mrs. Fellers keeps a neat little house. The men built it a few years

Small Farmers Try to Make Good

before when wartime prices for crops rose enough to carry them out of debt. Visitors may sit in the hallway on rockers made of white oak with matted seats of woven corn shuck, or they may come into the large master bedroom and toast their toes by the deep brick fireplace. The family eats in the kitchen, and the woman of the house cooks and serves all the food. She does not always eat with the men but takes a bite here and there during the preparation and serving, sitting down during dessert time and entering then into the conversation. She seems to let the men maintain the center of discussion when visitors are around, but she also has power around the house as can be seen by nods and frowns that accompany her husband's telling of a "tall one." Since most meals in Plantation County are served "family style"—large serving dishes of garden vegetables, fresh or smoked pork, beef, or chicken, and home preserved fruits and jams to go with corn bread and biscuits—the housewife can well participate in the regular meal. There seems to be a difference of opinion on the matter among the housewives.

The Fellers have adjusted to their situation by getting the most profit from their woods, by selective cutting rather than clean-cutting. They have achieved a balance in the production of cotton, corn, and higher grades of cattle. They "live at home" with an ample vegetable garden and a larder of home-grown meats and preserved fruits. Their many enterprises yield cash for extra expenses and purchases in town. These are the sort of people the merchants in town wish to remain in the county. Many small farmers are becoming like the Fellers by virtue of an educational and service program initiated by the federal government.

The boll weevil hit Plantation County about the time of the First World War. The postwar recession and finally the depression of the thirties found plantation owners and small farmers alike with their backs to the proverbial wall. Traditionally independent and of a *laissez faire* mind, these farmers were forced, at least temporarily, to acquiesce to the program of the New Deal. Its agricultural agencies became so familiar to them that they became almost divorced from the New Deal "socialism" the farmers continued to decry.

While the office of county agricultural agent antedates the New Deal by several years, his work has been made meaningful to the farmers only through the programs of the New Deal. This is doubly true of the vocational agricultural program in the secondary schools.

If the farmers had not received loans, credits, and subsidies during the dark days of the depression they would not have had a mind to listen to the scientific planning the county and home demonstration agents talked about on their visits about the countryside. The success of the county and home demonstration agents today is in large measure due to the financial backing given their programs by such agencies as the Agricultural Adjustment Administration (known locally as the "Triple A"), which has used economic incentives through subsidies, to encourage the planting of cover crops and other soil-building agents. The Soil Conservation Service surveys the land and advises the farmer how to make it produce best for profit and survival for generations. The Farm Credit Corporation and the Farmers Home Administration have loaned money at lower rates of interest and on greater risks than merchants or local banks would allow. These federal agencies have helped large farmers as well as the small farmers. In fact, the small farmers are quick to point out that the larger the operation, the greater the subsidies and savings to the farmer.

The county agent is an employee of the State Agricultural Extension Service, yet he is also a federal employee, since the federal government in part subsidizes the State College of Agriculture, the seat of the Extension Service. State politics and state-wide organizations for farmers like the Farm Bureau Federation have a lot of say in the activities of the Agricultural Extension Service and its personnel. To an extent this means that powerful plantation owners and larger farmers dominate the picture here. There is rivalry between this group and the federally controlled agencies like the Farmers Home Administration. The latter organization, in helping tenants become owners, tends to work contrary to the values of the plantation owner group.

The Veterans Administration vocational training program represents one of the most recent advances of the federal government into scientific agriculture. Since the program involves a younger element in the small farmer section of the population, it is of interest for us to note the procedure and success of the program. It is the measure of success of small farming among the present generation of young adults that will indicate a future for the small farmer in Plantation County and the plantation area.

The program in Plantation County in 1948 had some sixty white veterans and twice as many Negro veterans on its roster. Most of the white veterans already owned their farms, either in partnership with their fathers or brothers, or else through inheritance or individual purchase. The Negro cases are by far more significant since the majority have never owned land, and the small-farmer trend among Negroes is still in a developmental stage.

The Veterans Administration program has enabled Art Sims, a white veteran, to expand his holdings toward the purchase of a medium-sized plantation. Up until recently Art was farming his father's plantation, now largely converted to cattle raising. Art finds the scientific agriculture classes which are held twice a week a chore, but it gives him a chance to meet with the other veterans, who are mainly his buddies, and they talk over crops and plans for the future. The veterans' instructor wishes all his students were as well adapted to farming as Art. He seldom borrows beyond his means; he has built his own bungalow style home from the odds and ends of a tenant house; he is developing a fine herd of cattle; and his operations in corn and cotton are sufficient to balance the cattle and yield a nice cash income.

Mrs. Sims, a college graduate, is busy making their new home attractive and raising their little boy. Her educational background being somewhat on a par with the plantation women rather than the small-farmer wives, she participates in local women's home demonstration and cultural clubs with women of the large-farmer group. She has even taken a job in town to earn supplemental cash to carry through the plantation investment. The Veterans Administration program for Art, then, has accelerated his movement toward plantation management. Because he is a good farmer anyway, the training and subsidy have merely eased the early struggles to succeed in farm life.

Labe Waller perhaps represents the sort of veteran the program is most geared to help. The son of white tenants, he probably would have left for work in the city if the agriculture program had not been established for veterans. Labe has not had the financial or educational resources of Art. The classes at the training center teach him the latest about profitable small farming through diversification. The knowledge of how much corn, cotton, hogs, and cattle, and the recognition of the importance of the vegetable garden and the "live-at-home" program are all means by which the small farmer makes the adjustment to his situation. If Labe's new little cement block house which he constructed himself leaves something to be desired from an aesthetic point of view, nevertheless it is better than the unpainted plank cabin of his birth. With "outside work" during the winter months, probably at a sawmill, Labe should be able to provide for his young wife and babies in a modest way.

The government has helped the Arnolds since the depression, when Mr. Arnold was granted a New Deal Farm Security Administration loan to help him recover from a hog epidemic, the cotton market crash, and the general catastrophic events of the period. Being a good farmer and a hard worker, Mr. Arnold painted houses to make a living, and he invested his government loan carefully to buy good cattle and plant cover crops. Today the Arnolds are numbered among the few F.S.A. clients who have paid their debt in full. The prosperity of the war and postwar years has enabled the Arnolds to get on their feet once more. Their economy is strictly geared to diversification, and since labor is scarce, Mr. Arnold has introduced more cattle. In this work he is helped by his son.

Young Bill Arnold is an ex-G.I. who is studying under the Veterans Administration agriculture program. Although a good student and farmer, the veterans' instructor runs into difficulty because Young Bill is farming his father's place. Until Young Bill can set out on his own, his instructor does not feel he will gain the most from his course of study. An independent streak runs through the Arnold family. Mr. Arnold says he paid off the government so that they would stop "bothering him." It is assumed that Young Bill will soon be farming on his own in due time. If he meets a wife who is as good a homemaker as his mother, he will certainly be a success. Mrs. Arnold is busy with garden, chickens, preserving, cooking, and sewing. She contributes as much to the success of the farm as her husband. She has reared a family that includes farm people and a school teacher or two.

Independent to the point of avoiding the services of the county agent, the Arnolds seem to have the grit to succeed on their own. Although they do not like to admit it, only the government programs could have pulled them through. Since the depression was not of their making, however, can we say there is inconsistency in accepting government aid?

Not all the small farmers who participate in the government program are successful. Success comes from a desire to want to learn the newest methods and to apply them. Quite often the farmer is distrustful of the "government people." This was especially true in the earlier days of the program.

But time has had its effect, and the county agent, the Soil Conservation Service people, and other officials in Plantation County who are associated with the government have become familiar figures in town and around the country. As they participate in local affairs, their programs tend to be transmitted to the people more readily. Into a traditionally individualistic area, the federal government and its counterpart in the state have made inroads into agriculture. Originally these programs were meant to help a depression-stricken area recover financially; at the same time scientific agriculture has tried to promote long range programs to create a prosperous farming economy.

One cannot help but wonder how long it will take for the level of aspiration of the small farmer to be raised, so that he will seek wider fields of endeavor. This is happening to a degree among the small-farmer children—they attend consolidated school and mingle with the children from town and from the plantations. They attend movies, and the fashion plates of magazines flash at them from drugstore newsstands. New material needs are created by the mass culture. The small farm will have to strike a balance between increased subsistence and cash income. Increasing the size of the farms by adding pasture land and cattle is one way. Another is to have the women and younger sons work in small industry. The small farm of one hundred acres cannot hope to provide more than a subsistence economy.

If the previous discussion concerned white small farmers for the most part, it was planned that way to permit a special section for a new class of operators represented by the Negroes. Although the whites still outnumber them, the proportion of Negro owner-operators has increased at the same time that Negro tenants have decreased. Considering the low status of the Negro in general throughout the plantation area, the status of these farm owner-operators is as significant as it is novel.

To be sure, there are Negroes in Plantation County who have owned their farms for a generation or more. These few examples of advance over heavy obstacles are related in more than one way to the plantations from which their parents were freed as slaves. In the era before the New Deal the struggling Negro owner-operator made his way only by virtue of his frugality and determination, and with the blessings of white friends and plantation owners who sold him land or otherwise subsidized his early years.

Mr. Sampson, the white plantation owner, recalls several Negro tenants his father subsidized because they seemed to have initiative and know-how to succeed at individual enterprise. Such a plantation owner generally willed a forty acre plot or sold it for a small sum to a faithful tenant. In many cases, where mulatto children were involved, blood relationship was a motive for willing property to Negroes. But for every success there were several failures. Generations of ignorance and servitude were no help to the Negroes. They also labored under the suspicious and watchful eyes of white planters who, though kind to individuals, feared "lettin' the niggers gettin' to own the place before many years." Since the white man's say-so was a prerequisite for sale—with his control of deeds and contracts, and buying and selling—only the strongest and keenest Negro could survive as an owner-operator. Negroes who "knew their place" before the white man, yet who had internal fortitude said, "I'll show them," and they did.

And if there was success in the first generation, there was no guarantee of success in the next generation. The children of these struggling Negro farmers often succumbed to the temptations of spending their money before it was fully earned. Unscrupulous white men did not hesitate to get entire estates into debt by loans to one or many children. The instability of Negro families and questions of legitimacy tied up estates for years at a time, while weeds and the elements took charge of the farm. The Negro who could not write or "figure," but knew only how to plant cotton, was easily duped by those who profited in human weakness or who feared the too rapid advance of a subordinate group.

Old Neville, the son of Cindy, a slave woman, was given his start by a kindly plantation owner who noticed his ambition and appreciated his continued "good manners." Old Neville's first "forty" was the beginning of the Rum Road community of Negro small-farm owners in the county. Old Neville kept on good terms with "high type" whites, and these connections kept him safe from those who would take advantage of an otherwise "ignorant darkey." By saving his small profits, curbing the desire for fine clothes, and by educating his children, old Neville was able gradually to add to his original forty acres. His daughter kept the books, his sons helped with the crops, and before long Old Neville began to have tenants of his own. As a Negro, Old Neville had to control his tenants by virtue of his personality. He did not have the authority of race-caste like his white neighbor plantation owners. Because of his humble origin, Old Neville fraternized with his tenants and worked among them. His relations with some of the tenant women on the plantation were too "fraternal," however, and numerous "outside" (illegitimate) children added to the complications that resulted when Old Neville's will was read. (White plantation owners behaved similarly, but race-caste prevented claims on the part of their "outside" children.)

As a result of the boll weevil and the depression, the plantation was heavily in debt so that the contestants to the will were fighting over something that was of no use to anyone unless the land could be vitalized once more. Old Neville's second wife held prior claim over his children, which merely added to the dispute. Today the children are scattered, so the future of the farm remains in doubt. The widow is trying to bring it back to a profitable basis, but she is not well versed in farming. A large enterprise like Neville's may eventually be broken up into smaller farms if his children decide to sell through a real-estate dealer; or else the land may be added to neighboring plantations to be used for pasture and woodland.

The status of the Negro plantation owner is certainly a high one in his community, all things considered. He has economic security and a following among his tenants. But other factors are also important for status, namely education (or an interest in it for one's children), interest in the church, in community organization, and moral standards.

Brady Dean was fathered by a white plantation owner, and it is said that this is how he got his start in farming. Now he has a plantation with tenants. He spends a good deal of his time downtown chatting with old cronies, but he looks with an anxious eye at the disabilities of his race. As a mulatto, Brady chafes at his social position as a Negro. He is wealthier than many of the white men who sit and gossip under the pecan tree at the courthouse square. But he must sit on the curb benches in front of the stores with the other Negroes. He can afford a nice car. His wife is a school teacher and a refined person. His children are mostly college graduates, and they hold good positions in northern cities. But Brady is still regarded as a "nigger," and he cannot vote for the people who are subsidized by the taxes he pays, he cannot argue with the white merchant from whom he buys, nor can he move into a nice home in town.

Brady's position in the Negro community would be as high as his wife's if he took an interest in the church, or if he "let the women alone." The Negroes talk about Brady's "goings on." Furthermore, there is a feeling he considers profits above the welfare of his tenants. Mrs. Dean does not associate with the tenants; she has her friends among the Negro schoolteacher group. For this the other Negroes consider her snobbish, but she plays a typical Negro upper class role. While Brady fraternizes with his tenants more than a white plantation owner would, he is still primarily an employer, and as such is interested in maintaining his authority and profits.

The future of the Brady Dean plantation like those of white owners whose children have moved away is probably absentee ownership and failure or sale through real-estate dealers.

The number of Negroes who have become operators without the help of the federal government and its agencies is a small proportion of the total. For the three thousand Negro farmers in Plantation County of whom 20 percent are owners, the visits, organizational work, and encouragement shown by the Negro county agent have often meant the difference between failure and success.

The office of the Negro county agent is under the supervision of the white county agent in Plantation County. He has direct contact with the Negro College of Agriculture in the state, however. The Negro county agent's job is to deal with plantation owners' tenants and with Negro farm owners. Actually he spends more of his time with the owner group, since the white plantation owners prefer to look after their own tenants. When they wish to introduce a new agricultural program, however, they do not hesitate to call upon the Negro county agent. He tends to bridge the gap between white and Negro farmers, easing tension situations by his personality in dealing with each group. He understands the importance of keeping on good terms with the whites in order to gain their support for projects he aims for among the Negroes.

Two years ago the people of Plantation County, white and colored, heard about Frank Waters' return. The rumor spread like wildfire and was accompanied by sounds of jubilation. A visitor to the scene who asked about such an unusual phenomenon of simultaneous rejoicing among all the groups in the county was told, "Waters used to be county agent here before the war. He got promoted to a government district job, but the job gave out and now he's back with us." Whites mentioned his qualities somewhat as follows, "He's a nigger, but a smart one. Knows his place, and he sure can get the niggers to farm. He helps us when there's nigger trouble."

We might mark off Mr. Waters as another "white man's nigger" if we did not hear comments like these from Negroes: "He organized the colored farmers into clubs, got them to study how to farm properly, then got them to clean up their houses and barns; got them to buy cattle and taught them how to care for them. He's active in the church, and he goes around to all the country churches to visit with the folks. He's friends with the white people, and he gets them to sell land to a colored boy who wants to start farming on his own."

Like Booker T. Washington, whose picture hangs in his office in the Negro Activities Center near Plantation Town, Frank Waters believes the Negro will advance only so long as he maintains good relations with the whites. "The whites control property. They say who can buy land, and what land they can buy. They control credit and the taxes. If you have your feet on the ground you know you'll get ahead by playing with the white man and at the same time educating yourself to manage your own farm, build your house, and develop your community."

The Negro county agent is fighting generations of ignorance among Negro farmers as much as anything. Years of dependency on the white man have not created a group who can come together and cooperate on a community basis without sound preparation. Mr. Waters attempts to foster study clubs for adults, 4-H clubs for the school children, and other group activities on a local and county-wide basis. The new spirit of a community of purpose and a sympathy for scientific agricultural methods has resulted in cattle and saddle horse shows among Negro adult and youth groups. Mr. Waters furthers the opportunity offered to Negro veterans by the Veterans Administration program when he secures promises of land sales to veterans from the whites.

Mr. Waters feels deeply about the plight of the Negro in Plantation County. He holds a high position in the eyes of the whites since he is "trusted," and this enables him to plead with them to part with some plantation land which otherwise is considered too precious to sell. He impresses on the whites the economic value of Negro farm ownership. He notes that they will make better customers and they will not be subject to "alien isms" which the whites fear so much. For the Negroes, he sees land ownership as the first stage in their economic and social regeneration. He feels that other advances will come after this one.

Mr. Waters recognizes that the lack of local opportunity for educated Negro youth keeps only the unambitious ones in the county. He hopes his programs for small-farm ownership will keep some of the potential Negro leaders in the county, and will thus help the entire group of them. Both the Veterans Administration and the Farmers Home Administration programs are helping here.

Mr. Waters believes the plantation area and the South are entering a new era, where both the old plantation owner who exercised *noblesse oblige* and his faithful "darkey" servant are disappearing. In their place he sees educated whites and Negroes, each realizing the value of the other in the community. As Mr. Waters continues to develop the type of Negro he desires, he leaves it to the white man to carry out his part of the deal.

No other agency, government or private, has done as much toward establishing the Negro as an independent operator as the Farmers Home Administration, still known locally as "the Farm Security." In an area where the traditional status of the Negro has been that of tenant on the plantation, the Farmers Home Administration entered on the wings of the depression and established communities of tenant-purchasers on the very plantations where these people had been tenants and their ancestors, slaves. The plantations were heavily in debt; it was a revolutionary thing. Local white people today call it "socialism." Yet it has set a new pattern for the Negro and the small farmers in the plantation area.

Jim Slater, like the other hundred tenant families on the river plantation, formerly worked cotton and corn on shares with the plantation owner. He was encouraged to plant as much as he could; he was "advanced" when his credit gave out. Most of his money at "settlement time" was returned to the plantation owner through the commissary. Jim lived in a tenant cabin with fallen stairs and a leaky wooden roof. His children worked in the fields when they were supposed to be (by law) in the tumble-down shack that served as a school. The plantation owner helped Jim to sell his cotton and provided for his father's burial and his daughter's appendicitis operation. Jim did not have to worry about taxes or about buying and selling. He seldom left the plantation; his wants were few. The farm and the church were his life, and he and his wife, Amy, struggled together as best they could. There was apparent security in the Riverton community among one's kinfolk and with white folk seeing that nothing from the outside brought you to harm.

But an economic depression knows no limits. The plantation owner came to a point where he could no longer fulfill his obligations to the humble tenants on his place. After his death the creditors came to foreclose for the mountain of debts his tenants had innocently accumulated. Jim's kinfolk could not resist when men came to take away their hogs, chickens, scrubby cattle, bags of meal, and anything that seemed to be of economic value on the place. Jim, Amy, their children, and their neighbors, went on starvation rations. They had no understanding of the economic and legal forces that were operating from the great outside world against them. Their prayers were answered only when a Red Cross truck came with flour and sugar, but for the future, they did not know where or to whom to turn.

Unknown to the simple Negroes of Riverton, the federal government had purchased the plantation. Agricultural experts in Washington were drawing up plans for a new community, for bungalow style houses, a cooperative store, a new school, even a new church. A new boss, "the government," was preparing itself to take over duties and obligations traditionally assigned to the plantation owner.

At least this is what appeared to be the case when the Negroes of Riverton were hired to build neat little frame houses, to paint them white, to equip them with unheard of wire screening, and other paraphernalia quite foreign to them. Many people cut holes in the screens to let in the fresh air. The new store was finer than the old plantation commissary; the school building was modern; the church had a steeple that could be seen clear across the river. The Negroes thought "the government" was a fine boss indeed.

This turn of events during the late thirties was not to be a carry-over of the plantation system, however. For a time, the federal government and its agents appeared to act in a paternalistic manner to bridge the gap of transition. But gradually it was possible to strengthen self-reliance and community activity through an education program which was undertaken by the agricultural and home demonstration agents assigned to the local Farm Security Administration office. The old community had been an organic development arising from a common status as tenants on the plantation. This community was unable to cope with such powerful world-shaking forces as the economic depression, however. The old patterns of agriculture did not teach the tenants how to gain the most from their fertile soil or to market their produce at the best prices. The potential of the organic community was never tapped for improving buildings, hygiene and sanitation, educating children, promoting initiative and leadership.

The community-minded officials of the Farm Security Administration introduced new patterns. The commissary took on the form of a consumer cooperative so that all the profits from the store would remain within the community, either as patronage dividend shares or to purchase machinery for community use. The cotton gin and gristmill were also planned as cooperatives, to provide these necessary services at a minimal charge. The stages by which these simple tenant-purchasers learned the fine points of consumer cooperation were slow and are still very incomplete. There were no local people capable of managing the store or keeping the books. White men from Plantation County who were often sympathetic, but always aware of their white status, came in to care for the operation of the store. Business was good and some profits went for the purchase of trucking and tractor equipment, but profits were never high enough to please either the Farm Security Administration supervisors or the clients. Mismanagement in the office and behind the counter was evident. The patrons were interested more in their "bonus" (patronage dividends) than in improving consumer cooperation practices to net more returns. There was no program of education in the cooperative movement. The patrons felt that the commissary was certainly better than the old plantation store since it paid the "bonus," but beyond that it served the same functions—a meeting place and a convenient service center. There was little other incentive to induce loyalty to the enterprise. To take the place of commissary credit, loans were arranged in the commissary manager's office. These were actually government loans, but the function was similar to the previous loans of the plantation owner. Actually the interest rates were one-fourth those of the plantation owners; a semblance of cash trade was also preserved in the new commissary since cash from the loans was turned in for payment of goods.

Another attempt at cooperation, a medical care program, was less successful than the commissary, gin, or gristmill. The physicians of Plantation County during the depression continued to make calls on patients, but they received a fraction of their bills in final payment. The Riverton community was no exception; in fact, the community's isolation from medical and other services in the county rendered trips there least profitable of all. The government agencies felt that a cooperative medical program for the Riverton community would be an incentive to the physicians to come to the community, and at the same time it would render very real help to the people who had never received adequate medical care. The physicians entered the scheme because it meant some form of steady income, but they had their misgivings. Cooperative medicine is revolutionary enough in the United States as a whole, let alone in the plantation area. Service for Negroes superior to the service most whites were receiving went against race-caste beliefs as well.

The federal authorities sent a resident nurse to Riverton, and they embarked on a program of health education and maternal care through the schools and the home demonstration agent's visits. But the physicians did not reckon with a backlog of ills of all types which began to avalanche and brought complaints from pharmacists, hospitals, and others who hesitated to provide services for so many with inadequate coverage. The race-caste situation and the presence of an outside force, the government, also worked against the program. As the physicians were overburdened for their numbers (two active physicians in the county and about eight old or retired practitioners), they gradually had to whittle down the program under succeeding contracts with the government. At the same time the depression came to an end, and wartime prosperity for the local farmers enhanced their ability to pay for medical services when they were rendered. The Riverton clients thus did not prove as rewarding to the physicians during the early forties as they had been during the late thirties. The contract expired during the war, the nurse was dismissed, and today patients send forty miles for a physician or, more usually, drive by secondhand car or by mule cart to the physician's office in town. Home cures and herbology continue to provide many of the cures for ailments, but the impetus given scientific medicine during the few years of the cooperative program increased the awareness of the Negroes of the value of such treatment. Many of them drive miles to the maternity clinic. The clients likewise participate in the state and the clinic's venereal disease blood testing program (there was little venereal disease in Riverton before it was opened to the outside world during the thirties). They receive public health services, such as the examination of school children which continues through the local school with the cooperation of the Farmers Home Administration authorities. Congressional reaction against many of the cooperative features of the Farmers Home Administration program has reduced budgets and personnel. This, with plantation area objections, inhibits the development of any significant cooperative forms in this community. In the long run the development will result in a community of small individualistic farm families, unless there is retrogression and a return to tenancy under a large operator.

The tenant-purchase program is the most important new pattern introduced by the Farm Security Administration. After the federal government took over some defunct plantations, a local board, consisting of reputable white farmers, formed to pass on the applications of whites and Negroes for participation in the program. The board passed on the character of the applicants and their potential ability to become self-sufficient small farmers. A successful applicant was leased a tract of land, usually one hundred acres, and given the opportunity to build an F.S.A.–specified house and outbuildings, loans for seed, fertilizer, a limited amount of livestock, and other necessary equipment for a well-balanced diversified small farm. The tenant-purchaser was granted a forty-year long-term loan averaging $2500 at $3\frac{1}{2}$ percent interest for the land and buildings. He made annual payments in order eventually to become full owner of this property. Shorter loans were granted for operations, including equipment, seed, stock, and the like. The Farm Security Administration officials had the dual roles of educating the tenant-purchasers in good small-farming practices and also of seeing that the government received a financial as well as a human return on the investment. Depending on the personalities and interest of the agricultural and the home demonstration agents, this education and supervision took on aspects of plantation supervision combined with scientific education in modern small-farm practices.

The agents I associated with during my stay in Plantation County

Small Farmers Try to Make Good

were sincere people, native to the state, and really desirous of transforming these tenants into owners. The majority of the tenant-purchasers were Negro, since most tenants in the county were Negro, and the race-caste factor entered nearly every phase of the program. The agents were white men with a tradition concerning the Negro as subservient and of lower position, yet the program from Washington called for transforming these tenants into independent and successful small farmers. The problems of making the transition were complicated, therefore, by the previous condition of the tenants on plantations, the role of the administrators as white men and at the same time federal employees, and the attitude of local white citizens who saw in the program a challenge to the plantation area way of life.

The process of educating these tenant-purchasers to become self-supporting small farmers necessitated a program of motivating them to become owners and at the same time to realize the responsibilities that were inherent in ownership and management. The program consisted of weekly visits by the agricultural agent and frequent visits to the farm women by the home demonstration agent. The agents drew up farm plans with the tenant-purchasers, inspected their enterprises, encouraged diversification, soil conservation, and a "live-at-home" subsistence program. The two dozen whites on the program have succeeded fairly well, and most of them are now small-farm operators. The one hundred and fifty Negroes in the program are experiencing varying degrees of success.

Some of the problems that discourage the Negroes stem from the plantation heritage. They do not like rules which urge them to make payments in advance to provide for lean years in the future. They are accustomed to annual plantation rents and the possibilities of making a change the next year. They are used to credit and cannot adjust to long-term payment on leases, let alone paying on time in order not to lose the entire investment. They do not have a long-range point of view that considers land a permanent investment for themselves and their children. They tend to think in terms of more land for extensive forms of agriculture rather than intensive farming. Their children are attracted by advertising and education to seek more material goods which subsistence farming cannot provide—thus parents who work hard to purchase their farms face the possibility that their children will not wish to remain and take over after they become infirm.

These are some of the problems inherent in the radical change in pattern from tenancy to ownership under the federal government program. By and large, the tenant-purchasers are making the grade. The agents see the proof of success, however, in the reaction of the second generation. Better schooling, vocational agriculture in the schools, and the actual living experience of farm ownership may make a difference.

5

FACTORIES TO BALANCE FARMS

UNDER the plantation system the river was essential for carrying cotton from Plantation County to the ports and returning much needed goods from large wholesale warehouses located at the port. Credit was secured largely through the cotton "factor" who was a commission merchant between planter and buyer. The roads between plantations and town were so poor that country folk came to town on rare shopping trips, to county court, or for events like weddings, funerals, and church services (though county churches continued to flourish until the beginning of the depression). Crossroads general stores furnished the needs of small farmers; commissaries on the plantations took care of the needs of owners and tenants.

Small business and the inland trade grew at the turn of the century when river traffic was replaced by rail and then highway transportation. The orientation today is completely toward inland trade—local towns, county seats, urban centers—instead of toward the Gulf port. The improvement of mass communications, especially chain newspaper advertising, magazines, movies, and radio, has raised the level of material aspirations among people of the area, so that what once satisfied their ancestors no longer serves a cosmopolitanized younger generation. Plantation and crossroads stores are beginning to feel the competition of town, cities, chain stores, and mail-order firms.

The stores in Plantation Town serve a trade area of twenty-five miles radius with about ten thousand potential customers. Many of the stores are general variety enterprises, serving as groceries, clothing stores, and farming equipment service centers. There are also special stores for the handling of feedstuffs, hardware, drugs, shoe repair, and dry cleaning, and the usual barber shops, movie theaters, banks, and restaurants. Some heavier industry and other enterprises are located by the railroad; these include the ice plant, cotton gin, gristmills, and oil and gas service stations. Offices for government agencies and local law and medical practices are in separate buildings or above the stores. The importance of mechanization is seen by the many automotive sales, service, and filling stations in town.

All of the above businesses are owned and operated by white people. Some stores, however, cater more to Negro trade than white, and they are known as "colored stores" in polite parlance. Since Negroes constitute four-fifths of the county's population, they give local stores the major portion of trade and take-in. The more affluent whites are able to make frequent trips to cities where they purchase higher grade goods. But the increased distribution of national brands tends to level the distinction among crossroads, town, and city store merchandise. Local businesses utilize national brands boiler plate in newspaper and movie advertisement. Since the nature of the plantation system makes for large credit needs, town business is also characterized by the credit system with its attendant risks and high interest charges. Only the few chain stores insist on cash and carry. They charge lower prices than most other stores, and their increasing patronage reflects new patterns which are entering the plantation area. Local stores and local people resent their entry into the community.

There is some small enterprise in the town which is owned and operated by Negroes, but it is relatively insignificant. In the Negro section of town there are two cafés, a barber shop, a beauty parlor, and a vegetable curb market, all operated by Negroes. There are also a few variety stores here which are owned and operated by white people. It is obvious that the whites dominate plantation area business and industry.

Relations between town and country are social as well as economic. Until quite recently most merchants and service people in town either owned farms or plantations, or they had relatives who lived and worked in the country. The very beginnings of the towns came from the desire of plantation owners to escape the malaria-infested bottom lands and at the same time to maintain social contacts with their neighbors. The trade and service functions of the town came only after populations were sizeable. Many plantations still supply townspeople with meat and vegetables and dairy products.

The growth of towns as centers of services and trade today is due chiefly to the shift from river traffic to the railroad and highways. It is significant that only one or two really affluent families in Plantation County are entirely town-centered. These families came within the past fifty years, and they own no farm land. The older merchants and professionals in the county either were reared on the farm, or else they have close kin who own and operate farms or plantations. Many such persons actually derive the major portion of their income from plantation holdings.

Rather recently there has emerged a new group we shall designate "the newcomers." The growth of Plantation Town and the county has attracted small business and service people, many of them between the ages of thirty and fifty. These people generally come from other small towns in the state or the Southeast, so they assimilate easily to the culture. Their relation to the farming and the Negro element is largely commercial and is thus quite different from the older group of merchant-planters. The social orientation of the newcomers is town-centered. Likewise, in political affairs they concern themselves with town improvement. Some of these newcomers have married locally, and thus they have more extensive interests, but on the whole Plantation County is important for them only as a trade area. While the older business group in town has tended to limit local expansion in favor of county-wide programs, the new group points its program in the reverse direction. Yet since town and country are interrelated economically, socially, and politically, each group needs the other.

The buzz of sawmills can be heard in the woods of plantation owners and small farmers alike. These temporary mills exploit the rich growth of pines in the area. In the past they have caused concern among conservationists because of their clean-cutting or stripping activities. More recently, however, the larger companies have come to set an example and the forestry service has undertaken a widespread educational program. Farmers are coming to appreciate the desirability of selective cutting and replanting, and they are coming to regard their timber resources as a "crop"—a periodic and important source of farm income.

The major portion of Plantation County industry revolves about the timber and lumber industries. Most of these enterprises are small, but they are of growing importance in an area that has, until now, been considered strictly cotton and plantation country.

A small veneer mill manufactures doors. It is located right in town, near the white residential section. The odd location may result from difficulties in acquiring other suitable property and the fact that industrialization is too recent to make zoning laws seem necessary. The business is expanding modestly since its owner began some seven years ago with less than a thousand dollars cash and a Reconstruction Finance Corporation (federal agency) loan. Once more we find the government helping enterprise in a traditionally individualistic area.

The owner uses Oregon timber rather than the local product in his doors. His chief problem is transportation, since Plantation Town is on only a spur railroad track. The owner of the plant began with Sears Roebuck machinery and has expanded very gradually and cautiously. He is introducing specialized machinery which will benefit his expanding projects. He sells his product throughout the South mainly by advertising in trade journals. The plant employs about twenty or thirty workers, most of these veterans who earned about seventy-five cents an hour in 1948. There is a close relationship among the workers since they come from similar background, and they get along well with their employer, who is also a war veteran. The workers come from small farms generally. The manufacturer is participating increasingly in civic affairs as his business expands and is emerging as one of the younger leaders in the community.

A window-frame plant is also located near the white residential section of town. This manufacturer utilizes local lumber and employs some fifteen Negro veterans in semiskilled work. Most of these veterans supplement their income by subsidy from the Veterans Administration on-the-job training program. On a typical afternoon this group was observed working at their machines without supervision, a new pattern for Negro labor in this area.

Large permanent sawmills are found near Plantation Town and in different sections of the county, mainly near the railroads and timber centers. The wages for Negroes average five dollars a day, which is three times what they get from farm labor. It is little wonder then that farm tenants and laborers are deserting to the mills. We have already discussed the arrangement between plantation owner and sawmill worker. The early objection to the sawmills has been obviated since the plantation owners find cattle raising more profitable than cotton. They can have the labor of sawmill workers' families and their trade at the commissary if they arrange for them to live on the plantation. This arrangement tends to have an adverse effect on the saw-

Factories to Balance Farms

mills. Absenteeism is high. On the other hand, since sawmill work is seasonal, the pressure of unemployed hands is relieved if they live on the plantations. Perhaps the seasonal nature of work has retarded the development of extensive sawmill workers' settlements near the mills. Such settlements that do exist are breeding places of malcontent when there are seasonal shutdowns. The Negro sawmill workers' community near Plantation Town has not integrated with the old Negro community. The workers gamble and drink, and their wives have little to occupy their time except to do likewise. The children are attending school, however, which may be the beginning of their integration into the community.

The plantation system of worker-employer relations has been transferred to the sawmill also. The owner-operator and the supervisors are usually white men. A few of the specialists and most of the unskilled labor are Negro. The race-caste codes serve to keep labor very docile; there is a fear of unions on the part of management, but the employees are generally helpless even should they desire unionization. In the long run, despite wages superior to farm labor rates, the Negro's sawmill dollar does not go far. He does not raise much food at home; in town his material wants are greatly increased. The Negro employee, because of his position as unorganized employee and as Negro, has little redress in case he is fired or has an accident. He is subject to great insecurities, which may explain his addiction to drinking and gambling. Having few community roots, he and his family live for the materialistic moment.

We may strike an analogy between industry and the plantation by noting the activities of the Lumberton enterprise. Lumberton is a typical paternalistic company town just over the southern border of Plantation County. The operation began some thirty years ago when an enterprising lumberman from outside the plantation area noted the possibilities of the area for exploiting its timber resources. He began to invest in large timber tracts at a time when prices were low, since few of the local plantation owners or small farmers realized their value. The small farmers in areas like Cornwall eagerly accepted the prices offered for their poor farm land, and, before the plantation owners were aware of what was happening, a new force entered the economic life of the area. Lumberton was planned as a mill village in the midst of a wooded empire. Its relations with Plantation County developed through local people who settled in the mill village. Plantation County upper-class persons married into the Lumberton founding family, and their social activities are common to the plantation area and the neighboring Pine Belt country.

In Lumberton, the dwellings for white workers are spacious five-room single-storied plank structures, not unlike the Farmers Home Administration bungalows. These are all painted a deep green, and the community is so planned as to give a pleasant appearance at any time of the week or year. The dwellings for Negroes are quite inferior to those of the whites, but their two-or-three-room unpainted plank houses compare quite favorably with tenant cabins. The whites have interior plumbing, spaciousness, and decoration which the Negro houses lack. Yet the Negroes feel relatively secure with the wages they receive in Lumberton and the fact that their community has taken root. The paternalism of Lumberton for the Negro is quite reminiscent of the plantation, but the work is more interesting and there is greater opportunity for advancement in a semi-specialized occupation. The employers seem benevolent enough to the white workers also, and there are services provided here that would be more difficult to find and to pay for either in agricultural communities or in the cities.

The Lumberton operation provides a commissary as one of the services. One of the largest general stores in the area provides for most of the needs of the workers. At the same time it cashes checks and makes midweek advances to employees (in the form of silver dollars), so that business is sure to be directed there. Prices are similar to those in the small towns, and patronage seems to be spontaneous. The store functions as a meeting place for various groups, especially Negroes. It is profitable to the owners and convenient for the customers. The company, in addition to the store, provides medical, recreational, religious, and other services for a village of several hundred families.

The managers of the enterprise are the sons of the founder. The subordinate executives are white. Salary and housing in the community are correlated with position in the company, but, as far as housing goes, there is no great division between the housing for the owners and those employees, professional or industrial, who are a few echelons below. One finds a greater differentiation in income and in social interests, however. The owners have social and business contacts throughout the South; the employees' life is village-centered.

There is a friendly relationship between employer and subordinates, however, partially caused by the newness of the community and its ecological structure. The owners come from a family that began as middle-class, non-plantation stock. They have risen in status by virtue of their economic and financial achievements and success. This has led to marital and social ties with other plantation area upper-middle-class families, but they keep their simple ways.

The owners fear the entry of union organizers as do other operators throughout the county. They threaten to cease operations and live off the produce of the woods if union organization should succeed. While they retain close paternalistic and semi-formal ties with their employees, there is nothing the employee can do if the form of management should change with the generations, or if economic catastrophe should come. Dissatisfied employees have only the recourse of quitting. The mass culture, with its demand for "equal rights" and democratic privileges including collective bargaining, faces rough sledding in the individualistic plantation area. The plantation system carries over to business and industry many of the characteristics of American industry of the nineteenth century; the power of race-caste is an additional factor to complicate the situation.

The situation in agriculture in the plantation area has necessitated new considerations to meet the needs of the people. The plantation system and cotton are subject to an economic cycle that has brought ruin to the area for many generations at periodic intervals. The boll weevil has likewise been a factor in the economic depression of the area. Small farming, even if carried on well, is unable to meet the economic needs of people influenced by mass advertising. The annual exodus of young people from the rural areas has meant a loss of some of the more productive youth of the community. Yet these young people have not fared as well as they might because they lack the vocational training necessary to give them a fair start in urban life.

The stimulus for local activity has been only recent. The problems have come to a head primarily because of the economic depression of the thirties. The wartime prosperity has stimulated thinking on the subject because people, especially young people, have travelled, and they are aware of what other sections of the country are doing to meet similar needs. The experience of farm and city pulling together toward a victory during the war has drawn the two closer together in peacetime; there is now some effort to prepare rural youth for urban living and to introduce local industry to rural social and economic problems. The newcomer group has been another stimulating force by giving new leadership to Plantation Town and other communities of the plantation area. These people have been the first town-centered leaders to come to the plantation area. Their motives are largely economic. They have a "booster" frame of mind; unlike the plantation owners, the newcomers are chamber-of-commerce-type citizens. Their fraternity is nation-wide, or regional, with a geographic and economic emphasis rather than sectional or historical interest. They continually look ahead rather than behind.

The federal and state governments have aided industry mainly through the Reconstruction Finance Corporation. In a way this balances the governmental aid to agriculture which we have discussed previously. In industry as in agriculture, businessmen in Plantation County do not hesitate to accept such government aid, although otherwise they decry "socialism."

Three new projects "broke" during my stay in Plantation County in 1948. The three projects seemed to satisfy a felt need of the people. They stimulated community action as few other experiences in the recent past. All sections of the population were involved.

Scientific agriculture, after two decades of operation in the plantation area, has made definite inroads on the thinking and practices of large and small farmers alike. There is a general appreciation of new methods which raise the level of living of the farm population. One of the more successful techniques of scientific agricultural education has been the experimental station and the experimental plot. Farmers, who themselves cannot afford to experiment with new methods, receive valuable insight in the results of the State College of Agriculture stations. Locally, within Plantation County, some progressive plantation owners have permitted the State College to utilize sections of their land. The Farmers Home Administration agents have tried with varied success to convey such experiments to their clients. In 1948, however, it was felt that a larger station would be very valuable for the farmers from counties with soil and climate similar to Plantation County. The local politicians and their friends in the Extension Service therefore came together on the idea and made the proposition to the people of the county.

This project is of interest to us, not only because it was related to

Factories to Balance Farms

new patterns of scientific agricultural education, but because the results of the project raised issues in the area which in previous years would not have been acted upon with such vigor and community spirit. Many values which the plantation area holds dear were violated or changed completely during the heat of the argument.

The experimental substation required the county to provide a fifteen hundred acre tract of average land. Although land prices were very high during and after the war, the tradition of the plantation area has been for land to be retained and kept as an investment and heirloom within the family for all generations. This investment in land has been the main basis for the accumulated wealth and prestige of the plantation owner class in the area. The high prices for cotton in 1948 provided an additional incentive for persons to keep their land even though they supported the experimental substation in principle.

The county commissioners set up a survey committee to report a suitable tract of land and to enter into negotiations with the owner. The Blakely plantation was large and was located inland from the river four miles from Plantation Town. Of importance, also, was the fact that the plantation was in absentee ownership, the present owners living in a nearby city. The commissioners, who included large plantation owners and civic leaders, agreed that there would be a minimum of displacement and a maximum of benefits for the county if this land could be purchased.

The Blakelys were hardly to be expected to act counter to tradition, and indeed they saw no reason why they should sell the property. The situation would have reached an impasse if the commissioners had not considered a step which was radically opposed to tradition and precedent. They threatened condemnation proceedings, public appropriation of private property. The commissioners were uneasy about this step, but the public seemed behind them, and the rewards of the experiment substation seemed to be greater than the traditional value of an absentee owner's private property. Since the condemnation proceedings would net the owners only fifteen dollars an acre, the owners finally agreed to settlement with the commission at twenty-one dollars an acre. The price was high for the quality of land, but the commissioners were sincerely relieved they did not have to use condemnation proceedings. They felt that such a drastic step would create a dangerous precedent. Only the exigencies of the situation led farmers, who thirty years before had overturned vats of the government tick inspectors, to undertake the invasion of private property. Bitterness was engendered between the Blakelys and the townspeople, many of whom were their kin; they felt that they had been discriminated against because they were absentee owners. The commissioners felt that the price was high at the time, but eventually the land would become more valuable as the experiment substation began to work it.

The county courthouse was packed even to the window sills one spring afternoon in 1948. Sirens blew at two o'clock to announce the closing of all stores and a mass rally to meet with visitors from the State Board of Education. The new project involved establishing trade and vocational schools for young people in strategic regions throughout the state.

Plantation County people long noted that their young people found it necessary to seek employment in the cities because there was not enough local economic opportunity to support them. Yet these young people faced disadvantages in the cities because they were not skilled in the trades and industry. It was this need that caused plantation owners, merchants, small farmers, housewives, and all other white groups to assemble that afternoon. (The Negroes also were beginning to suffer this disadvantage, but their time had not yet come for public demonstration.)

The merchants sparked the project to locate the trade and vocational school in the county because it meant business from new teachers and students; the cultural leaders of the community felt the influx of teachers would benefit the social composition of the community; farmers were interested in their children's being trained. Five hundred additional acres near the agricultural experiment substation were offered to the State Board of Education committee. Local educators spoke of the large out-migration of Plantation County youth each year. Local real-estate men surveyed the possibilities for building houses for teachers and came up with promises of cooperative effort on the part of townspeople—this despite property holdouts in the past. A survey of part-time job opportunities in Plantation Town revealed over seventy. The local Chamber of Commerce, a newly organized body led by the newcomer merchant group, produced a brochure showing the strategic importance of Plantation County in its sector of the state.

Factories to Balance Farms

Few such community endeavors did so much to unify local sentiment and build *esprit de corps* and pride. Not only the production of data and the committee work, but the very presentation of materials, made the townspeople proud of their community and its possibilities. If the visitors made no commitments, they were at least duly impressed. Although the school has not been located in Plantation County, this effort has indicated the awareness of the plight of the county's young people.

When Plantation Town acquired the Levin sports shirt factory, another link was added to the chain of changing tradition. For a long time the merchants had felt that some industry was needed to balance agriculture. While the sawmills represented some progress in this direction, the merchants looked for something that would employ white farm women, work which would give this group sufficient income throughout the year and would represent an expanded source of customers for the stores in town.

The drive for the factory was led by the Ramsey brothers. Descendants of one of the oldest plantation families in the county, the Ramseys were continual misfits in the community. They were enterprising and visionary individuals, extremely conscious of the importance of money and good trade, yet antagonistic toward the traditional plantation preoccupation with land for its own sake. The Ramsey brothers liked to operate in real estate with a quick turnover of capital. To these ends, they purchased large acreages and reduced them to small lots. They were astute businessmen who sold to all comers—Negroes, whites, old citizens, small farmers, newcomers. The Ramsey brothers ruffled a lot of white feathers when they sold a plot of land in the center of town to a Negro funeral company. Their land sales to Negro veterans aided the latter to become small farmers. (The prices were high, but the sales were appreciated.) As outcasts from their ancestral class, it was not surprising that the brothers turned to the newcomer group. The newcomers were just achieving status and wealth. They chafed at the traditional land-based capitalism of the area and welcomed a tie with a group of old citizens who, themselves, had property or access to it for immediate sale.

Plantation County had been attracted to industry in the past, but somehow the community had never acted to bring it about. The local power company did not have enough power; the local hardware store felt it made enough profit and that expansion would do harm; the upper and the middle classes did not want a mill village growing up near their community; the plantation owners feared they would lose their labor supply.

Conditions had changed since the end of the war, however. The State Power Company extended its lines so that the local power company made a hookup. The plantation owners were anxious to convert to cattle and did not need as much labor. But more important, it was felt that industry of a marginal nature—to employ white women who would continue to live on their small farms—would solve the problem of merchants as well as small farmers. The plantation owners and other employers of Negro labor thus would not be affected. Furthermore, they wondered if the retention of white labor, while Negro labor received no new opportunities, might not reduce white emigration while Negro emigration continued.

The newcomers wanted customers who could pay for their goods. They were opposed to the plantation system view of paternalism and the dependence of plantation labor. Whatever Negro group remained, the newcomer element preferred it to be economically self-sufficient. If the first industry were to serve the white population, they also had vague plans for Negro labor. The newcomers satisfied the fears of the upper- and middle-class whites by providing for factories that would employ farm surplus labor to prevent the growth of a mill village.

The newcomers and the dissatisfied Ramsey brothers organized a Chamber of Commerce which had as its purpose the sponsoring of industrial enterprise for Plantation County. The new organization also represented a protest by smaller merchants who were either not admitted to the existing civic club or were subordinated to plantation owner members in decisions affecting the county welfare. The success of the Chamber of Commerce's negotiations with industrial groups eventually attracted the older merchants and even plantation owners to the new organization. But the dominant leadership and spirit of the group were newcomer and town-centered. The newcomers made overtures to the large merchants and the plantation owners for several reasons. These were the real leaders of the community, and their approval was necessary to inspire mass support. The old timers also had capital which had to be channeled from land into industry. Town and country thus remained united by symbiotic needs, if not by long range unified goals.

Factories to Balance Farms   85

The Chamber of Commerce formed committees that made trips to new factories that were operating successfully in counties neighboring Plantation County. The merchants, farmers, and professional people on these committees were pleased to hear from their neighbors the benefits they derived from the factories in their midst. This sparked the efforts of the committee, and led to the actual construction of the small sports shirt factory and an invitation to other enterprises to locate here.

The typical factory in the plantation area and the Pine Belt is operated by owners or managers from the North who like the South for its relatively cheap unorganized labor and the cooperation of local authorities in keeping out unions and recruiting labor. The local people feel it worthwhile to attract these factory owners by granting them a period of time tax-free and by assisting their building program with local loans and the issue of bonds. The plantation system with its paternalism appeals to those factories which are refugees from collective bargaining, unions, and high wages in the North. The factory owners and managers feel that the local rural people can be trained to do most operations; eventually they hope to train local people for managerial positions. Local towns benefit immensely from the new trade the factory pay rolls bring. The factory owners also donate to local charities and build public parks and other facilities.

The neighboring community where the main branch of the Levin sports shirt factory was located vouched for the value of the industry for the town and countryside. Mr. Levin and his family felt that Plantation Town was cooperative and offered a likely place for expansion. The Ramsey brothers offered a plot of land on the highway. An attractive red-brick structure, well-lighted with fluorescent light and employing seventy-five farm women and girls at sewing machines, now occupies a site which was formerly the town house of a plantation owner. The Levins have a local woman manager who hires the workers and grades them. The women were earning from fifty to eighty cents an hour before the 1950 minimum wage law went into effect. This has supplemented small-farm income considerably. Both the townspeople and the factory owners seemed pleased with the arrangement. There is no mill village; the pay roll is a weekly affair; there is an employee waiting list drawn up; there is no fear of unionization. (In a neighboring community union organizers are noted as they come into town, and employees who speak with them are warned through their families to leave the community or to desist from union activities.)

The Chamber of Commerce is undertaking an advertising campaign to promote the interest of additional industry in coming to Plantation County. One large textile company has evinced interest, and a mass rally, not unlike that for the trade and vocational school project, once more showed the support of the community behind the idea. If the proposed textile factory should be established in Plantation Town, it would employ some seven hundred white men and women at operations including sewing, dyeing, packing, and assembly.

The labor survey of the area extended to a radius of forty miles. Improved roads and bridges might make such commutation feasible. White residents still wish to avoid a mill village; they wish only to strengthen the white small farmer by such new enterprises. The community plans to purchase the Levin factory, perhaps to convert it to Negro labor, if the new and larger factory comes to the community. However, the new manufacturer hesitates to enter Plantation County for fear of disturbing the position of his fellow manufacturer. Propositions have already been advanced to the Negro schools to introduce sewing machine and assembly instruction. Attempts have been made, unsuccessfully at present, to bring in a work garment factory for Negro labor.

The Levin factory was merely in the idea stage when I left Plantation County in June, 1948. The additional developments above were seen firsthand on my revisit during January, 1950. I have had to revise earlier hypotheses concerning employment of Negroes in factory work. Apparently after the white labor market is exhausted there will be attempts made to find work for Negroes. This follows the race-caste attitudes of the newcomer group. They seek a strong white element based on the small farmer and his working womenfolk; they also seek a Negro population that is economically and socially productive. This will eventually be of benefit to the merchants and to the participants in industry. As for the plantation owners and their need for labor, the proposed cotton crop restrictions for 1950 will tend to hasten the conversion of land to pasture. If there is not to be a mass exodus of Negroes from the plantation area, some industrial opportunity must be found. The merchants in Plantation County seem to desire such Negro customers. A secondary prospect for the Negroes lies in an increased need for domestic service. Working white women will be in need of house servants on small farms, just as white women in town employ domestic help and still have a good sum left over from their wages.

The factory projects further bring to a focus the felt needs of various interest-groups both in the county and outside. The merchants who first fostered the projects wish to overcome the economic cycles of the old cotton-based plantation system and encourage economic stability among white smaller farmers and Negroes. Factory owners from the North find southern communities potential sources for labor and profit; the paternalism of the plantation system encourages similar employer-employee relations. Plantation owners, faced with cotton crop restrictions, no longer need large supplies of Negro labor, and they can afford to support local industry as an investment without hurting their farming interests. Small farmers can check the shock of low prices and can provide themselves with some of the material goods that mass advertising pictures as necessary. Negroes, threatened with eviction from the plantations, look to the new industry as a step to new opportunities and economic security. The upper classes look upon such change with disillusionment because the old way is disappearing; but industry offers some new opportunity for economic investment.

The plantation system still characterizes social and economic forms in the area regardless of the recent industrial developments. Race-caste relations, employer-employee relations, private enterprise, and other forms of *laissez faire* capitalism hearken back to the plantation character of the section. The introduction of industry could not have come about had not the merchant newcomer class received approval from the plantation owners. These leaders of the community control public opinion as well as the largest capital resources in the area. Only the conversion from cotton culture to cattle raising has permitted such a change in plantation owner attitude. State interference is still fought by these interests; only educational programs, credit services, and other governmental enterprises of direct benefit to this dominant group are tolerated. Plantation owners who are making adjustments to the changing conditions favor the new balance between factory and farm. The other group tends to remain conservative. As the factories prove themselves financially remunerative, it is possible that capitalists in land might participate directly in such new enterprises. They do not want to see newcomers take over the leadership of the plantation area.

6

WHEN WHITES AND NEGROES COME TOGETHER

PLANTATION COUNTY was settled after the War of 1812 by white people, mainly of Scotch-Irish ancestry, who had lived and farmed on the Atlantic seaboard. There was also a sprinkling of Germans and French among the early white settlers, the latter coming from the Gulf Coast area.

The early settlers brought their slaves with them, Negroes whose ancestors came from west Africa and other parts of the Dark Continent. They had been shipped to the New World in slave ships between the seventeenth and nineteenth centuries. The increase in plantations and cotton culture made it profitable to purchase additional slaves through the great slave trading centers in the area. By 1850 the Negro slave population in Plantation County outnumbered the white population two to one. Those whites who settled in the poorer hill areas had small farms and could not afford or did not need slaves. The ratio of Negroes to whites was four to one in 1900, and the proportion has remained approximately the same since then, despite large out-migrations by each group.

Although the close of the Civil War supposedly ended slavery, the period of the Reconstruction with its Union Army occupation, Republican government, and Negro-oriented regime produced such a reaction among whites in the South that relations between the two races became stabilized in a race-caste code of behavior that has endured in but slightly modified form since that time. The former Negro slave became a tenant on the plantation because it was economically feasible for both whites and Negroes to make such an arrangement. Yet this arrangement did not give the Negro much more freedom than the right to leave the place. In fact, the plantation owner no longer had to feed and clothe him. Memories of Reconstruction days are still deeply imbedded in the minds of the children and grandchildren of the Confederacy so that national and international attempts to create conditions promoting equality of opportunity between whites and Negroes are resisted.

The term race-caste seems appropriate to describe white and Negro interrelations in this area. While a majority of the Negroes, so-called, in the plantation area have some white blood in their veins, race, rather than culture, defines the group. As long as Negro blood is perceptible in a person he is relegated to the Negro group, his cultural condition notwithstanding. Of course, the inhibitions placed on Negroes tend to cultivate cultural specialties and alternatives that characterize a subculture, but this seems to be a consequence of the race-caste character of behavior rather than a survival from some African cultural ancestry. While the Negro is not so content with his lot as the member of a Hindu caste, we may characterize the unequal distribution of privileges and the organization of prejudices in plantation area society as race-caste behavior. Intermarriage is forbidden and mutual kin between the races are not publicly recognized. While miscegenation is actually practiced, no public recognition of it is sanctioned, hence the caste-like character of Negro-white interaction in the area. Membership in either group is determined solely by birth and there is no opportunity for individuals or groups to pass into the other caste, unless their physical features are such as to permit the clandestine act known as "passing for white."[1]

In a rural environment where everybody knows everybody else it is almost impossible for persons to "pass for white." Almost everybody's kinship is known by everybody else, white and Negro. Not only that, but in Plantation County there is such a cultural difference between Negroes and whites that the lightest skinned "Negro" is soon detected when he opens his mouth to speak. Negro and white subcultural differences are highlighted by vast differentials in education between the two groups; they are more marked in the plantation area than in southern cities or northern states where there is more equality of opportunity. In Plantation County I heard one story of the attempt of a visiting Negro girl to "pass" while seated in a white section of a train. When some white men escorted her to her destina-

---

[1] Cf. Oliver C. Cox, *Race, Caste, and Class* (New York: Doubleday, 1948), for an opposing point of view. Cox regards the Negro-white interaction situation as a form of Marxian economic class struggle. He defines caste only in the Indian sense of the term rather than the sociological. But the Negro seems too imitative of white capitalist values and behavior to be considered a proletariat.

tion they were chagrined to find her greeted by Negro friends. The white woman who told the story was surprised the girl was not punished for her deception. Some white men in a bus station in Plantation Town told a joke on another who offered to carry the bags of a woman who turned out to be a "white nigger."

We can best size up the various statuses within Negro and white society by utilizing ideal types to represent the ideal person who occupies such a status position, his varying roles, and his relations with other members of the social system.

Sam Eades is a "good Negro." He behaves strictly in accordance with the race-caste code when dealing with white people. He "gets along"; he "isn't looking for trouble"; he is humble above all. He is a "good Negro" if he smiles and appears happy. By inclining his head, Sam shows the white man that he acknowledges him as superior. He tips his hat to white men and women. He does not look a white woman straight in the eye. Sam treats all whites, from the "sorriest" poor white to the wealthiest "high type" white from the plantation, with the same deference. He waits until a white person is disengaged before approaching for conversation, even though his own business may be of more importance to each than some trivia that might be under discussion. He says "sir" or "ma'am" at all times, punctuating his conversation frequently with these titles of courtesy. He rarely proffers his opinion, especially when it is not asked for. White people say that Sam would not sit and eat with white people even if he were asked to—they say "he knows his place; he would be embarrassed." White people also feel certain Sam would be confused if he were called by anything but his first name. Sam is even careful not to call other Negroes "Mr." or "Mrs." before white people, although his inhibition here is declining. Sam waits in line until all whites, regardless of when they came, are served. He will go out of his way to do favors for white people, even if it inconveniences him. He tends to anticipate the behavior of the whites.

Although Sam may be considered a "good Negro" by the whites, his fellow Negroes may classify him differently. He can be a "good Negro" among his own people if he gets along with them and actually helps his group through his friendly relations with the whites. We have already seen how Mr. Waters, the Negro county agent, is such a person. A Negro who uses his position in the eyes of the whites to the disadvantage of the other Negroes is called a "white man's nigger." Such a person has status in the Negro community only in so far as other Negroes fear his powerful connections with the white man. Many plantation taskmasters had such reputations. The old mammies of pleasant white tradition gave their all for the whites and neglected their own offspring. Modern Negroes have little use for such persons.

"Good Negroes" like Sam receive the protection and patronage of "high type" whites. The "high type" white generally has high status in the white community. This gives him sufficient security to merit the *noblesse oblige* that is bestowed on the lower Negro race-caste. Such a white man may help a Negro in trouble if the Negro has not violated a race-caste code. He may lend him money, give bond, and generally protect the Negro underling from unscrupulous whites. The "high type" white tries to be fair and just within the limits imposed by race-caste etiquette. He pays his help on time and he keeps honest accounts. He expresses interest in the welfare of the individual Negro and his family. He gives help and encouragement to ambitious Negroes to enable them to better themselves, but he does not go beyond the race-caste limitations in so doing. It was "high type" whites who first gave Negroes small plots of land to farm for themselves after the Civil War. This group pays doctor bills, visits the sick and injured, replaces "burned out" furniture and clothing, and supports Negro churches and charities.

At the same time, the "high type" white man must maintain his status within the white group. He must also show "he knows his place." He must "act like a white man," or else both whites and Negroes will lose respect for him. This means that "high type" whites do not sanction behavior in violation of race-caste rules. They may condemn lynching or other punitive behavior toward Negroes which involve violence, and occasionally they take the stump against it, but if a case is obviously in violation of ingrained race-caste beliefs of the whites, they feel powerless to interfere. Secretly they may support a white group (usually lower status whites who have pent-up aggression to release) and allow them to "keep the Negro in his place." The "high type" white is fair and honest in his dealings with Negroes, but as a white man and an employer, he pays the prevalent minimal wages and feels that the Negro who is paid too much will "get strange ideas and get into trouble." He is confused by such trends as higher education for Negroes; although he would like to see "good Negroes" advance, he wonders if the wholesale advancement of the race might not lead them to seek equality with the whites. He especially opposes giving political favors of any sort to the Negro. As a white man, the "high type" white, like all the others, feels insecure in the threat of Negro numerical and socio-economic potentials in the plantation area. Locally, the "high type" white would like to see all Negroes remain "good Negroes." When they begin to strain this relationship, the "high type" white becomes anxious and withholds his favor.

There is a small group of whites in Plantation Town regarded as "high type" whites by the Negroes, yet regarded as "radicals" by their white neighbors. Elsewhere, these four or five people would be known as "reformers" or even "liberals." Almost none of these people steps far beyond the accepted sphere of Negro-white relations, but they are more outspoken than others in seeing that Negroes receive "fair treatment." These people are professionals, writers, and civic leaders. None of them calls a Negro "Mr." to his face, though a few use it on mail, especially to Negroes out of town. These persons were the only ones in the county to oppose a state constitutional amendment requiring voters to interpret the constitution in order to receive a franchise. None of them believes in the innate inferiority of the Negro. They view him as a person who has not been given the opportunities to develop and demonstrate his abilities. These liberals ally themselves with national and regional reform movements through church associations and professional societies. Although they support civil rights legislation in principle, they do not think it will work in the plantation area. They are willing to grant the vote to the educated Negro group at once, but they feel the masses should be educated before the vote is completely extended. These liberals are evolutionists; they are "liberal southerners," rather than "southern liberals" in the accustomed usage. They operate through existing race-caste behavior patterns rather than attacking them directly. Their status in the white community is sufficiently high to protect them from revenge by dissident whites. But their numbers are so few that they take care not to be known as "nigger lovers" and thence ostracized.

A "mean nigger" is a Negro who does not adhere to the race-caste rules of behavior according to white definition. In Negro society such a person is often also a "trouble-maker," in that he may cheat, lie, steal, or even murder among his own people. Such a person may act as informer to the whites in order to ingratiate himself with them. Neither group trusts him, and when the "law," in the person of the sheriff, catches up with him, the Negro community is not too surprised nor does it defend him strongly. Negroes who have status in their own community are defended by their people regardless of how they behave toward white men. But such Negroes make the entire community insecure so that every attempt is made by the responsible leaders of the older generation to teach fear and respect for white people. Young Negroes who cannot play such a role are forced to leave the area lest they "get into trouble." The situation is becoming increasingly intolerable to young Negroes who have achieved some education or who have travelled.

The "poor white" is often of low status and is the least secure member of the social system. Upper-class whites look upon persons who drink, fight, gamble, and take revenge on weaklings as a shame to the race. Negroes take their cue from "high type" whites in grading other whites, so they also hold the "poor whites" in low esteem. Negroes who have dealings with these groups adhere strictly to race-caste etiquette lest they arouse suspicion and invoke aggression. Negroes try to use "high type" whites as intermediaries with these groups as much as possible. The "high type" whites can thus play protector to the Negroes; lower status whites serve to keep the Negroes in check and at the same time divert aggression toward the Negro instead of against those who are really in power. These "poor whites" have the franchise and serve on juries; they guard white supremacy.

A new type of Negro is emerging in the plantation area who at the same time is a product of the mass culture. This type of Negro appears "uppity" to white people, for he appears to seek status beyond that which the local whites are willing to grant. These Negroes often attain high status in the Negro community by virtue of economic and educational achievements. They do not care to associate with the whites any more than necessary for they feel themselves to be as good as the whites, although they are relegated to an inferior position. They tend to isolate themselves from the majority of Negroes who are "good Negroes" and to form cliques of their own. They are highly race-conscious and read Negro magazines, such as *Ebony*, and the Negro newspapers from the North. When these Negroes find it necessary to come in contact with whites, they perform their expected race-caste role but make the encounter as brief as possible. Many of these persons are mulattoes. The group is bitter at being classified with the bulk of Negroes in the area and tries to compensate for it by showing achievements comparable to those of white persons. Since they are forced to be with the Negro race, they use their economic and professional position to influence the younger generation of the masses to be more like themselves than like their parents. Many of this group are the schoolteachers in the secondary schools and their pupils, and most of these students leave the plantation area as soon as they graduate from school. The group's dilemma is caused by the contradiction between American mass culture, preaching democracy and equality of opportunity, and the culture of the plantation area which preaches white supremacy. The situation for this group has become so intolerable all over the South and the nation that its members feel civil rights legislation and correlative local programs a necessity.

A new type of white is also emerging in the "climber." This person does not have plantation ancestry; his interests are generally town- and business-centered. He does not feel close to the Negro, nor is he secure enough to ignore him. The "climbers" would like to achieve economic and social power in their group. The ignorant Negro holds back all of plantation area society according to the viewpoint of the "climber." As merchants, the "climbers" would like to see Negroes put on a sound economic and intellectual basis, within race-caste limits, to enable them to become better customers. They would just as soon be rid of the mass of "darkeys." White supremacy for this group means economic, social, and political control by a capitalist class without the accoutrements of plantation society *noblesse oblige*. The watchword of this group is sound business methods and efficiency. The Negro, for this group, is accepted more on the basis of what he produces than on how he behaves, although race-caste limitations are kept. As this white group increases, the Negro will have to seek elsewhere for patronage. The federal government, as we have seen, has substituted for the paternalistic plantation owner to a large extent. The Fair Deal, including Civil Rights, represents these new directions.

The new trends in white and Negro race-caste types are significant for the future of race relations in the plantation area. Both the white merchant "climber" and the Negro race-conscious intellectual are on the increase. The "good Negro" and the "high type" white represent a traditional pattern in the plantation area that is declining as the conditions of the situation change. American mass culture is playing a significant role.

When Whites and Negroes Come Together

An outsider's observations on race relations in Plantation County are reinforced by conversation with the whites. White people in Plantation County are ever ready to expound and justify their beliefs about the Negro. These representations are important if we hold them against a mental background of deep insecurity and anxiety about the future. While no psychoanalytic techniques were used in this investigation, the materials lead to some hypothetical conclusions about basic anxieties in the area.

The whites in the plantation area have gone through a succession of crises that have rocked their world. There was the military and economic defeat during the Civil War, a hated Yankee occupation with Negro license, cycles of prosperity and poverty with the cotton market, the boll weevil, and recently the economic depression of the thirties. Civil Rights legislation and the general pressure of worldwide public opinion for democratic equality of opportunity reach the white man daily through his radio, newspapers, and magazines.

The contradictions of race-caste are proven by the numerous mulattoes about the county. These are proofs of clandestine relations between white men and Negro women. White women have borne the shame silently, but the actions of white men toward Negro males possibly suggests projection—do they desire white women? The whites feel insecure concerning the purity of the race, yet this may be a cover for their own miscegenation activities.

To the question "What is a Negro?" the white man will answer, "He is not a real human being like you and me. He smells bad; he is sexually promiscuous; he is filthy and ignorant; he is good only for work with his hands; he eats once a day all day; he can live on next to nothing; he is always happy like a child; he has no foresight."

If we ask, "Why is he that way?" the answers will vary: "God made him that way as a punishment; that is why the races must not mix"; "A colored person is what he is just because he is that way." A few "enlightened" people will say, "He hasn't had the opportunity to advance." But the majority feel, "He doesn't want to be any better, or he wouldn't be the way he is; the Africans never had any civilization; anybody who has ambition can get ahead." Then they cite a few cases of Negroes who have made their mark. The value-ideal of private initiative and enterprise operates here too.

When we ask, "Why do Negroes and whites down South act this particular way?" white answers are forthright. "The Negro is always trying to be like a white man. We know he can never be equal to us, but he tried once, during Reconstruction, and we have to keep him in his place. With the whites outnumbered four to one in Plantation County and ten to one in some parts of the county, you see the need for control, even force if necessary, to keep the Negro from taking over the country." "Taking over" presumably means a fear of the Negro conquering the whites physically by forced miscegenation; politically, by assuming political offices; economically, by taking over land ownership; and generally, by joining all social activities of the whites. The whites seem to fear as much for their power and property as they do for their racial purity. In light of the existing high rate of miscegenation, racial purity appears to be largely a defense mechanism. Whites say, "This is a white man's country, and it will always be so. We came here first and we mean to stay. If the Negro doesn't want to live here on our terms, he can get out."

With the above representations in mind, we can examine the action patterns by which the whites alleviate their anxieties and fears. We should also note whether there is consistency in their behavior, between what they feel, what they say, and what they do.

White supremacy is summed up in the expression, "keeping the Negro in his place." The behavior of the "good Negro" is the approved role in a white supremacy society. Whites, for their part, are also expected to "keep their place." This is done to a high degree, as we have already noted; even "liberals" observe race-caste customs.

White society has forbidden legal marriage between the races in order to keep the white race "pure." The whites maintain their racial "purity" by including all perceivable mixed-bloods in the Negro race-caste and refusing to legitimize their births. Occasionally a mulatto offspring is granted property or gifts, but on the whole whites try not to recognize the relationship between mulatto and their own legitimate offspring. If a mulatto looks obviously like a white parent or a white half-sibling, he is generally driven from the community.

While no systematic investigation of miscegenation rates in Plantation County was made during this study, both white and Negro informants seem to feel that if miscegenation itself has not decreased in this generation, at least mixed-blood births have been radically reduced. Some of the reasons given for this phenomenon are related to the influence of the mass culture, especially in the area of white women's behavior. Ante-bellum and Victorian restrictions against young women have been superseded by a general liberal attitude toward dating, courtship, and marriage. Observations on the sexual behavior of girls in secondary school and older girls in Plantation County bear this out—there seems to be a wholesome attitude between young men and women in the area. Older white people comparing the restrictions of their childhood days note with alternating approval and disapproval the changing pattern. There is greater freedom of movement in modern plantation area society—the automobile functions as a private meeting place. Then, too, the growing estrangement between Negroes and whites in their informal dealings with each other has been noted—there are fewer steady Negro domestics in white homes; white children do not play with Negroes except on plantations; Negro children form their own society in school, whereas they used to accompany their mothers to work in white homes.

Negroes have also altered their sense of values within the past generation. There is a growing feeling of race consciousness and race pride which has been fostered by mass media through Negro magazines and newspapers and a school curriculum heavily weighted with materials on Negro achievement. Negro educational advances have also played their part in introducing white patterns of moral behavior as an ideal. Negro men have been able to find more remunerative employment in local industry and small farming, so that their own security and responsibility in regard to family life seems improved. Both whites and Negroes have been subjected to education about venereal disease and contraceptive practice. This seems to be a contributory factor toward a decline in miscegenation, or at least in the products of interracial sex relations.

A striking consequence of miscegenation for the white man has been an almost obsessional fear that the white woman will be violated by Negro men and that Negro men desire sexual intercourse with white women. The sexual potential of Negro men and women is exaggerated by all white groups. White women have supported race-caste codes because they also fear Negro male advance; they are bitter over the presence of mulattoes in the society. It is usually embarrassing to white men and women to speak about them; they usually claim that only "low-class whites" have such offspring. When it comes to noting the parents of some well-known mulattoes about the county, however, plantation owner ancestry seems as likely to appear as any other. That

Negro men may be desirable love objects for white women is borne out by three examples reported to me—two of them took place several years ago; the third is a current topic. In each instance the Negro was killed and the white woman driven from the area. Both middle-class and low-class white families were represented in these affairs. No Negro in Plantation County has raped a white woman, but such fears are ever present and serve to keep race-caste behavior patterns operative. Whites believe that any breach in race-caste behavior will lead to "social equality," which to them signifies rape as much as anything. White women feel that they may become objects of rape, but at the same time they feel the security of a white mob that can always be organized to protect them. One white widow who lives alone relates how she has no fears whatsoever of "disturbance," for she knows there are white men all around watching out for her. Another fears the "buggeman" but knows that neither white nor faithful "darkey" will let her come to harm. It is significant that this woman will accept the protection of an old Negro man against possible harm from younger Negro men. White fears that Negro war veterans would not settle down peacefully after their experience with white women in Europe have been unfounded. Whites now point out that this proves races like "their own" best. White people invariably tell a northerner about seeing white women and Negro men together on subway trains up North—it "disgusts" them and "justifies" keeping race-caste codes down South.

We have already noted the intensity of economic motives for white supremacy. White people justify paying Negroes low wages by claiming Negroes are spendthrifts; this is easily noticeable in October and November after settlement time. But Negro love for material goods of the moment is conditioned by the insecurity of his position in society. Since he moves about considerably, there is little incentive to invest in objects of permanent value. One Negro domestic says, "If you save your money, the white man will find some way of getting it from you, so you might as well spend it while you've got it." A white man who sells land to Negroes and who arranges credit transactions remarks about the profit from such ventures: "The Negro may have money today to make a down payment on some property, but he won't have any money six months from now, and we have the property back." The plantation owner has not taught the Negro how to save; plantation conditions have rather encouraged the Negro to have his good time while he has the money for nobody knows what tomorrow will bring. It is this psychology which the Farmers Home Administration has to combat before it can create Negro small farmers. Local whites fear such a change in Negro attitudes toward money. While they praise the few Negroes who have managed to save their money and purchase land, the whites are also careful to note that general trends in this direction by Negroes must be resisted. White merchants sell all sorts of bicycles, toys, and radio-phonographs to Negroes in the fall; they invite them to borrow on credit. The dazzle of the new goods coming to the plantation area from all over the country causes most Negroes to lay their money on the merchant's counter rather than trust it to the bank or purchase some property. Besides, the whites control property sales, and banks have failed in the past.

The whites have also maintained race-caste relations through their control of the schools. A visit to white and to Negro schools in the county (they are segregated, as are all schools in the South) reveals the inferiority of Negro school buildings and equipment. An examination of Negro and white schoolteacher certificates reveals white superiority in teacher training and qualifications. While the budget for all Negro schools in the county (1949-1950) is higher than that for white schools, expenditure per pupil is much higher for white pupils. The white school board does not understand why Negro school principals wish to teach languages, social science, or higher mathematics in their schools. Whites are eager to increase the vocational training facilities in Negro schools as indicated by their proposal to install sewing machines and tool shops. They feel that the liberal arts, worse than being of no value to the Negro student's future in this area, "spoil" him and make him troublesome. Educated Negroes begin to despise their situation; they achieve white values as they become as educated as white people. They are frustrated, however, so they leave the area or else turn to their own people, as their teachers have done, and indoctrinate them with Negro values and achievements.

The whites control politics above all. Attempts from the outside to impose civil rights in the plantation area are resisted bitterly, and Reconstruction days are recalled. No Negro in Plantation County votes. The state has a poll tax and a constitution-interpretation law to qualify voters. While I was in Plantation Town a Negro veteran tried to register for the current elections. The sheriff told him firmly that Negroes "just do not vote" in Plantation County. The veteran noted the glances of white people near by and apologized profusely for "presuming" that Negroes could vote. White people downtown still laugh at the reaction of some other Negroes to a white man renowned for several shootings of Negroes. When he bellowed at them, "Where's that vet'ran who tried to register?" they all scattered.

When Negro leaders and average citizens are questioned about "all them doin's up in Washington," they nod their heads and say, "Civil Rights is all to the good, but who's going to enforce it down here?"

If you ask white people why they are opposed to Negro voting they come up with the following typical remarks—"They would elect their own; how would you like a nigger probate judge?" Perhaps the whites are again projecting and fear reprisals. Another faction of whites opposes the Negro vote because they feel any elected official (even if he were white) would be at the power of the Negro electorate and would have to serve them to the disadvantage of the white electorate. They cite the domination of northern politics by "minorities" as a proof of their argument. A third group says that ignorant Negro voters would be at the mercy of demagogues, and therefore they would not vote the way they really feel—actually several instances of politicians paying "poor white" poll taxes and otherwise bribing them are on record. One local official lost out during re-election because he served liquor to "poor whites" in a section of the county; the "better elements" thought this was scandalous. In order to vote, poll taxes that have been unpaid for many years must be made up. Local people wondered when certain poor people suddenly began to pay thirty and forty dollars in back taxes to vote in a recent state election.

The whites control the courts and the execution of the law. Only white men are called for jury duty. A friendly white man is of great advantage in securing justice for Negroes. In a case which I observed during one of the biannual sessions of county court, the testimony of ten white witnesses about the "fine character" of a Negro defendant in a manslaughter case secured him his freedom. All evidence presented by the prosecution and his Negro witnesses showed that the defendant had actually bludgeoned the deceased. While I was in Plantation County rumors spread about two white boys from a neighboring county who had forced a Negro man away while they raped his wife. The white community was shocked and urged that something be done. White people felt that the sheriff should show the Negro community that there was law and authority to protect them. But when the day for the boys' trial came, the courtroom was cleared of "all white women and colored people." While waiting with the other white men in the audience, I could see the lawyers bargaining and joking; the boys ultimately were convicted of assault, sentence suspended.

It is interesting to note that the Negro benefits in cases which do not violate race-caste codes. A major portion of the cases at county court involve distilling, and these are generally repetitive. Negroes are the chief violators. They are generally fined "costs" the first time; a jail sentence is imposed for a second offense. Many Negroes are never brought to court for offenses against the law such as drunkenness, theft, or even knife-fights within their own group. White people say such Negro behavior is "proof" that they are like children; they are "punished" by a night in jail or a fine. White people who are their employers or protectors generally bond them. The law feels it is better to keep the Negro working than to let him lie in jail. I have seen Negroes taken out of jail to mow the deputy's lawn, thus keeping them busy and giving them some fresh air.

White people admit that Plantation County Negroes are generally well-behaved and "know their places." Occasionally, however, there is a direct breach of the code, and white reaction is swift. A few years ago an escaped Negro convict killed a popular white deputy who set out after him. The whites in the community were enraged, and a mob was quickly formed to hunt down the culprit. That this was no ordinary mob is shown by the fact that among the leaders was a well-known professional person in town. When the convict was trapped and shot, the mob brought back the body and laid it on the ground before the courthouse as a warning to others not to tamper with race-caste limits. It is said that many white women also joined in the celebration and gazed upon the body. A local writer was nearly run out of town when he wrote up the incident for a national publication. Such incidents serve to remind the Negro community of the consequences of "fooling around with white folks."

The sheriff in Plantation County is respected by whites and Negroes alike. He spends his time protecting "respectable" people from the intrusions of drunkenness, thieving, and rowdyism. He thus maintains order in both the white and Negro communities. A great deal of his time is spent with the state police hunting local stills. The sheriff receives a bounty on each still that is captured, and he has an organized group of Negro and white informants to help him in his search. He enjoys quite a reputation, both among whites and Negroes, for detecting moonshine establishments. While the sheriff is supposed to maintain order in both white and Negro communities, in a real showdown his role as white man conflicts with his role as sheriff.

While I was in Plantation County two white boys beat up a Negro domestic without due provocation. The white community expressed its indignation, and several citizens requested that the sheriff "do something about it." The sheriff locked the boys up in jail for the night, but they were released later with no follow-up. The Negro woman's employer was not sure whether or not to prefer charges against the white boys, but in the end she was persuaded not to. A white lawyer said that while he sympathized with the victim, he would never take her case, because he felt all whites must stick together lest the Negroes take over. The white community continued to discuss the incident for several months, and there were repercussions between "liberal" and opposing factions which brought in religious and social divisions as well.

One Negro response to the situation is emigration. This is principally because of the lack of economic opportunities in the county. White supremacy is related to this also. The pull of the North and other sections of the country is largely sponsored by letters and stories about economic opportunities outside of the plantation area. Economics seems to be more important than race-caste restrictions, for large numbers of Negroes are tending to settle in southern cities as industrialization provides greater economic opportunity near by. Except for an increasing number of educated young Negroes, the majority still have an affection for their homes and for friendly whites; those who leave return for visits, and they write letters about their activities both to Negroes and to whites. Our foregoing discussion of the economic institution and trends shows that opportunity for Negroes, with a few exceptions, is becoming increasingly scarce in the plantation area. We might therefore expect continued emigration,

Another form of Negro response to the situation is acculturation.

When Whites and Negroes Come Together 103

Negroes are becoming more like whites all the time. My white landlady, listening to a wire recording of a Negro church service, remarked that she could tell little difference between this service and a white church service. White people who attend Negro high school graduation exercises have noted the dignity and bearing of the occasion. For these white people, the increase in secondary school graduates symbolizes a change from the older ways. White people are continually saying, "Who'd ever expect it from a colored person." Actually, white people in Plantation County have little opportunity to observe and meet many educated Negroes. Local Negroes tend to leave because their very education creates new wants and needs which cannot be satisfied in Plantation County. Negro teachers and the few government workers in the Negro community contradict white ideas about the innate inferiority of the Negro. This proof is disturbing to many whites also; while they admit that the Negro of today is not at all like his humble ignorant father or grandfather, they fear the increasing challenge of Negroes to white supremacy.

Negro family life seems to be more stable than it was in the recent past. Negro men are earning higher wages in local sawmills and their crops have brought in more money also. Negro women do not find it necessary to work outside as much as they did formerly. White women wonder what Negro women "do with all their spare time." The full-time Negro domestic servant seems a thing of the past. A white woman feels fortunate if she can get good part-time help. Negro women are able to work for two or three white persons a week if they wish to; they earn as much from one part-time job as they did from full-time jobs before the war (wages average six or seven dollars a week for full-time work, three times pre-war wages; servants come at breakfast time and prepare dinner and the "cold" supper). Nurses are no longer faithful mammies; in their place we now find Negro adolescent girls who play with small white children and care for them as best they can. Yet, increased employment of lower-class white women is creating a new demand for Negro domestic help.

Negro women can now devote more time to their younger children. Children of school age are more frequently in school than they were years ago. An old grandmother used to care for the children and do cooking while her daughter was out working for white folks. Siblings have always been charged with care of the little children.

Negro women in Plantation County are still slow to participate in organized recreational activity during the day. There are church circles for religiously inclined folk, but other women, notably sawmill workers' wives, fritter away their time gossiping and occasionally drinking and "raising a rumpus." White women seem to have organized their leisure time much more formally in civic clubs and adult educational activity. As Negro education and leisure time increases, however, it seems likely that the women's activities will follow those of whites. The Negro upper classes already evidence such behavior.

Negro families have hitherto been female-dominated. Men, since slavery times, have functioned for sexual relations with small emphasis on their role as parents. The Negro upper classes have followed white patterns progressively more as economic opportunities have opened up for Negro males. Likewise, small-farmer Negro families are male-dominated, since the male head of the household is the breadwinner and manager of the enterprise. The Negro families on Farmers Home Administration projects function very much as white families. Economic stability and a feeling that the male member of the family has a definite role to play as husband and father bring Negro family life closer to the preferred white patterns. Negro schools, churches, government workers, leaders, and literature have combined to promote such trends.

The Negro class system seems based on the values of white society. Those Negroes who are the most like whites achieve status. Negro status groups are described in detail in the next chapter.

A third pattern of Negro response to his situation, after emigration and acculturation, is in-group aggression. The following patterns are noted—direct aggression against fellow Negroes involving violence; mistrust of Negro leaders and preference for white leaders; betraying Negroes to whites; emphasis on trying to eradicate white objections to Negro behavior, and other manifestations of self-hatred.[2]

The sheriff and the physicians report highest rates of Negro ingroup violence on Saturday nights at frolics, or parties, where there is liquor, free sexuality, gambling, "hot" music, and often knife-play. Both officials, however, note a decline in this violence. They feel that the worst Negroes have left and that education is having an effect.

The white physician in town feels that Negroes do not yet have

---

[2] Cf. Kurt Lewin, *Resolving Social Conflicts* (New York: Harpers, 1948), especially Chapter 12, "Self Hatred Among Jews."

confidence in their own leadership and prefer whites as leaders. He was unable to keep a Negro nurse in attendance at the maternity clinic some six years ago. For similar reasons the social welfare department in the county does not hire Negro case workers, though some have applied for the job, and there is a local shortage of workers. Rural Negroes, especially, have had little contact with educated Negro professionals or leaders. They are accustomed to the white man having power and doing things for them. To an extent, however, the whites are responsible for the situation, since they control the entire power structure. Therefore, there is no local opportunity for Negro professionals. The success of the Negro county agent and Negro school teachers perhaps proves that white contentions are not entirely founded. Given the opportunity, it is possible that Negro professionals in Plantation County would be as successful as they are elsewhere in the South. Negro education and the distribution of literature advertising the achievements of the race tends to increase Negro racial solidarity.

Negroes aggress on members of their own group in favor of white people when they relate anecdotes about Negro infidelities, violent action, and other unsavory incidents of Negro life that cause white people to justify their stereotype of the Negro. Yet it is significant that younger and more enlightened Negroes are ashamed of such behavior, and they are also trying to convey this feeling to the whites. Whereas older generation Negroes used to laugh off such foibles before whites, Negro ministers and teachers speak of it to their congregations and classes as a blot upon the Negro race.

A more subtle result of this feeling of shame, however, is actual self-hatred for being classed with ignorant and immoral Negroes by whites. Certain Negroes, unable to escape their condition, become crusaders to show the white race that the Negro *can* achieve stature by white standards. In their zeal they condemn lower-class behavior. They often isolate themselves from the masses of Negroes because they cannot stand to be near them or to be thought of as associating with them. Many Negro intellectuals thus have a vested interest in the situation—they hold jobs as teachers in a segregated system, yet they despise the ignorance that segregation enforces. This group is extremely confused and bitter. They are marginal men who are fully acculturated to white standards yet who live from the products of racial segregation and discrimination.

The last form of Negro response to the situation is aggression directed toward the whites. Direct violence against whites is rare, but modified forms of aggression include lying, cheating, thievery, and other patterns which tend to justify the stereotype of the Negro in the minds of the whites. Negroes also gossip about whites, bear tales, do inefficient work, quit without notice, and do other things to vex white people and show independence. Whites shrug their shoulders and say, "What more can you expect from a Negro?" Direct and obvious Negro aggression is crushed as a challenge to race-caste. The modified forms of aggression are no less challenging, but the whites feel them to be less of a threat.

Of the four forms of Negro response to the situation we have discussed, acculturation seems to be the most positive and dynamic force operating in the plantation area and beyond. It is forcing the widest breach in white beliefs in race-caste. Emigration relieves certain population pressures, but it is a negative reaction to the situation. It does not alter the white man's beliefs in race-caste. Aggression within the Negro group and that directed toward the white group provide temporary relief at most. Aggression does not alter the conditions of the situation; it merely fights symptoms. All four responses by the Negro are manifestations of insecurity and anxiety. While acculturation tends to alter the conditions of the situation, the trend is proceeding more rapidly than the whites are willing to accept; this accounts for a piling up of frustration and aggression among young educated Negroes in particular.

In this changing area of race-caste relations, certain institutionalized patterns have fostered change. Acculturation has proceeded through the school, the family, the church, and the mass culture. Economic conditions have fostered both emigration and, secondarily, acculturation. Aggression has taken place in all the institutionalized areas.

Certain institutionalized areas have likewise retarded change in race-caste relations. The plantation system of paternalism has been extended to business and industry. White supremacy is evident in the educational and political structure of the plantation area. Negro economic insecurity, in addition to social and psychological insecurity, has retarded acculturation. The emigration of more educated and ambitious Negroes from the county also retards acculturation of the rest. White insecurity, itself, is a cause for conservatism in race-caste relations. This is manifest most strongly in political and economic affairs and secondarily in education. In the realm of religion there are those who try to "prove" that God created the Negro innately inferior to the white man.

The war and postwar periods have brought race-caste relations in the plantation area and the South to the attention of the entire United States and the United Nations. In order to change the situation, however, national leaders must understand the roots of the problem and the many forces operating both on and beneath the surface. For the consequences of race-caste behavior in the plantation area affect the entire position of the United States in international relations. Likewise, the activity of world opinion affects the people of the South and the plantation area in a chain reaction.

7

STATUS IN NEGRO AND IN WHITE SOCIETY

PEOPLE in the plantation area rate each other as higher or lower in status according to certain culturally defined criteria. Associated with such status we find certain expected patterns of behavior, certain rewards, rights, and duties. People who occupy status positions in the society play roles. Since there are many institutionalized areas in the structure, we are likely to find statuses associated with the institutions and concomitantly institutionalized roles. We shall call the constellation of statuses which a given individual occupies his general status. The manifestation of general status is role behavior and the public personality. Role behavior may be conflicting, in which case the performer makes decisions about which role to value the most. Cultural values and individual preferences in specifiable situations cause individuals to play one role before another where there is conflict. But such conflict influences personality. A culture which so defines status and role as to create great conflict is a culture wherein the personalities of its members are not integrated.

In the plantation area, as in other societies, we notice certain groups whose members occupy similar statuses and practice similar patterns, or subcultures. In the previous chapter we discussed Negroes and whites as race-castes. Within each race-caste, moreover, there are subgroups which have their own value systems and which practice certain well-definable specialized patterns of their own. We are justified in calling such subgroups classes since there is a hierarchy of goal-directed patterns of activity and cultural objects for each subgroup within a race-caste. In other words, within each race-caste in the plantation area we find a stratified class society.

Our concept of class is more than a conceptual scheme. People in Plantation County readily classify certain people as better or worse, richer or poorer, religious or irreligious, moral or immoral. While the race-caste barrier leads to a dichotomous division of plantation area culture, we can find parallels at each level within white and Negro groups. We must retain the concept race-caste distinct from class as long as birth determines forever one's social station in Plantation County and there is no mobility between the two groups. Class implies achieved as well as ascribed status and vertical mobility up and down.

While throughout the South and the plantation area there are universal criteria and patterns at each stage in the stratification system, the peculiar situation in Plantation County requires attention to local peculiarities. On the whole, the stratification system in both Negro and white society in Plantation County is fluid and loosely organized. Both historical factors and the structure of the community are responsible for this. I believe it is worthwhile to utilize the upper-middle-lower class outline to describe stratification in Plantation County.[1] But the reader must consider that there are differences in criteria, rigidity, and outlook on life between Plantation County and other areas in the South or, for that matter, the plantation area.

The white people who came to Plantation County after the War of 1812 represented a second wave of settlement in southern history. Most of their ancestors came from Europe before the American Revolution and settled the Atlantic seaboard states in the South. The second wave of settlement included yeoman farmers and small planters; the more successful planters stayed behind. The families who came to Plantation County, therefore, did not include aristocratic "first families" as we know them in other sections of the Old South.

The typical plantation in Plantation County is four generations old. The grandparents and parents of Plantation County adults were simple, hard-working farmers who cleared their land, built log or plank housing, and began their operations with little or no Negro slave labor. The planters who prospered on cotton purchased slaves to work their expanding enterprises; by the decade before the Civil War many of these plantations had fifty to over a hundred slave families, but the majority of hill farmers rarely attained a dozen slaves,

---

[1] For previous studies using a more or less complex conceptual scheme of class see: Hortense Powdermaker, *After Freedom* (New York: Viking Press, 1939); John Dollard, *Class and Caste in a Southern Town* (New Haven: Yale University Press, 1937); W. Lloyd Warner and Paul S. Lunt, *The Social Life of a Modern Community* (New Haven: Yale University Press, 1941); Allison Davis, Burleigh B. Gardner and Mary R. Gardner, *Deep South* (Chicago: University of Chicago Press, 1941).

Plantation County

CRITERIA FOR PLANTATIO[N]

Criteria	Upper Class	Upper Middle Class
ECONOMICS	Large prosperous plantation or business. Financial security. Leisure time in old age. Women need not work.	Large- or medium-sized plantation or business. Men may be professionals. Women may work part-time, but do not have to (professional or white collar).
FAMILY	Importance of the extended family, heirlooms. Intermarriage within the same class throughout the state. Democratic family, but old women retain symbols.	Immediate family more important than extended family. Few heirlooms. A democratic family with husband and wife exercising equal authority.
RESIDENCE	Old style plantation home, in town or on plantation—may be reconstructed. Antiques and modern furnishing.	Old style plantation house or modern frame house. More modern furniture than antiques.
RELIGION	Presbyterian, Methodist, some Baptist. Church membership more for social reasons than theological conviction. Church leaders.	Presbyterian, Methodist, Baptist church leaders. Social reasons for church participation, some theological.
COMMUNITY	Regional as much as local interests; leaders in both. Mixed and separate men's and women's groups. *Noblesse oblige* toward the Negro.	More local and less regional participation and leadership. Less *noblesse oblige* toward the Negro. Opposed to lower class whites as vertical threat; envious of upper class whites.
EDUCATION	Usually college. Only professionals are intellectually inclined.	
MORALITY	May provide equivalent to urban "country club set" among younger married couples. Liberal Protestant religious values combined with plantation tradition paternalistic race-caste values. Clandestine drinking, miscegenation, infidelity. Women protected.	
MOBILITY	Upward—to society in the region; through marriage, economic gain, appropriating symbols of upper class (antiques), home. Downward—through loss of wealth (takes two or three generations for a complete fall, since widows are protected).	

OUNTY WHITE CLASS STRUCTURE

Lower Middle Class	Lower Class
Medium or small farmers, or work for others. Women may work in service occupations, or trades. Have to work all their lives. Some debt.	Small farmers or tenants; work for others. Women may work in service, trades, agriculture. Men and women may not desire to work at all. Heavy indebtedness.
Emphasis on the immediate family. Endogamy. Emigrants may sever contacts with home. Increasing male dominance in the family.	Clannish in rural areas. Migrants sever contacts at home. Endogamy; male dominance; unstable family relations, infidelities, aggression.
Bungalow or rural plank farmhouse. not much plumbing, ornamentation. Mail-order furniture, old furniture. Rooms function for many purposes.	Unkept plank house or cabin; few rooms, items of furniture or conveniences. Old furniture; lack of order.
Methodist, Baptist, some sects. Leadership only in some rural churches and in sects. Many non-churchgoers.	Emotional sects or non-church goers.
Not much participation in community activities. Conscious of "keeping the Negro in his place." Feel themselves to be "as good as the next fellow."	Isolated cliques and clans. Mostly one-sex friendship groups. Take out aggressive tendencies on other poor whites and Negroes.
Elementary school; some trends toward high school. "Practical." Fundamentalist attitude toward the worldly "pleasures," yet clandestine breaches fairly often.	Quit school early. Public flouting of the mores.

Upward—with education, good job, successful marriage, improved morality, community participation, leadership.
Downward—where publicly oppose the mores of the community (morality), especially in areas of economics (industry), education, drink and indulgence, sex.

if that many. Frontier patterns remained among men of the plantation area, and we have seen survivals to this day. The Civil War halted the flourishing culture of the planter class of the second area of settlement, so that there was no opportunity to develop an aristocratic culture, tradition, or class comparable to the Atlantic seaboard.

While many Plantation County families are well educated, have high incomes, display "good manners," and even preserve heirlooms from ancestral homes back East, they are only three or four generations removed from the frontier, and they are not a true "aristocracy." They still support the universal patterns of church attendance and temperance; there is no high church in Plantation County; in order to qualify for "society" within the state, individuals from these families have to achieve such additional status as professional fame, political power, or fortunate marriage to leading families in the urban communities of the state. The leading families of Plantation County tend to be regarded as "country cousins" of high society in the state. They are the people who stayed behind, while other members and branches of the family got high political appointments, entered industry, or joined the "country club set" by moving to the state capital or other large social and cultural centers.

We may say that Plantation County has an upper class among the whites if we remember that these are people who have large plantations, property in land or in large businesses, social contacts with leading families elsewhere in the state, college education, and a love for tradition and for the extended family. But this upper class is relative to Plantation County only; within the state it would have to achieve additional prestige and would especially have to turn from a local provincialism and support of local mores and institutions to a more cosmopolitan outlook, much of which might violate local mores. In the following section we shall indicate such a case in the person of a local writer and educator.

The majority of Plantation County white society is a middle-class bourgeois society. Many of the universal patterns of American middle-class society and the values of the mass culture are to be found here. Most Plantation County whites have steady work and income, they own their own homes, attend church regularly, read popular newspapers and magazines, participate in community and civic affairs, and hold to middle-class Protestant Christian ideals of morality. Life in Plantation County is so intimate that "everybody knows everybody else." "Everybody" attends weddings, funerals, club meetings, and the other semiprivate or semipublic activities. The gradations we find in Plantation County white society can be measured by cliques and by the degrees of social participation of certain subgroups and subclasses—certain weddings are more exclusive than others; one may participate in common at a church meeting, but dinner invitations are more selective; certain individuals and groups hold higher leadership positions than others; housing values and appearances differ.

On the basis of such gradations and indices as housing and residence, family prestige, church affiliation and attendance, occupation and income, education, value system and morality, social participation and clique organization, we shall discuss the division of the white society into an upper-, middle-, and lower-class stratification system. The middle class is so large, and gradations here are so indicative of the need for dichotomy, that we shall describe an upper middle and a lower middle class. The upper class, as noted above, will represent a group that is very wealthy and enjoys the highest of prestige among all classes and races. We shall note the existence of a lower class in Plantation County that is distinguished by poverty and shiftlessness, the lack of desire to participate in middle-class culture, with a value system at odds with the value system of the power groups in the society. This class might be larger but for the fact that the Negro constitutes a large laboring race-caste with which whites cannot compete, so they have to leave. The race-caste setup encourages white advance and achievement, so that there is a constant upward mobility from the lower end of the stratification scale. The lower-class whites represent those who prefer to remain poor and ignorant and lazy. They are not a proletariat because they have no sense of class solidarity, leadership, or common goals. Those who wish to improve their lot advance into the lower middle class; the others are content to compensate for their condition by behaving immorally before the other white classes or avenging themselves on the Negro when somebody whips them up to it.

Sunday dinner at the Joe Starlings represents a gathering of some of Plantation County's leading families and personages. First of all there is Mr. Starling, a plantation owner and also a director of the Plantation Town utility company. Mrs. Starling is a professional writer and an occasional schoolteacher, in addition to her duties as housewife and mother of three children. Professor Walker, one of the guests, is descended from plantation people, but he is particularly noted for his professional achievements, his social connections with statewide upper-class circles, and his reputation for the bon mot. The young Presbyterian minister is recently arrived in Plantation County, but already his interest in antiques and genealogy earns him ready access to people who care about such things. Mr. Starling's brother is a leading merchant in town. The oldest Starling son attends college where he is active in the fraternity in which plantation area young men predominate. The younger children are in public school. (Their mother has set up a table in a neighboring room where the cook serves them.)

Professor Walker and Mr. Starling, the host, begin to reminisce about their boyhood days. Mr. Starling says, "Remember how you used to be a bookworm while I sneaked off hunting and fishing every time I could. Never could sit down to a lot of reading. That's more for women, I think."

Mr. Starling's brother is inclined to agree with him and adds, "And those parties we had during college week ends; I met my wife at one of those fraternity dances. Joe knew Martha from the time they were kids, but I think I've done just as well from the week-end angle."

The minister begins to remind Mr. Starling about their obligations to attend the Boy Scout conference at Black Belt City next Wednesday; there is also a meeting of church officers next week. "It seems as if once people around here find out you can handle one job, they soon begin to load all other sorts of work on you. Most of the members of these clubs do nothing but come and sit."

Mr. Starling's brother adds, "I suppose those of us with means ought to feel a responsibility for seeing that things go right. It's the same way with the colored people. One of them came up to me the other day and said, 'Mister Jim, can you give our church some money to help with the convention plans for next month?' Of course," Mr. Starling emphasizes, "I had to give him something. Father always saw to it that they kept happy in their church-doings. Keeps them from getting into trouble."

At that, Mrs. Starling breaks in, "Speaking of trouble, dear, don't you get into anything with those roughneck friends of yours on that fishing trip Friday week! I don't see why you want to go fishing with them anyway!"

Her brother-in-law is quick to answer, "My dear, we are only amateurs compared to Mac Slater who always brings home some whoppers. He may only know how to run a one-mule farm, but he can hunt and fish better'n any white man in these parts. You've got to recognize leadership when you see it."

The professor notes, "I suppose so, but I prefer sitting in a cool parlor drinking iced tea or something stronger and reading about such trips to actually going on them. Next week I'm taking some of the Women's Study Club to visit the old plantation house down by the river. They're looking forward to visiting some antique shops along the way."

Mrs. Starling's sister-in-law sighs, "I suppose men will be men, and we women glad of it. At least you don't bring those roughnecks home with you. I'll spend the day visiting Aunt Becky—she has some new bushes to show me."

After a pause, the professor asks, "Did any of you read about the latest goings on at the capital? I hear they've got a new law up about regulations for voting."

"I didn't read about it in the paper, but Joe told me something about it," Mrs. Starling says thoughtfully. "I don't have much time to read the paper; are the niggers trying to start trouble again?"

"I only get to read the society page," Mrs. Starling's sister-in-law adds. "There's so much going on these days; all you hear about is trouble with the Reds and the darkeys. Why don't those northern troublemakers leave us alone? Seems like they've always got something to say about how we treat our darkeys down here. Up there a nigger hasn't got a friend. The communists talk, but when it comes to helping out a 'burned out' colored family, show me one who'd lift a finger! I've just finished collecting clothing for my cook's sister's family. Poor things lost everything."

The men of the plantation area are predominately farmers; they derive great sport from the frontier-like activities of hunting and fishing. Their womenfolk are proud homemakers and keep up plantation day traditions. Men of the upper class mingle more than women with other classes of the community—in their business and in their recreational activities. Women tend to associate with those in their own cliques.

The upper-class home reflects a culture partially bourgeois American and partially of the plantation tradition. There are usually some antiques, a coat of arms, and cuttings of camellias or other flowers in season. The housewife supervises cooks and nurses and yardboys; she shops downtown to meet her needs for food but also to visit with friends and to "see what is going on." The upper-class housewife has her afternoons free for meetings—the United Daughters of the Confederacy (U.D.C.) or the Daughters of the American Revolution (D.A.R.), church circles, the bridge club, and shopping trips to the city. These women drive their own cars, and they are exceedingly mobile. Like their husbands, they take leadership in community activities—cultural clubs, church groups, and the Parent Teachers Association (P.T.A.). They give time to Red Cross and cancer drives; they aid worthy causes among the Negroes.

The upper-class home has more books and magazines than middle-class homes, yet they are quite "average" middle-class American in taste. The most popular magazines in Plantation County are *The Readers' Digest* and *Life*, women's journals (like *Good Housekeeping, House and Garden*, or *House Beautiful*), and news magazines such as *Time* or *Newsweek*. It is rarer to find a *New Yorker* and still rarer to find *New Republic* (probably one subscriber part time). Then there are the journals of numerous clubs and societies to which the family belongs—church, school, civic, farm. The book shelves in upper-class homes contain a few sets handed down from generations before, but most of the books come regularly through Literary Guild or Book of the Month Club selections. Women seem to have more time and inclination than men to read. The men are tired after the day's work, and they prefer outside life.

People like the Starlings marry both for love and considerations of family. While parents do not formally select mates for their children, they direct relations between boys and girls by giving parties where only children from preferred families in the plantation area are invited. It is not unusual to find many of these guests from out of town. In this way a state-wide characteristic is given to upper-class society. At college, fraternity and sorority functions continue to keep upper-class young people in the same company.

People like the Starlings have economic security; their status is more or less assured. They can afford to be liberal toward religion, race-caste, the lower-class behavior. Most members of this class are "high type" whites. The upper class belongs to the Presbyterian church in Plantation County (there is no Episcopal church). They do not place much emphasis on theology or fundamentalism, though many of their parents did in the heyday of Protestant fundamentalism, revivals, and Victorian morality.

The upper class in Plantation County differs from the aristocracy of the Atlantic seaboard, however.[2] They mingle with the local middle class and marry into it. They participate in church activities and conform to such restrictions as center about the pleasures of drink or women's smoking (they may smoke in private). There is no country club set in Plantation County because the community is small (there is one in River City near by, but Plantation County people rarely participate). One member of the upper class in Plantation County threatened to disown his son because he was attending too many cocktail parties with his college friends. College fraternity parties release young men and women from local restrictions; those who cannot bear to return to the cloistered life of Plantation County leave for the cities where they join the country club set.

There is mobility both upward and downward in the upper class. The upper class provides for its own when they lose their wealth. Since many of the people are kin to each other the ties are close. Many widows and spinsters have lost their wealth by not keeping up with the changes in cotton culture and the plantation. Middle- and lower-class people call those who continue to put on airs "decadent aristocracy." These women try to retain their status within the upper class by working at white-collar jobs or clerking in stores. Some of them live off pensions provided by relatives. The younger generation among such poor relations soon lose status, especially if they marry much below their station or cannot afford to attend the functions of the upper class. They usually work at lower- or lower middle-class occupations which net them incomes too meager to keep up a pretentious home. By the third generation one notices the family name as the sole reminder of such a past.

On the other hand it is possible to rise into the upper class in Plantation County by economic achievement and marriage. This class is more fluid in Plantation County than in the southern cities or in the

---

[2] Cf. Davis and the Gardners, *op. cit.,* for a description of upper-class values in a large city on the Mississippi.

area of first settlement. The "carpetbag" families who own plantations and large businesses in Plantation County today have economic wealth and prestige. They sealed their status by marrying into the families of the old upper class. Since southern planters fared ill during Reconstruction days such marriages were not resisted too much. The newcomer merchant and industrial group in Plantation County is entering the upper class through marriage. Lineage is important to the upper class, but it takes wealth to maintain it.

The middle class in Plantation County is the majority class, but within the middle class there is such a gradient with differences in values and achievements that we may conveniently divide it into upper middle and lower middle classes.

The upper middle class lives in the same section of town as the upper class and participates in many of the same activities. There is extensive intermarriage between the two groups. The main distinctions are in economic security and general authority and prestige which the upper class enjoys over the upper middle class.

The Anders cannot be considered upper class because they were not born into the upper class, and both husband and wife have to work to support the fine old plantation house they have just purchased. The Anders are schoolteachers. They participate in some of the informal and formal activities of the upper class, and they belong to a church which contains many upper-class families. Their lineage is acceptable to the upper class; their children play with upper-class children and will probably attend college with them. But essentially, the Anders are in a transitional stage. Their income is insufficient for them to travel extensively and they do not have much leisure time. They are intellectually inclined, but this is inherent in their occupations. They have some ancestral plantation property they are trying to develop, but it is a small enterprise. If their son takes advantage of the grooming his parents are giving him, he may marry into the upper class. Otherwise, the Anders family will continue to provide upper middle-class leadership to Plantation County.

Professional people are generally assigned to the upper middle class because they are fairly well off financially, they have intellectual interests, and they provide active leadership in community organizations. One of the physicians in town is counted upper class because his forebears were upper class. He has an upper-class town house, a plantation, considerable income from outside his profession, and state-wide social and professional relations. Other professionals, like the Anders, remain in the upper middle class, but they provide opportunity for their children's advancement. Merchants who are newcomers to the community rise in similar fashion.

The Mercers are an example of how leadership activities, belonging to the right church, and working at the right job are as important assets to status as wealth, family, or housing. The Mercers have a beautiful plantation-style home and they have the means to keep it up. Their community leadership activities are generally in political organizations (a fact which also gains them enemies) and in associations of secondary importance for prestige (e.g., a local church circle, Sunday school, and their social clique). The Mercers do not display *noblesse oblige* toward the Negro or toward the lower-class white. Mr. Mercer is a small merchant who also dabbles in other economic activities about town. His wife works occasionally to help him in the store. Although she was a schoolteacher in the primary grades, she is more interested in keeping house and caring for her children than in intellectual or leisure-time pursuits. The Mercers border between a solid middle class and upper middle class.

Mr. Mercer's brother married a woman who was born into an old upper-class family in the county. She did not forfeit her position by marrying a member of the middle class, even though her previous marriage had been into the lower middle class. She retained her plantation and the home and membership in patriotic societies, church, and club groups. The marriage to Mr. Mercer was upper middle class, but the wife retained her upper-class status, especially after she inherited a large fortune from an upper-class ancestor. The children of this second marriage are accepted somewhat in upper-class circles by virtue of their mother's descent. The mother tends to dominate her household which also explains why she is able to retain her status even though she cannot raise her husband's.

Mrs. Mercer's daughter by her first marriage has had a much harder time. She married a young man of the middle class. Her husband's job involves working for somebody else; his income is average for a skilled worker but less than a small businessman's; he associates with other young men of the middle or lower middle class but rarely with upper-class young men. This daughter works part time to help support the family in a manner befitting somebody who has been given a fine old house by her mother. Even though her children may inherit a portion of their grandmother's estate, they will struggle to keep in the upper middle class. It is easier for the first generation to retain status after a lower status marriage than for the second generation to be ascribed the higher status.

Members of the lower middle class may be close kin to members of the upper middle and the upper class, but individual circumstances account for their position. Tom Hersey is the grandson of a well-known plantation owner on his father's side. His father was a drunkard and dissipated his share of the inheritance. His mother is a woman of the middle class but not a leader in local society, nor does she come from a family with special status. Tom is shiftless and associates with a lower middle class crowd almost exclusively. His aunts and uncles of the upper middle class are ashamed of this branch of the family. They feel it is a cross they bear. For the young man's part, he avenges his low status by mocking his upper middle-class kinspeople and embarrassing them with his very presence in the community. Rivals of the family point to the fallen branch as proof that the upper middle and the upper class also have weak marks. There is an old saying in Plantation County that every third generation sees a shift in status.

The Branchleys are a typical family in the lower middle class. They earn a fair living; they have purchased an old plantation-style house which they have remodeled. But Mr. Branchley is a "back-yard mechanic" who repairs automobiles and does odd jobs at his home and out on calls. His home is in a neighborhood which has declined during the past thirty years. The Branchleys do not belong to one of the local churches; they say there is too much emphasis on dress and form in the church in town. Mr. Branchley's sister is a member and founder of a sect which meets in the country. Mrs. Branchley says this group has "real religion" since they concern themselves with teaching about God rather than with "show." Mr. Branchley is occasionally seen drunk in public, but otherwise he is a good citizen and provider. He is the absolute boss in his family. The Branchleys' education is of primary level, and their children will probably finish high school. The Branchleys are middle class by virtue of their income, housing, and general integrity; they are at the lower end of the class because of poor education, the manual nature of their work, and most of all, because they do not participate in community affairs.

People can rise in Plantation County society if they strive for leadership in the church and in community associations. Plantation County lacks ready leaders, and volunteers are quickly taken up. Leadership activity in approved associations gives persons connections for jobs and may also allow them to enter into profitable marriage unions. The upper and upper middle classes call such people ambitious "hardworking" people; they accept their young people in marriage. Families like the Branchleys who remain aloof from community affairs are called "honest folks who'll never get ahead."

White women in Plantation County often work to bring added income into the home and to provide certain luxuries or maintain an old house. The type of work and the necessity to work help determine status. Schoolteaching and white-collar and clerical work in stores are acceptable for upper middle-class women. Restaurant and factory work are considered lower middle-class women's occupations. The ability to stop work and still maintain status is what differentiates an upper middle-class working woman from a lower middle-class woman. Negro domestics are available for housekeeping, cooking, and child care, so working wives are more numerous in the plantation area than might be expected.

While most of the white people in Plantation County are middle class, we can see that there is a gradient within the class. The type of job is as important as the amount of income; community participation is a significant criterion; ambitious people rise by putting forth efforts to associate with higher strata. The middle-class individual is less secure economically than the member of the upper class; he is less tolerant of the lower class of whites and of Negroes in general. The middle class is not always willing to grant the upper class prestige without reminding it of its own weaknesses. The "climber" is especially intolerant of those who would bar his path upward.

The lower-class whites live in isolated rural areas in the poor hilly country where a small farm does not yield much of a living and where there is not much contact with the larger towns or cities. Poverty makes these people insecure. Because Plantation County has such a large Negro population, we find fewer white tenants here than in other sections of the South. The white planters prefer the Negroes, since they can be kept in check by race-caste rules. This attitude of the upper- and upper middle-class whites also gives the lower-class whites a sense of inferiority. The power groups keep the poorer whites from taking revenge on them, however, by whipping up white supremacy values and allowing the poorer whites to express their feelings at the polls and in occasional mobs organized to hunt down delinquent Negroes. The Negroes, for their part, keep away from the poorer whites as much as possible, and they reflect the dominant white attitudes towards the "poor white" group in their own conversations. Because the class system in Plantation County is fairly fluid, it is possible for the poorer whites to advance by leaving their barren farms and going to work in the cities—actually most of the present generation is doing this, and the lumber mills are taking over the area. The small group that remains seems to have little ambition or inclination to seek improvement in its lot.

People call the drunken and irresponsible sons of Mrs. Morrell, a small-farmer widow, "poor white trash." They do not participate in community activities; their home is unkept; they drink, gamble, fight, and violate other mores quite publicly. While this very lack of inhibition is a compensating factor for the low prestige of the lower class group, the cause-effect dilemma of poverty, low status, and irresponsibility is never broken.

Women, such as those around Cornwall, still dip snuff and chop cotton. They may conceive babies before they are married. They are dominated by their menfolk, at least outside the actual running of the kitchen. These women care for the wants of their husbands and bear them many children. They do all their own housework, being too poor to hire Negro household help. They think the Negroes are becoming "uppity" about their labor.

Many forces are making it easy for persons to leave the lower class. Government scientific agricultural workers teach them how to get the most from their soil. The educational authorities are making it worthwhile to keep children in school by giving programs designed to make boys and girls more useful on the farm or for city work.

Since family reputation is often a drawback, young people achieve status after they emigrate. This reflects back home, however, where it adds to the prestige of the parents and gives younger siblings ambition.

The lower class of whites, like the other classes, is relative to the situation in Plantation County. The presence of lower status Negroes gives all classes of whites advantages over Negroes. Agents and media of the mass culture and the federal government are making national values more attractive to all classes, and so we see a constant vertical mobility among the lower-class whites.

Both whites and Negroes in Plantation County are aware that there are differences within the Negro group. The whites have less knowledge about Negro class structure, however, than Negroes have about white class structure.

The majority of Negroes constitute a great middle class. The standards and criteria for this class differ considerably from the white middle class; the Negro stratification system and the criteria for class are drawn from the peculiar situation of the Negroes as a race-caste. Just as race-caste behavior is in transition, the internal structure of the Negro group is likewise fluid. Also criteria for classes in Plantation County differ from such criteria among Negroes in urban centers in the plantation area or in other parts of the South.

In the previous chapter we noted how acculturation among the Negroes brought them closer to participation in the total society. The upper class of Negroes is a small group of a dozen persons in Plantation County. Yet this is the group that is most highly acculturated to white values and actually serves to carry white culture to the lower strata of Negro society. The lowest class of Negroes, on the other hand, is least acculturated to white values. The goals of acculturation tend toward American middle-class bourgeois values.

Because of the peculiar situation of the Negroes in Plantation County, we find those values and criteria of class emphasized that will lead to maximal acculturation, e.g., education, morality, working for oneself. The lowest class on the other hand fits the white stereotype of the Negro—shiftlessness, immorality, dirty habits, ignorance.

Likewise, the numbers in each class among the Negroes of Plantation County vary directly with opportunities granted Negroes by the whites. The small number in the upper class is the result of lack of opportunity for Negroes in independent trades and professions. The whites have retarded Negro education as well as economic advancement. The consequences of white supremacy have been discussed already, so there is no need to elaborate here. As the presence of the Negro has enabled an upper-class white planter group to emerge, so the presence of an exploiting white group has kept Negro status low.

CRITERIA FOR PLANTATIO[

Criteria	Upper Class
Economics	Professionals (teachers), some small plantation owners.
Family	American middle-class values. Father earns a living; wife does not have to work, though usually does. Children attend school (high school and college).
Residence	Bungalows or frame houses in midst of Negro community; or on campuses of secondary schools.
Religion	Missionary Presbyterian, Lutheran, Methodist, Baptist affiliation locally or in home towns.
Community	Most interests outside Plantation County. Temporary residence here. Leadership in education, government work. Try to be independent of whites or else utilize them to aid Negroes. Foster race pride.
Education	College and high school; liberal professions. Acculturation to middle-class American values.
Morality	Fundamentalist Protestant ideals; some clandestine inconsistencies.
Mobility	May rise if move to a city or other region and keep professional status.

OUNTY NEGRO CLASS STRUCTURE

Middle Class	Lower Class
Elementary schoolteachers, domestics, farm owner-operators, artisans, steady workers, tenants. Some indebtedness.	Shiftless workers or tenants; wander from job to job as means for subsistence. Eternal indebtedness.
Unions stabilized after many liaisons. Both men and women work. Children work at least part time. Increasing education. Women as dominant or more so than men.	Unstable liaisons. Women dominate household with children. Child labor.
Own (a few) or rent frame homes of plank or log cabins. Live in crowded section of town, on farms; plantations.	Rent plank cabins on plantations or in town; log cabins. Slovenly; bedrooms dominate.
Methodist and Baptist church workers and leaders. Younger generation seeks more educated ministry; also attracted to secularism.	No participation in community churches.
Leaders in the local community. "Good Negroes" are befriended by whites. Occasional lapses and brushes with the white man's law.	Get into trouble with local Negroes and (rarely) whites.
Increase in secondary school attendance; elementary school still dominant.	Hardly any schooling.
Fundamentalist Protestant ideals with much lapse in behavior.	Lack of inhibition; publicly flout the mores.
Rise with education, higher status occupation, community activity, stable family life, church participation, morality, acculturation to white values, American middle-class values.	Rise if take on middle-class criteria and norms.

Since the majority of educated and ambitious Negroes leave Plantation County it is not surprising that the educated upper class consists mainly of outsiders. Because they are outsiders, they do not share in community activities to the extent that the white upper class does. The upper-class Negro generally has social and professional contacts outside the county. There are professional superiors, fellow alumni from the Negro College of Agriculture, and friends and relatives from the home county.

The Negro upper class in town consists of the Negro county agent, the Jeanes Supervisor (superintendant of Negro schools), and some teachers in the secondary schools. They own their own bungalow-style homes which are located among the other houses in the Negro community. Although they can afford to pay, they have no telephone service; they pay taxes on their homes, but they, like other Negroes, have no public water system or sewage disposal unit. These upper-class Negroes participate in local church and civic activities when they are in town, but the mainstays of Negro community activity remain the native middle class.

There is a clique of upper-class persons among the secondary school principals and teachers who board at missionary schools for colored students found in three localities in Plantation County. Because their work and social interests are similar and congenial, these persons tend to keep to themselves and are not considered part of the general Negro community. Since they are not native to the area either, they participate even less in church and other Negro community activities. Parent-Teacher Associations connected with these schools are poor, because the teachers are cliquish and they are unable to establish rapport with the semiliterate parents of their pupils. The students look up to their teachers and try to emulate them. When they reach the stage of wishing to be more like them, they begin to despise the environment that frustrates their efforts and quit it. This is what keeps down the membership of the upper class and empties the county of Negroes who might possibly be an asset.

Education and morality count more for Negro upper-class status than economic condition. This is because the white people place so much emphasis on ignorance and promiscuity in characterizing the low status to which they relegate all Negroes. Brady Dean, the mulatto plantation owner, has lower status than his schoolteacher wife because he is not educated and his morals are not high. He associates with middle- and lower-class Negroes while his wife keeps to an upper-class Negro clique. The Dean children live away from home and are educated and successful; they are upper class according to Plantation County Negro standards, though elsewhere they might be considered in the American middle class.

An incident took place during my stay in Plantation County which illustrates the differences between the values of the Negro upper and middle classes. Norma Frye was the daughter of the largest Negro property owner in Plantation Town. Her parents were not educated beyond elementary school; they associated with their Negro neighbors of the middle class, and generally they bore all the marks of the Negro middle class except, perhaps, for their wealth which was in real estate. The criteria by which Norma may be rated upper class include the fact that she was a graduate of a school of social work; she associated with the schoolteacher upper-class group in Plantation County; she had her baby in a hospital and continuously brought it to the doctor's office to have it examined (lower status Negroes use the maternity clinic; they have their babies at home).

Norma came home to live when her husband got a job teaching at the Negro secondary school near by. Her peace of mind began to be disturbed when rumors spread about her husband "seeing" a woman teacher on the campus. Although her parents felt it was a passing thing, Norma quit her husband for this. She valued the sanctity of marriage in a way different from the majority of the Negro community. The neighbors pointed out that such infidelities could be expected from any man and that nothing could be done about it.

The Negro upper class in Plantation County cannot bear to have whites feel that the Negro is sexually and morally uninhibited. Morality is a vital issue; the teachers utilize the schools and the churches to teach the younger generation Protestant Christian values, and they emphasize that Negro race pride necessitates erasing the whites' stereotype of the Negro. Although lapses in the ideal moral pattern occur among the Negro upper class, these are done clandestinely, as among the white upper and middle classes; lower-class Negroes and whites publicly flout the mores, which accounts for their low prestige in the eyes of the leaders of the society.

Morality, Negro race pride, education, economic independence, and even social independence from the whites are criteria for the Negro upper class. This is conditioned by the peculiar position of the

Negro in the plantation area and by the frustrating conditions under which the educated Negro group operates. Yet these Negroes seek to acculturate white values which yield prestige both in the plantation area and outside. The agents and media of the mass culture place highest value on middle-class American white values, and to these ends all the white and Negro lower status groups aspire. Because they are blocked from participating in white society, even after they are acculturated, upper-class Negroes who remain in the plantation area withdraw to themselves and rely on Negro race pride as a *raison d'être* for acculturation. They also react to their rejection by the whites by becoming the leaders of the Negro acculturation movement; the white stereotype of the Negro becomes a chief target for attack.

The majority of Negroes in Plantation County who are "good Negroes" in their own eyes and in the eyes of the whites are the middle-class Negroes. While there is diversity in occupation and income, in general literacy and ambition, in family life, or in religious beliefs the following characteristics are universal enough to constitute these Negroes as a category. They attend church more or less frequently as leaders or simply members; they have steady employment at farming, the sawmill, domestic service, or the small trades; they send their children to be educated; they eventually "settle down" with a wife or a woman even though they may have spent many years "sowing wild oats"; they put their small savings into burial or sickness insurance; they try to buy their own land in the country or in town and build a little house.

These Negroes do not have the education of the upper class, but they look upon education as a means by which their children can rise in the society. They are not as moralistic as the upper class, but they preach morality through the church, at least. The men and women of this class are not ashamed of hard work. They want steady work so that they can care for their simple economic needs. Of course, if they live beyond their means, which many of them do, they are likely to end up in debt and thus no longer be in the middle class. These Negroes realize that the white man is in control of the situation, so they get along with him as best they can. They behave themselves, and earn reputations which bring white help when it is needed. They do not isolate themselves as so many of the Negro upper-class people do. These Negroes find release through the church, lodges and secret societies, gossip groups, and a partial giving over to the immoralities they preach against in church. They likewise have a safety valve in visions of a heavenly paradise where they will not have to work and where all their needs will be satisfied.

The inconsistency of Negro middle-class belief in education as a panacea is borne out by a greater dissatisfaction among the upper-class Negroes with their situation than among the middle-class Negroes. The children of middle-class Negroes who attend school find their level of aspiration nearing middle-class white values; frustration by race-caste rules leads them to emigrate or otherwise to aggress against their own group or, more rarely, the whites. Traditional Negro middle-class safety valves become inoperative with Negro acculturation.

The sawmill workers in Plantation Town can be classified in the Negro middle class, but their situation is a peculiar one. Their work is fairly steady and their pay is as good if not better than that of Negro domestics or farmers. But this group is new to the community and has not yet established roots. The members do not take as much interest in education as the older members of the Negro community; they have not put their savings into property (rather they gamble and drink it away); they do not attend church; their family life is unstable. We seem justified in including this group with the middle class, however, because the trends, especially among their children, indicate a middle-class development: the children of sawmill workers attend elementary school; their attendance at church Sunday school is a beginning in religious training for the group. As the children of this group become acculturated, they will tend to conform more to Negro middle-class standards. This may also bring their parents closer to community activities, but it will take time to strike roots. The industrial picture is less clearly patterned for Negroes than the agricultural pattern where there are generations of tradition to go by. But agriculture holds less promise for the Negro in the future. His best bet for economic and psychological security lies with industry.

I did not have a firsthand association with many lower-class Negroes. Most of my information comes from middle- and upper-class Negroes and from whites. The lower-class Negro seems to be correlated with the least acculturated Negro, and the white stereotype of the Negro race as shiftless, ignorant, dirty, and immoral.

Since Negro society is very fluid, and vertical mobility is quite simple if people follow the rules, the Negro lower class consists of small elements of the population who have no incentive to improve their lot. They do not emigrate nor strive for economic or social gain. When a lower-class individual wishes to work he can always find odd jobs. White men can usually be found to clothe and feed such persons when they perform yard work or other unskilled tasks.

The lowest class of Negroes excites the envy of the whites at the same time they condemn. The lower class is relatively free from inhibitions. This same class is viewed with disdain by the other Negroes because the members justify the white stereotype of Negro inferiority. The lower class of Negroes, as a consequence, comes to rely on white protection rather than on Negro upper- and middle-class leadership. Many "mean Negroes" are unpopular in the Negro community because they fight and "cause trouble." But they have white protection, because they inform for the white man and do his bidding when it seems advantageous. Such white interference in Negro community affairs stirs the resentment of acculturated Negroes who wish to see equal justice for both groups. While other classes of Negroes try to emulate white ideals, lower-class Negroes remain more or less content with their lot, giving vent to insecurity feelings by aggression against the Negro group and by maintaining few inhibitions.

Though there are stratification systems in both white and Negro societies, the general lower position of the Negro group lowers each of its subcategories in proportion to the white classes. The criteria for each race-caste group likewise vary, class by class.

The white upper class values lineage, economic wealth, and display. Housing, furnishing, clothing, automobiles, and other material goods come under this category. Stability in the immediate family is important to upper-class white society, but extended kinship seems more important. Education at the college level is desirable, especially for the younger generation, but it is not mandatory. The Negro upper class, on the other hand, stresses the values which will signify acculturation of white middle-class values—education and morality are the greatest barriers which acculturation has to overcome, hence they receive the highest values in Negro upper-class society. Lineage is of little importance at this time because the Negro is only two or three generations removed from slavery. Economic wealth and material possessions are also attainable by less acculturated Negroes, hence they are not valued as highly as education and morality. As more Negroes achieve the educational and moral standards of the white middle class, we may expect economic considerations and lineage to play a greater role in differentiating Negro middle and upper classes —this has already taken place in urban centers of the South. The situation in Plantation County is such that acculturation becomes a primary goal for the advancing Negro.

The Negro upper class is insecure because of the race-caste situation. It tries to lead the lower classes to acculturate, yet it does not feel comfortable participating directly in Negro community activities. Upper-class Negroes withdraw to themselves to seek the companionship of other acculturated persons since race-caste patterns forbid participation in white society on even a professional plane. The white upper class is secure enough to be able to dispense *noblesse oblige* to the poorer whites and the Negroes. The situation in Plantation County is structured so intimately and fluidly that the white upper class finds it advantageous to take direct leadership roles in community affairs. If class boundaries were more rigid in white Plantation County society perhaps the white upper class could survive in seclusion; in older areas of settlement they seem to behave with less conformity to the mores of the community.

While the white middle class is the backbone of white society and its bourgeois values dominate both white and Negro groups, the Negro middle class is actually on a rung corresponding to the lower- and lower middle-class white groups. But this condition springs more from historical factors than from Negro volition or long range goals, so we may note a similar middle-class correspondence in aims if not in achievements.

White and Negro lower classes are both unstable and nonconforming to the patterns set by the middle and upper classes. The white lower class is small because of historical conditions and the possibility for upward mobility. The Negro lower class is becoming smaller as opportunities and incentives for acculturation become greater. The white lower class relieves its anxieties by in-group aggression, by uninhibited behavior, and by aggressive action toward the Negro group. The Negro lower class concentrates on aggression within the Negro group, by uninhibited behavior, and aggression against the higher Negro classes. White lower-class society is less secure than Negro lower-class society, however. Both white and Negro groups look down on lower-class whites because they have had more opportunities than Negroes, yet they remain in a position equal to or below many Negroes. This is one reason for white lower-class aggression against Negroes. The Negro lower class, on the other hand, has only recently had opportunity to rise. The white upper class still protects this group because it contributes to the stereotype and proves the upper Negro class wrong. The white upper class actually manipulates the entire society, since it plays off lower-class white against Negro rather than against itself; it uses upper-class Negroes to keep middle-class Negroes in line. In turn lower-class Negroes threaten both upper-class Negroes and lower-class whites.

The trends in Plantation County should increase the size of the white upper and middle classes since new economic opportunities are opening up for these groups. Economic values may come to play a greater role, but lineage can close the doors of advancement if the upper class can retain its wealth. Economic conditions, on the other hand, will force more Negroes to emigrate. These will continue to be middle-class and potential upper-class Negroes. Those who remain should be able to make the transition from lower to middle class if the rewards are sufficient. Acculturation may raise Negro class standards closer to corresponding white standards; yet the lack of opportunities for Negroes in the plantation area will continue to send upper- and middle-class young people to other sections of the country. The Negro group will continue to be subordinate to the white group for this reason among others.

8

THE CHURCH AND THE BELIEF SYSTEM

IF YOU PLAN to stay in Plantation County for any length of time you should not be surprised if you are approached and asked what church you belong to. This is the most general form of welcome to Plantation County. If the visitor takes up the invitation he will find himself at once in the midst of a situation that will give him social status almost immediately and may further his acceptance into the whole society. The social function of the church is probably as important as its function for theological and ethical belief.

There is a relation between the churches in the plantation area and the stratification system. Negroes and whites have their own churches, and even though they claim similar denominations, there are differences in emphasis and interpretation for each race-caste group. Within race-caste, likewise, there are churches which cater predominately to the upper, middle, or lower classes. Since religion is one criterion for status and class, we must relate the two in our study of the churches and the specialties of the belief system in the plantation area.

The white settlers of Plantation County brought Protestantism with them. Their belief system interpreted man as having a body and a soul. Man was created by God in the image of God. The flesh was mortal; the spirit lived on after death and was immortal. The Old and New Testaments of the Bible constituted the basis for the belief system. As Christians, these white settlers of Plantation County believed that man had sinned by eating the forbidden fruit in the Garden of Eden, but God sent His Son, Jesus Christ, to earth to atone for the original sin of man. Man could benefit from this sacrifice of Christ by declaring his belief in God and Jesus Christ as the Saviour through baptism, communion, faith, and good works. Some of the means for achieving salvation involved public worship and membership in a church (or other religious body or group); prayer consisting of the adoration of God, thanksgiving and supplication; a minister and other church officials to help interpret God's word to man; missionary activity to spread God's message; and various other rites and rituals.

The peculiar situation in Plantation County took on the ideal belief system of Christianity and adapted it to the needs of the people. Thus, Negro slaves were converted from various African pagan beliefs to Christianity because white planters were convinced by the clergy that it would be a good deed to save more souls; Christian principles such as those which stressed humility, industry, and honesty would encourage loyal and hard working service. To the slaves, Christianity provided a belief system which promised reward for faith in a better life after death. The rituals, hymns, and prayers of Christianity served a felt need of the slaves. While white plantation owners feared the consequences of Negroes gathering for public worship, the clergy assured them that the belief system would promote Negro mass acceptance of their condition on earth. The Negro churches did make the lot of the Negro on earth more acceptable by virtue of the social function of the church as much as the theology.

Within the white community the fundamentalistic interpretation of Scriptures justified white supremacy over the Children of Ham. Calvinism served the frontier capitalist by promoting the virtues of industry and thrift. It also enabled the upper class to consider itself chosen by God since its worldly possessions were evidence of predestined salvation.[1]

Atlantic seaboard prototypes gave Plantation County its particular churches. The Episcopal and Presbyterian churches came first, followed by the Baptist and Methodist. Methodism and Baptism prospered on the frontier. The itinerant ministers did not hesitate to leave the sheltered towns of the East; their prayer and preaching were highly emotional and colorful. Episcopal and Presbyterian clergy tended to be too educated for the rude frontiersmen; they did not penetrate the sparsely settled frontier country. Their hymns and ritual were not sufficiently emotional to serve the needs of people who craved moving songs of faith and hope and required the fervor of the revival tent meeting.

---

[1] Cf. Max Weber, *The Protestant Ethic and the Spirit of Capitalism,* trans. Talcott Parsons (London: G. Allen & Unwin, Ltd., 1930); R. H. Tawney, *Religion and the Rise of Capitalism* (London: J. Murray, 1926) and (New York: Mentor Books, 1947).

The Church and the Belief System

Methodism and Baptism served folk who protested against worldliness and luxury, of which they had little. The frontier, itself, was a protest against the old society. In religion it was the protest of the sect against the denomination.[2]

Sect and denomination are ideal types which serve as useful sociocultural constructs. The sect is a small loosely-organized religious body which is generally otherworldly, protests the existing order, has few officials, is emotional in the content of its services, and is localized in nature. The denomination is a well-organized religious body which places more value on ethics and morals than on the fine points of theology. It has a hierarchy which is nation-wide, at least, and it is more or less at peace with the ideal goals of the existing order. Its members have more possessions than the members of the sect; they are also more worldly and "liberal" in outlook. Most denominations of today began as sects—even the Episcopal and Roman Catholic churches. It is possible to measure the evolution of sects to denominations. In Plantation County we shall note this for the Methodists and Baptists who, during the early nineteenth century, could certainly be classified as protesting, localized, more or less emotional religious bodies. The consequence of sects becoming denominations is to leave a void for those groups in the society who continue to be emotionally starved in an increasingly materialistic world in which they have only a small share of goods and prestige. The consequences during the twentieth century have led to the formation of new religious protest groups, or sects, and the process continues.

The frontier disappeared in Plantation County before the middle of the nineteenth century. The Methodist and Baptist groups were also on their way to becoming denominations—the fervor of "getting religion" through visions and protracted meetings, sermons on the Devil and sin, and expulsion of members from the church for "backsliding" (participating in worldly "pleasures") began to decrease, especially in the towns.

There seems to be a positive correlation between status and denominationalism in religious affiliation. The upper and the upper middle white classes in Plantation County belong almost exclusively

---

[2] Cf. the distinction between denomination, or church, and sect in Leopold von Wiese and Howard Becker, *Systematic Sociology* (New York: J. Wiley and Sons, 1932), pp. 624-28; Liston Pope, *Millhands and Preachers* (New Haven: Yale University Press, 1942), pp. 117-40; Elmer T. Clark, *The Small Sects in America* (rev. ed.; New York: Abingdon-Cokesbury, 1949), pp. 6-24.

to the Presbyterian and Methodist churches; an increasing number are members of the Baptist church, but they represent *nouveau* groups. There is no Episcopal church in Plantation County though there was once a denomination. Roman Catholic and Mormons in Plantation County are not truly sect groups since the parent churches are ecclesia and denominations, but the local churches and membership belong to the lower middle class and take on aspects of the sect. The Church of Christ, Russellite (Jehovah's Witnesses), and Church of God Holiness groups are sects in all senses of the word. They are protesting, independent, emotional, loosely organized, lower- and lower middle-class groups.

Negro slaves took on the religion of their white masters. This gave a preponderance to the Baptists and Methodists, with a sprinkling of Presbyterians. The emotional otherworldly nature of nineteenth-century Baptist and Methodist religion suited the Negro quite well. He continues to practice Methodism as otherworldly long after the whites have ceased to do so. Likewise the Negro Baptist Church retains much of the character of the white church of some fifty years before. While the Negro Methodist and Baptist churches in Plantation County have been taking the same road toward denominationalism as the white churches, they have not proceeded so fast that new sects need to be introduced. In neighboring cities, where the Methodist and Baptist churches of the Negroes have already become sophisticated, such sects as the Church of God Holiness have arisen to fill the need of lower-class groups for protesting, otherworldly, emotional religion.

More significantly, Negro drives to acculturate to white values through education have introduced three denominations in the plantation area directly connected with parochial missionary school systems. These are the Presbyterian, Lutheran, and Roman Catholic churches. We thus note a parallel between acculturation trends in the stratification system and acculturation trends in religion. The Presbyterian and Lutheran missionary schools in Plantation County are the most advanced Negro schools in the area; the teachers, equipment, and curricula are chief agents in Negro acculturation. Likewise, the parochial chapels, the ministry, and the religious services are denominational and appeal to those groups who desire to be affiliated with acculturated bodies. (The Roman Catholic parochial schools are in a neighboring county but serve the same function as the Lutheran schools in Plantation County.)

The Church and the Belief System

The Episcopal church in Plantation County existed during the nineteenth and early twentieth centuries, but it has since closed down for lack of members. The former members have since participated in the religious services of relatives or friends; or else they attend Episcopalian services in the city when they visit there. The Episcopalians were nearly all members of upper- or upper middle-class families who came from the Atlantic seaboard as plantation owners. Theirs was a denomination with much emphasis on ritual and ceremony, vestments, and a church hierarchy. Plantation County people regard Episcopalians as "high toned"; protest groups consider them close to papists.

The decline in the Episcopal church in Plantation County must be explained by the conditions in the county rather than a situation in the church or the beliefs of the church. Plantation County life is very intimate and social mobility is fluid. While the various church groups each have their particular beliefs and rituals, in actual practice church membership is more conditioned by lineage, status, and marriage than by outright support of a particular theological system. In the case of the Episcopalians, the group disappeared because individual members married Presbyterians, Methodists, and Baptists and began to attend those churches. Either the non-Episcopalian partner was more religiously inclined, or his church group appealed more to the Episcopalian partner in the marriage, and it was decided to rear the children in the other faith.

There are two white Presbyterian churches in Plantation Town, one of them the Southern Presbyterian church and the other the Associate Reformed Presbyterian church. The most noticeable difference between the two churches is that the latter does not sing hymns but sings only Psalms. In Plantation County the social status of the membership of each church is similar—plantation owners and merchants, for the most part—the clergy are seminary trained, membership is intimate and small, and the ritual is quite similar. While there is the difference between hymns and Psalms, the Associate Reformed Presbyterians do not feel that hymn-singing for other denominations is actually sinful. They sing hymns when they visit other churches though they would rebel at the idea of singing a hymn in their own church.

The Presbyterians differ from the other religious groups in their espousal of predestined salvation. But present-day members of the Presbyterian churches in Plantation County do not consider such theological questions too deeply, nor do they press the point in maintaining the superiority of their own denomination. This is characteristic of the Presbyterians as a denomination. When they were a protesting sect several centuries ago, they argued theological matters more. The Associate Reformed Presbyterians were a sect during the nineteenth century, but in Plantation County they have become a denomination. Although A.R.P. (as they are called) church members exist among lower middle-class elements in the southern Piedmont (ancestral home of Plantation County members), the local group has prospered since migrating to Plantation County. Although elsewhere considered more conservative than "regular" Presbyterians, it is noteworthy that the local A.R.P. church supports as its pastor the leading and most articulate "liberal" or "radical" of the community.

Secular considerations also dominate the white Methodist church in Plantation Town though rural churches in the open country during the last generation were less worldly. People do not now join the church as in the old days because they have "experienced religion." The Sunday school indoctrinates the children of Methodist parents in the basic beliefs of the church. Like Presbyterianism and Baptism, however, more emphasis is placed on over-all Protestant values in the Sunday school than on denominational values. There is cooperation among the four white denominations in Plantation Town, which may be demonstrated by "fifth Sunday" union services at alternating churches during summer months, by extensive visiting among the churches when there is a "free" Sunday (no preaching in the home church), and by high rates of intermarriage among the denominations.

If theological matters are relatively unimportant for the white people of Plantation Town what sustains each denomination? The answer seems to lie in history and in the need of the people for social outlets related to status, kinship, and prestige drives. The Baptist minister keeps a separate young people's group while the Methodists and the two Presbyterian groups have united. The reason lies in the vested interest of the minister in his job; in the belief of a theologian in his denomination's superiority over others; in the desire of Baptist laymen for an outstanding church choir and Sunday school system; in the reward of office; and in the desire of many people to be leaders, to command attention and the prestige of a following.

It is true that the Baptist belief in immersion for joiners and their

The Church and the Belief System

disbelief in infant baptism divide them from the Presbyterians or the Methodists. Many also believe in a closed communion, i.e., communion as an experience between a baptized member and Christ rather than an open communion as an experience between the members of a group and Christ. Yet in a community as small as Plantation Town, theological considerations appear to this investigator secondary to the secular considerations mentioned above.

The parents and grandparents of today's white adult churchgoers in Plantation County took their religion more seriously. It was an emotional and vivid experience for them to participate in revival meetings under a tent. They disputed theological matters. This was the era before Darwin and Hollywood. American culture at that time did not emphasize science, technology, or materialism. Today the revival meeting is merely a regular church service which takes place daily for a week. Most young people join the church because they attend the Sunday school where their parents send them. People laugh at the idea of visions and at other forms of emotionalism. The fact that the young people of Plantation Town have shifted attendance from the Methodist church to the Baptist church on Sunday nights is explained by the moving atmosphere of the hymns and the sermon and the efficient organization of the Baptists. Sunday dating by attending church and then going out in automobiles is approved. Sunday night movies, if permitted, might offer competition to the churches; sin can be related to competition for church attendance.

The white Presbyterian and Methodist denominations in Plantation Town have a combined membership smaller than the Baptist church. Likewise, their Sunday schools and church organization are less efficient. But these denominations will persist as long as certain families keep attending and send their children to the Sunday school. There is a loyalty to the church of one's father and grandfather. If there is religious conflict with intermarriage, the more religious partner or the denomination with higher prestige usually prevails.

The efficiency of modern religious organization can best be summed up in the Plantation Town white Baptist church where the sect has become a denomination quite recently. The Baptist church is more the "people's church" than the others; membership and attendance are both high; the minister keeps his statistics up to date and on display. His lieutenants are laymen of all social classes, selected at random; they derive great satisfaction in seeing who can bring the most new people to Sunday school and to preaching service (Sunday school in town is at ten; preaching is at eleven almost every Sunday of the month). The children's Sunday school classes are kept lively by young women teachers who entertain them with coloring books and new hymns. A fourth of the members of the old men's class wear ear phones, but they likewise feel an air of "saving lost souls" when they bring in new people.

The Baptists sneer at the exclusiveness of other denominations and claim they increase their own membership through "good old-fashioned preaching and singing." Actually, the driving spirit of the minister is responsible for much of the success—he is a good preacher, partially on the emotional side, and he leads the singing better than his lay song leaders. The preacher urges his Sunday school leaders to seek out the "back yard" mechanics as well as the new sawmill owners. While the other denominations joke about the Baptists and their concern for fundamental points like immersion, the most recent members of the Baptist church are newcomers whose donations outmatch the tightfisted Presbyterian plantation owners by far. Money furthers the saving of souls by building new Sunday school buildings, painting the preacher's house, and sending missionaries overseas. Many Baptist members actually tithe their income (give one-tenth of their income or an appropriately large share each week). The "little man" is proud to belong to such a "hustling" organization as the growing Baptist church in Plantation Town. He can sing the old-fashioned hymns and either be soothed by them or exercise his vocal powers; he can compete for membership prizes; he can have fun at Sunday school class fish fries. He rubs shoulders with the newly rich who also like to sing hymns and do not mind going to church without coats on Sundays in the heat of summer. The old-fashioned church run in an efficient way satisfies.

In a few isolated rural communities Negroes still attend a white church where they sit in the balcony just as their ancestors did during slavery times. But most Negroes have their own churches, box-like frame structures which have tottering steeples and are painted white with green trim. The rural churches have less sophistication about them than those in town, but loyalty is high and the spirit is just as significant. As with white congregations, Negro ministers from town visit rural churches during the afternoon or evening on certain regular Sundays of the month. Interdenominational relations are good, so Methodists attend Baptist preaching when their own church is not in session, and both come together to provide hospitality for a convention or a big recreational program.

The Negro Baptist or Methodist church (they differ significantly only in that one immerses while the other sprinkles, and the Methodists have a hierarchy which appoints the minister) is an all-Negro institution despite the fact that the theology and the rituals come from the white culture. The Negro has fashioned the church so that it serves his many needs. In his church the Negro is among his own group; he is preacher, choir director, secretary, treasurer, deacon, or usher. He may hold an office and derive the prestige of office. In the world outside which is dominated by the white man he starves for such association. He "politicks" and he votes; he can praise and shout all he wishes. At revival time a visiting preacher brings a message from the Negro world outside. At regional conferences Negro farmers and city dwellers come together in all-day and night sessions. They board at each other's houses, sing the old favorite spirituals, and exchange the latest news. At one convention which I attended in Plantation Town, I noted the simplicity of the local people compared to their city guests (who came from near-by Black Belt City). They tended to look down on the simple countryfolk who were not such good speakers, were less lettered, and who contributed a smaller share to the collection. Young people from Plantation Town envied the city "swells"; the older people (the generation that had stayed behind in the country) shook their heads at such arrogance and pompousness.

But the trends of acculturation toward white patterns are affecting Negro church life in Plantation Town as well as other areas of life. Spirituals are reserved for special gatherings. The prayers of old men who sit in the "amen corner" are getting shorter, and the grizzled old mammies and faithful "darkeys" in the front row are dying off so there is less "Praise the Lawd!" and "Amen!" Young people with their educated ways demand a preacher who is more than a country farmhand who got a "calling" one day and began to "feel a lightness and a oneness with God." The present Negro Methodist minister in Plantation Town has some seminary training.

Acculturation is bringing the religious ideal and everyday reality closer together. Preachers' sermons about "doing right by your wife," "not coveting what is thine neighbor's," or "workin' hard so's you can get someplace" are actually being practiced to a greater extent these days than formerly. People say there are fewer scandals involving preachers and their female parishioners. The parochial schools are offering stiff competition for the membership of school children. The Negro churches still harp on the sins of drink, dancing, and gambling, which the white churches have begun to de-emphasize, but Hell and the Devil are gradually giving way to more lofty ethical sentiments.

The following is an extract from a partly acculturated Afro-Methodist sermon on faith which was obtained by wire recorder—

A few months ago we were selling government bonds and the people bought them by the millions, by the thousands of dollars. People bought them. Now why did they put one thousand dollars in just a small piece of paper? They put their money in it because they had faith in the government. They had faith in the United States. That's what pays her bills!

The farmer has faith. Faith in the soil, faith in the seed. But when we curtain (*sic*) all these different types of faith, his faith goes beyond the seed. It goes beyond the soil. And his faith is coupled up with Jesus Christ. He realizes that fact that Paul may water and Silas may plant, but the increase must come from God. It's necessary to have faith.

The sermon is one of the high points of the preaching service. Bits of wisdom which are centered on the Bible and also the everyday life experiences of the farmer and the artisan tend to color the Negro preacher's message to the people. If the preacher tends to be bombastic and uses polysyllabic words, of which he does not really know the meaning, his congregation drinks in the euphony, nevertheless; the members care little about semantics and know even less.

The poverty of the Negro is utilized to social advantage in the ritual which surrounds the offering, the collection taken up for the minister and the support of the church. The choir chants softly, then rises in crescendo as the minister prays and exhorts the congregation to come forward with their dollars, or silver, or copper coins. The parade of the more faithful, the cooks and carpenters who subscribe some silver weekly, files up to the table where a secretary records the gift and hands the coin over to the treasurer. The hymn is chanted over and over again. The choir, which is made up largely of women who wear black dresses covered by white robes, keeps a rhythm in time with the marching feet of the donors. The count is finally made, and the collection reads seventy cents short of the goal. The chant is taken up again, ushers rush up and down the aisles to elicit nickels and pennies from children, from holdbacks, or from visitors. The presence of a white visitor (who is requested to sit in the front of the congregation) is usually the occasion for an extra collection for some widow or a family that has been "burned out." The "rich" white man is expected to give at least a silver dollar and to make up the collection goal with his nickels and dimes. The minister makes the final report, the goal may not have been attained but a satisfactory offering has been gathered. He thanks the congregation, blesses them, and closes the preaching with a last hymn.

The officers work hard at their many duties, and the preacher has to be a showman of the first order. But this is what makes him popular, and the size of the congregation is a measure of his popularity. The Negro preacher usually has a greater circuit than the white preacher since his churches are poorer and it pays to have only two services for a single congregation in a month. While white preachers usually work full time doing pastoral work and studying between preaching services, the Negro minister is still largely a part-time worker. After preaching is over he proceeds to the next church or visits about before he returns to his farm or his job. The stronger churches in Plantation County are beginning to acquire more permanent preachers, but because of general poverty they still cannot pay adequate salaries. There is usually some sort of preaching going on in the community, however, since different denominations try to schedule circuits to complement one another.

Hymns in the Negro churches are still "lined out." The preacher recites one line, and the choir and congregation sing out after him. This practice began in the white churches a generation or two ago when books were scarce and many persons could not read too well. By the time they reach adulthood, however, churchgoers generally know the familiar hymns; they sing them during work and play. Hymns are a tie with the promise of a good life after death. They remind one of childhood days among friends and family in church and at home meetings. Secular songs have come into the community through radio and the movies, but churchgoers shun these transitory tunes for the more permanent and satisfying old hymns. Negro spirituals, for some reason, seem too sacred for everyday service; they are reserved for special gatherings.

The Negro church is about a generation behind the white church in many of its patterns, but even in revival meetings the old tent and camp meetings have given way to meetings in church for a week at a time. Revival time is tied in with the economic institution and the agricultural cycle. One round takes place during the August season when the crops are near the end of "laying-by time." A more profitable cycle takes place in September when the crops are harvested and more cash is available. Twitching, shaking, and convulsions are still part of a "good old-fashioned" revival or church service, and I have seen this at the Negro Baptist church in Plantation Town at a regular Sunday service. But "such goings on" are now condemned by most groups, and Negroes as well as whites are beginning to join the church as the result of Sunday school indoctrination rather than "getting religion." The vacation Bible school for children which takes place during the summer for one week brings in more young members than the old-style revival meetings did.

Dinner-on-the-ground has not gone by the boards. The best cooking in Plantation County comes to the fore when there is a convention, a protracted meeting, or a cemetery cleaning. The local committee of women shares the work, and tables are loaded with fried chicken; baked chicken; chicken stew with dumplings; Brunswick stew (ground meat, tomato sauce, hot pepper); cold pork; country ham; barbecued mutton, pork, or chicken; deviled eggs; potato salad; cole slaw; banana pudding; all sorts of cakes and pies—in other words, the epitome of southern cooking at its best. No person (including the resident social scientist) who has eaten southern restaurant cooking should pass judgement on the southern cuisine until he has been to a dinner-on-the-ground. This is the occasion for visiting with friends and kin from far-off places. Old childhood friends reminisce on days gone by; young people meet and frolic together. The various churches present their own interpretation of Scripture and the good life, but the dinner-on-the-ground is a universal custom in the plantation area.

The growth of sects in white society can be laid to the increased dissatisfaction of lower- and lower middle-class whites with their churches. The white Baptists and the Methodists have become denominations; sects have sprung up to protest their worldliness. The Church of Christ has no music at its service; the Russellites (Jehovah's Witnesses) have neither a church proper nor a paid ministry —they meet in a converted store to study the coming Kingdom of

The Church and the Belief System 145

God; the Church of God Holiness condemns smoking, drinking, dancing, gambling, and other worldly pleasures and temptations, and promises hellfire for sinners—it feels superior to other denominations because its members speak in unknown tongues and "feel religion all over" through trance-like shakes and shouts which penetrate the meetings.

The theology of these sects is a protest against worldly pleasures which, incidentally, the poor groups cannot afford. The social status of the members of these churches is a sign that the larger denominations do not satisfy their needs—the church officers and the other members wear finery, hold their missionary circle meetings in nice homes, and give large contributions to many "causes." Lower- and lower middle-class people feel uncomfortable.

Both the Russellites and the Church of God Holiness are recent sects in Plantation County. They were introduced by young women who happened to participate in their services in other areas and became converted. They returned to Plantation County and began to attract other dissidents. The Russellites drew the major portion of families from a former Methodist rural community into Kingdom Hall, their meeting place. There the members study Scripture and the writings of the sect's leaders. They rotate the leadership of meetings since every man is deemed a potential leader. The millennial emphasis of this sect serves a need for poor small farmers who have eked out a hard life on earth. Likewise, the otherworldliness and strict fundamentalism of the other sects serve the needs of the members. I do not believe, however, that the actual sect is as important as the general form of all these sects. In counties neighboring Plantation County, Hard-Shell Baptists, Methodist sects, and others fulfill similar functions. In numbers, the membership in sects in Plantation County represents a small fraction of white church participation. This is because the majority of white people are in the middle classes, and denominationalism in the Baptist and Methodist churches has been rather recent in rural areas similar to Plantation County.

The small Mormon group in Plantation County (Church of Jesus Christ of Latter Day Saints) is older than the sects mentioned above. During the end of the nineteenth century Mormon missionaries travelled in pairs throughout the plantation area. They stayed overnight at hospitable farm houses and managed to convert a few families who found this religion more to their satisfaction than the predominating church groups. These Mormon families are generally small farmers who are somewhat isolated from community activities. They hold meetings in each others' homes occasionally and are visited by missionary leaders. They believe in Scripture and the prophetic Book of Mormon which describes a belief in the coming of the Messiah; this religious belief is American in its orientation. The present Mormon families in Plantation County do not seem theologically inclined, and since their sect is small (I call it a sect because it remains distinct from the main denominations in Plantation County in protest of their worldliness; Mormonism is a denomination in Utah), they are gradually losing members to the other denominations as mixed marriage increases.

The small Roman Catholic group among the whites is also missionary in origin though some of the families came to this area from regions which are more heavily populated with Catholics. The group meets twice a week at a member's home, and a priest visits them to instruct and to present the ritual. There is widespread anti-Catholic feeling among the Protestants of the plantation area, but it does not spread to the local group because it is very small and does not particularly seem to be ultra-religious. The members intermarry with Protestants and occasionally attend Protestant meetings; they keep their numbers because children are required to be reared as Catholics in mixed marriages. The native Roman Catholic families are of middle and lower middle class. Some local people of the upper middle class have married Catholics from elsewhere; they rear their children in the Catholic faith, but their Catholicism is rather loosely defined. Anti-Catholic feeling in the area reached its height during the 1928 political campaign. Al Smith was identified with the papacy (it was feared the Pope would rule the country) and with the "Wets." (All the Protestant denominations were staunchly prohibitionist.) In Plantation County it was a struggle in conscience between political history (hated Republicanism, the Civil War, and Reconstruction) and religious conscience. The Democratic vote carried Plantation County, but many Protestant congregations were split on the issue and one minister was dismissed. Other sections of the state further removed from plantation area tradition voted Republican for the first time in their history.

There are no Jews living in Plantation County though there were a few families thirty years ago. (Mr. Levin, the shirt factory owner, lives in a neighboring county.) These people were small merchants; one family was so well liked that the son was sent to the legislature by the predominantly Protestant community. The population of Plantation County have some contact with Jews in Black Belt City and River City—these are mainly merchants in the clothing business. There is mild anti-Jewish sentiment which stems from theological teachings, primarily that the Jews did not accept Jesus as the Messiah. There is also mild anti-Jewish feeling since they seem to dominate certain economic sectors in the cities. However, Plantation County people tend to be tolerant toward groups whose members abide by most of the culturally approved rules; some prejudice that might develop toward the Jews is drained off in the direction of the Negroes.

Among Negroes the trend toward acculturation is accelerated by the introduction of Presbyterian, Lutheran, and Roman Catholic (in the neighboring county) denominations. The old Negroes continue to support the informality of the Methodist and Baptist churches; but the young people want better organization and an educated ministry. Since most of the upper class Negroes in Plantation County are teachers in the missionary secondary schools, it is to be expected that they are also the leaders among the new denominations. This is especially true of the Presbyterian church since more of the secondary schools are Presbyterian sponsored. The Lutherans and Roman Catholics maintain primary schools in the open country and secondary schools and hospitals in neighboring cities. They attract children who attend these schools and sometimes their parents. Whether they retain these members depends on how much education the children finally attain and where they eventually live. The major portion of primary school students who return to the country to work on farms never join these new denominations. In the cities, local Negroes attend those churches where the other members seem most congenial. Their income, occupation, and general status control this choice. While missionary activity is tremendously successful in giving local Negroes an education and in accelerating acculturation trends, their success in religious change cannot be measured because the economic outlook for local Negroes is too uncertain. One indirect effect of the parochial chapels is to teach young participants the value of an educated ministry, hymnals, and ritual. If they do not accept or abide by the new theology, the students at least return to their Methodist and

Baptist churches and hasten acculturation to white patterns, which means denominationalism.

The theology of these Negro missionary denominations is of less importance to the participants than the ritual. Organ music (their local churches have old pianos), vestments, silver service, an elaborate sacramental system, and melodic hymns make an impression on these youngsters. The chapels are of simple pine board, but they are decorated in good taste. Children's art work, vases of flowers, harmonious coloring, and other aesthetic objects make the atmosphere inviting. The minister also is a teacher—there are white and Negro ministers and priests—and the Sunday school class is conducted by Negro seminary students or teachers. There are adequate texts, crayons, and coloring books.

As the Negro becomes more acculturated the impetus fostered by the missionary denominations will influence the Baptist and Methodist churches locally, even if he does not flock to the new denominations. If the old Negro churches become as denominational as white churches, can we expect new sects to appear among Negroes in Plantation County? I would venture to guess, from observation of other Negro groups in plantation area cities, that new sects will arise to meet the felt needs of oppressed groups.

Superstition and, to a secondary extent, magic are means of invoking divine intervention outside of and alien to the church. The prevalence of magic and superstition is correlated negatively with the extent of education among the different status groups in the area.

Unfortunately the very secret nature of magical practice prevented me from having direct contact with a conjure man or voodoo specialist. The Negroes seemed very suspicious of inquiries as well as ashamed of admitting that such persons existed. Upper-class Negroes and upper- and middle-class whites looked upon magic and superstition as either fraudulent or a sign of ignorance. I requested the Negro elementary schools to submit essays on the subject, and received to my surprise a collection written entirely by the teachers. These teachers represented middle-class Negroes who were in the main high school graduates. The essays were quite sophisticated and claimed that it was the duty of the school, as a believer in Christianity and science, to stamp out the vestiges of superstition in their midst. They will have a difficult time of it, however, for a folklore contest which I sponsored among Negro and white schools brought in over five hundred different superstitions which are current in the area. The students hunted down the superstitions by asking grandparents and other old people for the most part. This collection covers such varied subjects as weather signs, omens for good and evil, numerology, and cures. Most of these beliefs are popular elsewhere in the South, and most seem to be derived from European origins. The interested reader can find most of them in any good collection of sayings and superstitions about the South.[3]

Negroes tend to believe in "hants" and ghosts more than whites. These spirits are generally evil and are related to the wandering souls of dead persons who are being punished for some wicked deed they did during their lives. Certain marshy areas, where the mist rises in the night, is said to be haunted, and superstitious people stay clear of them. Dreams and visions about the deceased have a variety of meanings to the dreamer. I was unable to collect specific anecdotes about such dreams; most of them tend to have universal meaning throughout the South, however.

While the church condemns such superstition and magical practice, the two are closely related to organized religion. One anecdote, which was submitted for the folklore contest by a white girl, told of a Negro woman who had been "turned out" of the church for some misdemeanor. She was not allowed to return until she had dreamed a dream that would satisfy the elders of the church. The woman dreamed that the white Farm Security Administration agent carried her across the river on a white horse. The woman was readmitted to the church on the basis of this story. The significance of the signs of the dream are not made clear through the anecdote; it is possible that the white man and the white horse represent power, prestige, and goodness. This projection of white values seems to be significant. Religion also plays a role in the commercialization of superstition and magic. A Curio Catalogue which hails from a Chicago novelties company and which is subscribed to by some Negroes in Plantation County advertises the following magical herbs—John the Conqueror, Devil's Shoe Strings, and Adam and Eve. These roots are supposed

---

[3] Cf. N. N. Puckett, *Folk Beliefs of the Southern Negro* (Chapel Hill: University of North Carolina Press, 1926) for a comprehensive collection; my collection is on file in the Institute for Research in Social Science, University of North Carolina, Chapel Hill.

to give power to attract or repel, to insure love, peace, power, and money.

The Curio Catalogue advertises frankincense and relates it to the use of incense in Biblical times:

MANY of our customers like to burn this FRANK-INCENSE COMPOUND and offer Prayer at the same time. Some of our customers have burned this Incense and read at different times PSALMS 4, 8, 10 AND 26, or if you wish to use this method of PRAYING and at the same time BURN FRANK-INCENSE, you may read any Psalm that you wish or cite any Prayer that you should Desire. Even though it is well known that some people like to BURN INCENSE and OFFER A PRAYER, we make no claims that reciting any of the Psalms or the Burning of Incense or that Prayer will produce any supernatural effect or be of any value. We sell this FRANK-INCENSE COMPOUND only as a fine incense.

Curing is also related to scientific medical practice. A white physician in the community some thirty years ago had quite a reputation as a conjure-breaker. A Negro woman was walking down the street one day when a man jabbed her in the back. She took to her bed, became very ill, and said she believed she was going to die. She felt she was conjured, that the conjure man had caused a lizard egg to be laid inside her. It had hatched and the lizard was running around inside her. The Negroes could not help her, so they sent for the doctor. Taking no chances in the case, the physician made elaborate preparations in advance. He brought a live lizard and some cutting instruments along. Instructing the patient to turn over while he made an incision at the point of swelling, he then allowed some blood to fall on the lizard (out of the patient's sight) and released it before her eyes. He quickly stepped on it, then wrapped it in a newspaper, and instructed the patient to keep it under her bed for three days. She was to bury it in the garden and never dig it up again. The patient gradually began to regain her equilibrium and feel safe. She soon was walking about town again completely restored to health. The old physician, unlike white doctors of today who are too busy to handle such cases, had performed a service possibly related to psychosomatic medicine.

The equipment with which one can combat the spells of a conjurer includes a "jomo," or conjure bag. Some of the good luck pieces that go into the bag include a buckeye, the right hind foot of a rabbit, lodestone filings, balls of hair, and cats' bones that can float upstream. One white informant tells of a Negro acquaintance who bragged that his good luck at gambling was caused by a New Orleans jomo bag he kept at home (New Orleans is the center for hoodoo specialists). One day he began to lose heavily and returned home to discover that his wife had opened the bag out of curiosity, thus destroying the power of the jomo. He drove her out and took off for New Orleans to earn money with which to buy another jomo. A white blacksmith in Plantation County says the Negroes come to his shop for iron filings which they use in the good luck bags.

Education through the schools and the mass culture have reduced the desire for "curing." Some children and adults continue to wear asafetida bags around their necks to ward off a cold. Old midwives know the secrets of herbology and such unscientific practices as putting an axe under the bed to cut labor pains. The midwives are careful, however, to subordinate these practices to those they are taught by the educational program of the public health department. Science, itself, has come to fascinate both Negro and white youth. They build terrariums in elementary school; science-fiction stories cover the comic book and magazine stands at the drug store. A more extensive knowledge of the world around has weakened the belief in magic and superstition among all groups.

9

GROWING UP IN PLANTATION COUNTY

"How long you been comin' here?" asks a young Negro woman who is obviously in the later stages of pregnancy.

"Been comin' to this here maternity clinic now for two and a half years," answers an older woman. "What I mean is this is my second maternity clinic baby. Before these here clinics come, I'd jes wait my time and holler for the granny woman (midwife). Like as not the young'un 'd come afore the old woman."

"I've been thinking of having mine in a hospital. They say it's cleaner, and they treat you so nice at the Catholic hospital in Black Belt City. My husband's now working steady at the sawmill, so guess we can afford it."

The older one shakes her head. "You're lucky. I had no man around for the first two or three. And now—well, since the county folk's been training the granny woman how to boil out things and such, it's not so bad. When old sister Iris died, she had herself buried in her blue and white uniform. The old midwives are dying out, but they're sure proud of those uniforms! You make sure they put an axe under the bed at that hospital—cuts the labor pains, you know."

"Oh, they won't do that, I'm sure. And they don't tie up the cord with a scorched rag either. I'll be glad when the midwives are gone and they have nurses around here. I want all my babies to live and grow up. The doctor's helping Frank and me to plan our family."

The older woman shakes her head some more. "Times sure are changing. I jes *had* mine, man or no man. I loves 'em all jes the same too—those that have growed up."

Things are changing even in the customs of having babies. In town the white people of the upper and the middle classes began to have their babies in hospitals some ten years or so ago. More acculturated Negro women have also begun to use the Catholic missionary hospital in Black Belt City. The County Department of Public Health opened two maternity clinics during the recent war. The clinic helps check venereal disease among mothers, and it initiates cure. The resident physicians and nurses give prenatal and postnatal care to the mothers and their offspring. A new clinic building has been opened in Plantation Town to service a wide segment of the population with up-to-date medical services of all kinds. Ignorance, filth, and venereal disease have been as responsible for high infant mortality rates among the poorer groups as malnutrition or a lack of understanding of infant processes. The maternity clinics mainly service Negro patients; country and town whites visit the doctors in private, or else they go to the city hospitals. On Wednesday mornings mule carts and old trucks bring Negro folk in from the country to visit the Negro Activities Center. The women go to the maternity clinic which is held in one room; the men visit with the Negro county agent and lounge about town gossiping with old comrades. The Negro Activities Center is the only place in the county where there are public washrooms with flush toilets for Negroes.

Infant mortality is being combatted by public health education through the clinics, the schools, and the agricultural extension services. There is a slow dissemination of contraceptive information by the doctors, the druggists, and the social welfare and agricultural extension workers. Such information is usually requested by a client and then spread to neighbors. The upper- and middle-class whites and the more acculturated Negroes already practice family spacing. The Agricultural Extension Service and the schools are fostering better balanced diets among the country people and residents in town. They are also creating an awareness of more scientific health practices; the response has been good.

On the part of the people, much of this change has been possible because incomes have increased since the end of the depression. Pellagra, rickets, and the general malnutrition that characterized this section of the country before the New Deal have almost disappeared. Small farmers have been encouraged to increase their garden space; housewives have been taught how to preserve and to can foods. The Negro as well as the white man can now afford to purchase a variety of different foods at the groceries in town—the mass culture has diversified diet in the plantation area as well as in more urban areas. Negro family life has been stabilized because men can find employment; acculturation has also made marriage more permanent—the

Farmers Home Administration, the Veterans Administration, the public health registry of births, and other governmental agencies base their program on the family unit and encourage family stability.

Almost everybody in Plantation County likes infants and children. Families are proud of them even when they are "outside" (illegitimate) or when they come unexpectedly. Expectant mothers begin to prepare tiny garments which they stitch carefully or knit with tiny needles. If they have steady employment, expectant women quit about two or three months before they expect the birth. Higher-class whites and acculturated Negroes wear stylish maternity dresses to hide the obviousness of pregnancy. Women do not feel any shame in appearing in public even in advanced states of pregnancy, however. The father is as pleased as the mother about the expected event even though it means additional economic responsibilities. After the birth of his first child, one young white friend of mine said, "My hat's off to a woman who is brave enough to go through that!" Birth is looked upon as quite natural, and no informants seemed to express a fear of pain or the aftereffects of bearing children.

Breast feeding still predominates among rural whites and most Negroes. The infant receives the breast whenever he wants it, and the breast is also used to pacify infants. Not many years ago the infant was kept in its mother's bed at night so that it could be fed or pacified when occasion demanded. Modern parents prefer for the infant to have its own bed. Bottle feeding has been encouraged so that mothers need not watch over infants constantly; it also enables mothers to work out and leave infants with grandparents or siblings. Bottle feeding thus has progressed considerably among lower status groups, especially Negro domestics.

Sanitation surrounding infant and child care varies with the status of the parents and the home environment. The whites, on the whole, have facilities for keeping clean—they have plumbing, larger homes where each room serves a different function, screening, and above all, the knowledge of how important sanitation is. The county sprays the entire area annually with D.D.T. to check the ravages of flies and mosquitoes. Malaria and typhoid, formerly scourges in this section, have been reduced considerably. Negro living conditions are not conducive to healthy surroundings for infant and child rearing. Entire families live in one or two rooms—they cook, eat, sleep, and play in cramped quarters. Open wells, open privies, and an ignorance of the importance of cleanliness create conditions for high infant mortality during the first few years of life, if not at birth. The situation is improving, however; governmental agencies are taking the lead in educating all sections of the population.

There are variations in the type of family milieu that surrounds the new born infant and plays such an important role in his personality formation. In upper- and upper middle-class white families there is usually a steady Negro nurse. Formerly, before labor became scarce, a middle-aged Negro mammy provided for most of the wants of the white child under her care. Today nursing is becoming a part-time occupation, and inexperienced Negro adolescent girls are called in to play with younger children part of the day. White mothers and fathers are away from home much of the time, at work or attending club meetings. Their children, therefore, see their nurses almost as much as their parents. Mothers and fathers are home for most meals, however, and they supervise the feeding even if the nurse is there. White mothers spend more time training children than fathers; they also instruct the nurse concerning her responsibilities. The Negro nurse gives the white child an early awareness of the biracial society. Memories of one's nurse are usually pleasant ones; this is generally extended to nearly all old Negroes of the "darkey" type. Plantation area paternalism is closely related to the ties between the nurse and the white family. The nurse's children and her personal problems are considered within the realm of white obligations toward loyal Negro help. The Negro nurse is usually an untutored person; she conveys the superstitions, dialect, and many anecdotes and values of Negro life to young white children. They retain these to a certain extent even after they come under the influence of white playmates, teachers, and their own family.

White mothers are responsible in the main for the training of their children; they punish them for minor infractions of the behavior rules. Fathers are respected more than mothers since they are seen less often; they are also the ultimate arbiters for punishment when behavior among children is extremely bad. Father dominance and distance seem to be declining, however, both with the passing of the old Negro nurse and with the democratization of white family life with an increasing role for women in economic, political, and social life.

The Negro infant receives a different upbringing from the white child. Frequently there is no father living in the home, and the mother works for white folks most of the day. The infant is left to the care of an old grandmother or older siblings, either children or adolescents. The Negro infant does not receive the strict toilet training that white middle-class children receive; meals are not as regular or diets as well-balanced. While there is love and affection among the members of the Negro family, the daily routine is not very well-ordered, so it is possible for there to be over-solicitation, pacification, or neglect depending on the surrogate in charge. Negro family life, however, is becoming more stable, thanks to an improvement in economic conditions whereby men can find employment and the women are not forced to work such long hours outside the home. Conditions which foster Negro acculturation also make family life more like that of the white middle classes. It is surmised that child and infant care patterns will follow suit.

Infant feeding patterns involve the gradual introduction of mashed foods—either home-grown vegetables or prepared baby foods—after a few months as the infant is able to digest them. Favorite mashed foods include turnip greens, corn bread crumbs, Irish potatoes, and especially the vegetable juices called "pot liquor." Some old white informants mentioned the possibility that their mammy nurses might have premasticated food for them, but no direct evidence on premastication was obtained.

It is felt most desirable to wean infants between the ages of one and two. The bottle-feeding complex enables a quicker transition from breast to bottle (first month), then to glass for water, and eventually milk. Breast feeding lasts longer though successive births force the infant to give way to a younger sibling. Some old practices used to wean infants from the breast include applying soot, quinine, or other ill-tasting solutions to the breast. Infants might be boarded at the homes of friends and relatives at night to keep them from their mothers' breast. Shaming is used to wean children over the age of one and a half or two. Some mothers, however, prefer to pacify their youngsters with a nipple and bottle to keep them quiet. Some rural Negro and poorer white mothers occasionally nurse their infants by breast in public, but on the whole breast feeding is done in the privacy of one's own home or in women's groups. Weaning might be called moderately severe in this culture. Feeding habits associated with the bottle-feeding complex are more regular and severe than the traditional patterns.

Toilet training is also moderately severe, being more compulsive among upper-status parents and offspring than among the lower classes. Modern parents use soft cloth diapers and latex panties, and they change soiled diapers as soon as they are noticed. The material for more isolated rural infants is coarser, or the infant wears only a robe-like garment with no special covering for the uro-genital areas. This is especially true during hot weather. These infants also fail to be cleaned as regularly or as often as infants in higher-status families.

Modern parents train their infants to regular bowel movement by placing them on a toilet seat or pot at scheduled intervals during the day, keeping them there until they make a movement. Infants are taught to call attention to their needs for relief as soon as they begin to understand speech. Persistent punishment for soiling or wetting usually begins when the child understands speech. While some mothers are lax about patterned toilet training and punishment, others may punish children who "forget" themselves, especially if the parent is in a bad mood. Children learn what is expected of them by example, praise, corporal punishment, or shaming. Most children are nearly fully trained by the age of two or two and a half years. Modern parents tend to be more compulsive and regular about toilet training than old-fashioned parents.

Modern parents bathe and clothe their children with a higher regard to health than old-fashioned parents. Years ago the children of affluent people were generally overdressed in winter. Store-bought infants' clothing is of light-weight material. Poor parents may use local cloth which is coarser. In summertime infants may wear only a diaper cloth or, among Negroes in the country, go bare-bottomed. Sex differentiation in clothing begins after the first year or so; boys are soon put into shorts or little overalls; girls continue to wear dresses. Special clothing for little boys and girls usually depends on the family's ability to include it in their budgetary means.

Infants' hair and fingernails are cut around the first birthday. There is an old superstition that cutting them before this time brings bad luck, but most parents pay no attention to this. White boys have their hair cut short and parted; the crew cut is popular among some groups. Negro boys' hair is cropped closely. White girls have their hair curled or cut with bangs and combed straight. Negro girls invariably have their hair platted and twisted into pigtails.

Sleep is considered important for infants. The most modern parents schedule infant sleep and include napping in early childhood years. The traditional pattern is to let the youngsters sleep when the rest of the family sleeps and whenever they feel tired enough to sleep during the day. I have observed infants as young as two or three weeks old carried to the movies or to a softball game—they appear to sleep in these close environments about as well as they do in their little beds, or so their parents feel. Young children are also kept up late by most groups, especially if the family has visitors or is attending a community function. Only parents who are trying to raise their children "by the book" send them to bed at early and regular hours. When the child joins a play group it is difficult to isolate him from playmates who stay up late and play together. All people in Plantation County go to sleep early in wintertime and late in summertime.

Babies are loved and fondled. They are caressed on the head, the small of the back, or on the buttocks. They are bounced on their father's knee or tossed into the air (as long as they do not show signs of fear or cry). Babies are the center of attention at a family gathering. Mothers and fathers talk about their development and their antics. Babies are usually carried in their parents' arms or against the chest. Not many baby carriages or strollers were observed. Babies are encouraged to walk as soon as possible. They are held by adults, and their first steps are approved.

Babies first begin to speak by imitating adults around them. Adults try to encourage them to say simple words and eventually to form sentences. Baby talk is frowned upon by modern parents. Children learn extreme forms of the southern dialect early; the influence of Negro nurses and association with Negroes affect white speech at all ages. White adults resort to Negro dialect and expressions in dealing with Negroes. The plantation area dialect is a source of regional pride, and foreign accents (northern United States or European) are quickly noticed and meet with disfavor. The homogeneity within white and Negro groups in the plantation area and their ethnocentrism make them intolerant of "foreign" dialects.

Corporal punishment for offenses begins as soon as children understand speech and can convey their needs. Mothers generally administer these earlier punishments; fathers punish boys as they become older. Most children in Plantation County are fairly well-behaved, however, and only a few "real good switchings" are administered during a lifetime. Punishment by withdrawing favor is usually effective among younger children; older children are denied things they value highly.

Infant status depends on the status of the family, on the sex of the infant, and its order among the children in the family. The oldest son is regarded as an assured heir for the family property although inheritance is divided equally among all children. Hence if the first child is a boy, it is an occasion of great joy. If the first child is a girl, it is felt that the mother will have an easier time of it when other children come along since there will be somebody to help her care for them. Additional children bring lesser jubilation. The youngest, however, is given some special attentions though he may at the same time be the inheritor of hand-me-down clothing or the frustrations felt by displaced siblings. The child that is named for the father or grandfather is the favorite of that person. There is no godparent system in this culture, but certain relatives and friends of the family have favorites, especially if children's names, physical features, or personality make-up appeal to them.

Naming assures the infant status in the society. Births are registered at the public health office, along with the date and parents' names. Illegitimate children have their mother's name listed only; if the mother marries later, her husband's name may be added whether he is the biological parent or not. It is usual to name one child after the father; other children are given names common to the family. Negroes name their children after favorite white people in the past. Biblical names are popular, but certain names peculiar to individual families are also noteworthy. In order to avoid confusion among the generations, a son is frequently called by a middle name and his father by his first name; another solution is to add "little" before the name, e.g., Bill and Little Bill; the father may be called Mister Bill.

The status of one's parents is perhaps as important as anything in the development of the infant's status and personality. Each status group in the plantation area has its way of rearing children. Young children are ascribed status according to their family background. The security of one's parents and their ability and desire to give the child every chance to make good are important for the developing personality. Ascribed status remains with people in the plantation area as long as they live. Achieved status becomes important from the time of childhood, but the status of one's family enhances or limits the opportunity for the individual to achieve status.

The infant becomes a child when he learns to walk and to talk, when he has been weaned, and when he has had his toilet training completed.

While the mother is important during the child's early years, other surrogates now begin to assume importance. The father may administer corporal punishment; he teaches little boys how to perform tasks about the farm. A Negro nurse or playmate may be introduced at this time for middle- and upper-class white children. Older sisters and brothers take care of little children, protect them from harm, and teach them the lore of the child world and the grown-up world. The child begins to differentiate relatives and friends of the family who visit. The play group begins to assume some importance.

The young child is taught the first rudiments of self-reliance at home so that he will be prepared to meet the trials of the outer world. He learns to dress himself, to play, to be curious and ask questions, and to explore nature and the world about him. Yet there are restrictions on his behavior. He begins to learn that there are right and wrong ways of doing things. He learns which clothes are appropriate for the occasion, which foods are good for him, what places are safe to play in, which children he may play with. These are the beginnings of institutionalization and role-playing for the child. He is rewarded with approval and the satisfaction of his wants. He is punished by scolding, spanking, or derision, or he finds that his misdirected behavior is not rewarding. People begin to assume statuses in the child's world—friends and enemies, nice people and bad people, grown-up people and playmates, family and strangers. The child soon learns what to expect from each of these persons and groups, how they must be approached to meet his needs.

Children are given little tasks to do about the house or the farm to keep them busy and out of mischief. Children soon become useful by doing small chores; Negro plantation children begin to pick cotton at the age of four or five; they become full hands by the age of twelve. Participation in the adult world and a feeling of responsibility which is engendered early in children may be responsible for the good manners I observed in Plantation County. Children say "sir" and "ma'am" to their parents and to other adults; they recognize authority. Yet the children are not cowed, and they have plenty of spirit among themselves.

Sex differentiation increases with maturation and includes dress and adornment, tasks performed about the house, the selection of playmates, and types of reward and punishment.

Little boys are urged to be hardy like men; they are expected not to cry. They go outside to play, to hike and to fish, to capture insects, and to seek out small animals. The boy's father introduces him to the chores of the farm. The play group initiates him into competition for status in his own age-sex group. He begins to look upon women as weak creatures and persons to be avoided as much as possible; but he is supposed to protect them and to show them deference. Women try to keep little boys clean and well-mannered; boys are supposed to resist, however, or they become "sissies." Their mothers secretly admire this resistance for men are supposed to be independent of women. The old men of Plantation County who sit under the pecan tree at the courthouse square think the boys of today "don't raise nearly as much hell" as they did generations ago. Mechanical devices and other material comforts of life tend to make people generally soft. One by-product of the increasing technology is the augmented mobility children experience and the intellectual curiosity aroused by science. They learn more about how other people live than their parents did. This tends to break down intolerance among the new generation in the area.

Girls by tradition are supposed to be "sweet" and "nice." Their mothers teach them the little things that have to be done around the house. Girls are not supposed to "roughneck" or "get into trouble." Yet, just as the mechanical age has made a change in the boys' behavior, so also girls have become possessed with an egalitarian spirit, and they play softball, basketball, and other sports formerly reserved only for boys. Girls wear dungarees, and they go barefooted in warm weather (the privilege of every youngster in the area regardless of his family's status). The girls are in general less genteel than their grandmothers were supposed to have been. (Yet from some grandmothers' stories, this gentility was mainly a mask for very mischievous activities that went on behind the scenes.) Girls take care of the younger children; they are more interested in domestic affairs than boys. But girls' groups function in a similar manner to the boys' in teaching the lore of childhood and youth in the world beyond the home.

Status differentiation is recognized later in childhood. The early beginnings are birthday parties and visits to the homes of children approved by the mother. After the child attends public school and gains a wider range of friends, mothers have a problem controlling friendships. They employ family gossip about the parents and relatives of the new playmate in question and try to impress the child with the value of choosing one's companions wisely. By the time of adolescence and dating, children define the status of all their acquaintances and select close friends with this in mind.

Recognition of race-caste comes early. In one case I was acquainted with, a two-and-a-half-year-old white boy embarrassed his parents when he pointed at some Negroes and yelled, "Hey niggers!" The parents spanked him. They think he might have learned the expression from his Negro nurse (who would use it toward another Negro in anger) or from themselves. They did not realize that a child so young could distinguish between the races.

Negro children learn how to behave in the presence of white people by observing the behavior of their parents and by hearing conversation about race relations. Negro children now play with white children only on the plantation. There is some slight deference shown white children here, but the children play and tussle together without regard to the full implications of race-caste they will learn when they grow older. White people may call Negro children's attention to "good manners," but they do not punish them.

White children also learn their race-caste role by observing the behavior of adults and by listening to talk of race-caste relations. Certain Negroes, like the nurse or the yard man, are held in special esteem by the white youngster, and he only comes to associate them with the entire Negro race later. Even when he is an adult, however, he will address such close Negroes as "Aunty" or "Uncle." Negro and white children do not play with each other much any more, because Negro children attend their own schools. Domestics no longer stay all day at white homes and so do not carry their children with them to work. White children from the country can stay in town and play with other white children since transportation has improved, and the consolidated school provides many new playmates. I never observed white and Negro children in Plantation Town playing with each other. White children ignored neighboring Negro children who skated on the sidewalks in front of white homes. White adults told them to go away because of the noise they were making, but they would have reacted the same way toward white children.

The child who becomes five or six years old finds his world expanding to include other institutions beside the home—the play group, the public school, the church, and later the part-time job. The

Growing Up in Plantation County

child begins to spend much of the day outside the home and becomes the charge of the entire community. It is the community which teaches the child the rules of behavior expected of him, the community that rewards and punishes him depending on his willingness to conform. Throughout this period of tutelage the home and the family continue to give the child security and to encourage him to conform. The family is always considered the last refuge of adulthood and old age. Friends are also considered close confidents, and they help out in time of need, even when the family is incompetent to offer succor.

The public school expands the child's competition for status within his own age-sex grade which was begun by the play group. The authority of the teacher introduces a new surrogate in the life of the child, who previously has looked to parents and relatives as sources of authority. The public school forces the child to achieve status. It broadens his world outlook; he learns new patterns and values which may also conflict with old values taught in the home or in the play group. This may raise anxieties in the mind of the child that lead him to consult parents and friends. He will try many ways and will usually choose the approved patterns as the result of trial and error, reward and punishment. The rewards for achieving the approval of one's teacher and classmates may go against family values and may lead the child to revolt against family ways. In Plantation County this conflict is strongest in families which are poor and illiterate. Some students look down on their families. On the other hand, pupils who are loyal to the family's way of life may revolt against the school and its authority, and they will prefer to remain at the family's low level. Social mobility develops when the child begins to seek the values of a group which is above his previous family condition—it begins in the public school and follows through adolescence in relation to his job, dating, courtship, and perhaps marriage. Making new friends also is a means of achieving status and moving up the status scale.

One function of the public school as an institution is to inculcate the folkways, mores, and the values of the society on the child and the student. In Plantation County there is segregated education for the races. Both Negro and white teachers are usually from the plantation area or the South; they instill southern and, for the most part, plantation area values in the pupils. But recently there has been an increase in the influence of mass culture. This is represented by a heightened interest in science, technology, and even social and political issues. Negro schools have introduced Negro history and literature; this has bolstered Negro race pride and has combatted the effects of race-caste subordinating behavior patterns.

The white schools have been consolidated for the past several years since the New Deal supplied funds to build central secondary and primary schools. Fewer one-room school buildings open their doors each fall, but there are still several of these little schools in isolated communities. The various two-room schools which remain in the county are able to provide a little better facilities. There are three large brick buildings in most of the towns, equipped with classrooms for primary, junior high, and high school classes, laboratories, libraries, gymnasiums, and sports fields. Consolidation has had a deleterious effect on the communities that once counted on the school as the center for intellectual and social activity. Consolidation has benefited the pupils, however; they have been brought in contact with superior teachers and teaching curricula. The pupils who come from poor isolated small farms are beginning to lose their shyness, and they go about town more—this tends to unite the sections of the county, especially when there is intermural athletic competition and vocational agriculture club meetings.

The curriculum is strongly influenced by the State Board of Education which trains teachers in normal schools, conducts county-wide teachers' meetings, requests teacher certification, and conducts summer courses to bring old teachers up-to-date. The state also attempts to equalize the financial burden of schools by contributing to county school funds. The State Board of Education, which has contacts with the National Education Association, adapts the newest ideas in education to the needs of the state and tends to reduce the intellectual differentials among areas within the state. Several generations ago the schoolteacher controlled her class and taught what she thought best; today the teacher is controlled by superiors in the field of education. In a way these leaders in the state educational bureaucracy also help the schools to revolutionize the communities, since the state money is needed by counties who otherwise would be able to dictate educational policy more than they can now. Teachers coming from outside the county are able to carry through such new ideas much easier than numerous older teachers who are married and have families in the county (but the current teacher shortage slows down acceleration of the schools toward newer educational methods). Many of the white female citizens of Plantation County today came as schoolteachers, liked the county and its people, and married local young men who were glad to see new womanhood come their way. They teach during the current shortage or substitute when needed. Being parents, themselves, they are more understanding of children's ways, and they tend to control the children more like parents; whether they are better teachers or not depends on the individual.

The story of the Negro schools and Negro education in Plantation County is an epic of the struggles of a slave group to achieve status coequal to the dominant whites. Negro schools in Plantation County, as in all parts of the segregated South, are vastly inferior to white schools in all respects. We can discuss this situation and conclude that the Negroes are not getting "separate but equal services." However, there have been changes in opportunities which indicate that there has been vast improvement in Negro education, with a trend toward closing the gap between the supposedly equal services. These changes have consequences for both Negroes and whites in the area of race-caste relations. The gap is still far from being closed, and we should recognize the forces at work both to close it and to keep it from being closed.

There is contrast between small one-room frame buildings that stand or lean beside old Negro churches on the plantations and the neat frame Rosenwald and Lutheran schools and the Presbyterian missionary secondary schools, equipped with libraries, workshops, playgrounds, assembly halls, and dormitories. The number of Negro children in Plantation County is over four times the number of white children, and they are widely dispersed throughout the rural areas. Consolidation has advanced slowly because there have been no funds for building large schools (the three large Negro schools were all built by philanthropic interests). Adequate funds are not supplied for school busses; committees of the white schools are not satisfied that the Negroes need such consolidation; Negro schools are crowded and poorly equipped. The teachers do not meet state-recommended standards for good teachers. Despite the fact that the total budget for all Negro schools in Plantation County has recently surpassed the total white budget, per capita expenditure for Negro pupils is much less than for whites. The county has only recently taken over a few of the missionary schools; on the whole the best Negro schools have been those not originally under county jurisdiction.

Race-caste is at the root both of segregation and the present condition of Negro education. The future of Negro education in the area is also dependent on race-caste trends. Under slavery there was no formal education because it was thought it would lead to insurrection. There was occasional instruction in Bible, or house servants were tutored by willing masters or mistresses. Missionary societies and kindly plantation owners started the first Negro schools. Begun with such disabilities, it is surprising that education for Negroes has made such advances; yet in light of modern democratic American values, the mass culture asks why it has taken so long for Negro education to reach the stage it has and why segregated education survives. This is the dilemma that faces both whites and Negroes in the plantation area as well as the American public. The value system of the plantation area in this respect is being bombarded by the American value system which preaches equality of opportunity and one class of citizenship for all. There is conflict, anxiety, insecurity, and guilt feeling among the whites; the Negroes are likewise insecure and they are frustrated. We need not repeat our discussion of race-caste here other than to note that in education it receives a primary test of strength or of weakness.

Despite the inequalities between the white and Negro school systems, both serve to socialize their pupils. White school teachers take the place of parents during a large part of the day; they are women in the primary school and women or men in secondary school. Since they are all of middle class, the teachers tend to inculcate middle-class values on the pupils. In this manner they influence many poorer children to strive for middle-class values. The school committee has as one of its policies making the school rooms as attractive as possible, so that pupils who come from poor homes will have some experience with aesthetic surroundings. Yet such experiences as this stark contrast between home and school may also discourage poor boys and girls and lead them to withdraw or aggress because of frustration. In trying to compete with children who come from homes where their parents read to them or where visitors are widely learned, poorer children must put out more effort in order to succeed. Intelligent pupils from such surroundings are encouraged both by their teachers and by the community; the Parent-Teachers Association and the women's clubs give an annual scholarship to college. Quite often successful pupils go on to college and then inevitably leave the community to begin life anew in a higher status. They reflect well on their parents too and help the parents improve status. This applies especially to Negroes where the difference in status between teachers and parents is so marked. The teacher for the Negro pupil often becomes a singular ideal; since other jobs at this status level are not plentiful many Negro students seek to achieve status by going into education. Teachers are the leaders in acculturation trends among Negro young people.

The school exposes the child to the world of scientific agriculture in contrast with the family's emphasis on traditional agriculture. Thus the school cooperates with those governmental agencies which are trying to transform the agricultural ways of the area. Most of the agricultural extension people feel that the younger generation which has received scientific agricultural education during its early years will prove the ultimate success of the entire program. The youngest pupils participate in 4-H club projects such as raising chickens or calves, and planting gardens. In the Future Farmers of America (FFA) and the Future Homemakers of America (FHA), secondary school pupils actually cope with farm problems through projects involving the handling of larger animals and keeping cost account records. These clubs also seek to train young people in public speaking and in organization work. The emphasis is on agriculture as a total way of life. Young people who become leaders in their clubs at school, if their families are among the community leaders, most certainly represent the future farm leaders in the area. For those whose families are not so successful, the experience of participation in the clubs stands them in good stead in whatever occupations they enter. While the scientific agriculture program in the school is democratically organized, parental status influences the effect the program has on the student. Some parents cooperate more with the projects than others; some have more means than others. The pupil is never quite on his own to develop entirely within the school program.

The school gives the child opportunity to achieve status as a leader in the group. Children from varied backgrounds compete fairly equally for popularity and leadership on the sports field, in dramatics groups, or in literary activity. Home background is both help and hindrance, inspiring and equipping pupils to participate in these activities. But it seems that the school is also a world in itself where competition may overcome home background and some status can actually be achieved. A glance at the leaders of the junior and senior class at the white high school in Plantation Town reveals little correlation between home environment and leadership ability in the various aspects of school life.

But there is also a source of frustration and conflict when the pupil from a low-status home who is a recognized leader in school seeks to carry his newly achieved status into the social and the economic world outside of school. One boy who was the local football hero was extremely popular with the girls, but the local banker forbade his daughter to date the boy. Many girls and boys drop out of school because the parents cannot afford to send them or because they are getting no encouragement at home to continue. This number is declining, however, because of a compulsory school attendance law and the growing appreciation of formal education as equipment for competing in a more highly technical society. A great many boys and girls dread graduation day when they will have to go out into the world; then the honors they achieved in school will count for little.

The decision or the necessity to leave school after the sixth or eighth grades colors the entire future of the boy or girl. Although there is a strong trend among whites and Negroes to stay in school to take the vocational agriculture and home economics programs, the value of child and adolescent labor on the farm or plantation is too high to warrant most Negro and many white small farmers keeping their children in school.

The Negro and white boys and girls who leave school at the age of thirteen and fourteen participate in the adult world and its responsibilities almost immediately. The boys begin early to experiment with sex, going around in gangs to communities or houses where sex is to be had easily. At the same time they begin to take on a full work load, first working with their parents, then gradually desiring to strike out on their own. If farming does not appeal to them, they emigrate by the age of sixteen to eighteen to seek work in town or in the cities. They are ill-trained to do skilled labor of any sort, so they become common laborers or occasionally they learn mechanics on the job. Their cultural and social interests are limited to the job and to going around with the gangs. They organize into sports teams; in small communities they may participate in church activities; and eventually they pair off with girls who have generally also quit school early. They marry when they feel they are economically settled—when they have a place on a farm or can purchase a farm, or when they have a steady job in town. By the age of eighteen or nineteen they are often parents. Their status becomes fully adult at this time, and they begin to participate in local church and farm organizations. It is seldom, however, that this group (in these modern times) assumes leadership, for the breadth of view of the young people who stay in school is greater, and they inspire a wider following. The former group may continue to lead and to participate in cliques of the lower and the lower middle class. Such persons and cliques may actually isolate themselves from community and civic affairs which are dominated by the middle classes. Social contact between those who stay in school and those who leave is very small during the time the first group is in school. It begins to increase after the other group reaches adulthood, but it is never as close as during primary school days. Status differences and values become too marked.

The group that desires to stay in school after the age of thirteen or fourteen presents a problem to parents who need the labor of as many members of the family as possible to maintain farm and home. People today admit that children are an investment that does not necessarily pay dividends. It is especially difficult for the tenant Negroes to keep their children in the schools. Most of the children of Negro tenants have a high rate of truancy throughout their primary school years (despite a compulsory school law which is more or less enforced). They are absent at cotton picking time; during bad weather they do not have the proper clothes, nor is there sufficient transportation to carry them long distances to school. Neither the plantation owners nor semiliterate Negro parents encourage the children to stay in school. In such a social environment there is little incentive to study while friends are earning money as wage hands on the farm or in town. The desire for material goods is greater than the prospect of future rewards.

Among whites it is becoming usual to allow children to stay in school and to study vocational agriculture. The parent who withdraws his youngster from school is under the pressure of teachers, relatives, and neighbors to permit him to continue. There is an increasing realization among most of the whites that education pays off in the long run. Whites, as a whole, are also more able to forego the labor of their children than Negroes. Among Negroes, the small independent farmers are more inclined than tenants to value education for their children. If the children wish to quit school, parents may or may not permit it, depending on how much they value education. The over-all trend among both groups is toward lengthening education. Children help out on the farm after school hours and during vacation periods.

The group that remains in school, on the whole, continues to remain economically dependent while at the same time it is maturing physically and intellectually. Although most Negro and many white students work every afternoon, and hold Saturday and summertime jobs, their parents are still denied the full-time labor of their children while they have to maintain them in food and clothing.

With physical maturation, adolescent activities are channeled increasingly to involve both sexes. There are parties, dances, dating, and eventually, more direct sexual activities. Even in sports, the boys play on the field while the girls cheer from the side lines, each trying to support and impress the other. These mixed activities are encouraged by the school, the church, and by family and friendship groups. Schools try to ignore social classes more than the other organizations. Sunday school activities and parties held in homes are socially selective. Parents sometimes feel it necessary to include school friends in parties in order to appear democratic, but among upper- and upper middle-class families, especially, dating is closely supervised so that young people may maintain class distinctions. While church parties are supposed to have some religious basis, they are predominantly secular in orientation. There is high spirit at wiener roasts and watermelon cuttings; this contrasts with the perfunctory manner in which the more religious aspects of weekly youth meetings are carried on. Dating seems to be a leading motive for church attendance on Sunday nights.

Animal life on and around the farms influences Plantation County people to regard the physiological processes, including sex, as natural and therefore wholesome. On occasion, some of the oldest generation of white women seem somewhat Victorian, but this tends to be the result of an element in the culture that affected all America two generations ago. The Negroes and lowest-class whites are accused of being promiscuous by higher-status whites, which is not necessarily true; however, one effect of their presence is to make sexual activity

Growing Up in Plantation County 171

more realistic to all sections of the population. The presence of mulattoes in the society is indication of illicit sexual relations between whites and Negroes.

Boys of both races are able to have sexual experience with lower-class Negro girls at the age of fourteen or fifteen. Upper- and middle-class girls of a few modern families are instructed by their mothers about menstruation and reproduction, if they have not already gotten the information from their older friends. In the old days these girls would have been told nothing at all beyond what an older sister or more often a whispering group might divulge. Mothers and teachers of the present generation are less embarrassed about telling "the facts of life." In addition there are both scientific and fiction books replete with sex to supplement such formal instruction. Girls of the lower classes may enter into direct sex relations at the ages of fourteen to sixteen; girls of the middle and upper classes engage in sexual play in the form of kissing and petting. Girls are supposed to show discrimination in whom they go out with and how far they allow their boy friends to go. The worst thing for a girl's reputation is to become known as "an easy make." Boys who thereafter go out with these girls are presumed to have sexual intercourse as the sole objective in mind. Boys who are conscious of their reputations may be somewhat secretive about going out with such girls; but they brag about their exploits to friends in their own circle.

The first experiences of boys with sex come during childhood. When I asked some white men about rumors concerning a "peeping party" in which some young middle-class boys had asked girls to strip for photographing, they laughed and said these were new techniques compared to the old ones of hiding behind bushes when girls went swimming or hiding near old privies. Men joke about sex in the company of adolescent boys and sometimes younger boys but never in front of girls (except the young low-class women known to be promiscuous).

There is no intentional infant masturbation. As it exists, masturbation is felt to be a natural phenomenon or urge if kept within limits. Some boys told me they heard that excessive masturbation led to sterility or insanity, but it seems to be merely a device to scare them into limiting it. No observation was made of excessive masturbators, nor were any persons noted who held such a reputation. The relatively free thinking about sex and the early possibilities of direct sexual relations may be one reason for limited masturbation.

A boy is expected to prove his virility around the ages of fifteen to seventeen. There is supposed to be an aura of secrecy about such exploits, especially between upper- and upper middle-class boys and the adult community. "Tomcat" expeditions may involve a few boys and take place on week ends in neighboring towns and cities. The automobile is a convenient and private vehicle for all stages of sexual pursuit. Whites have no sense of chivalry toward Negro women, but they also discuss their exploits among white girls quite frankly in their own all-male groups. It is considered poor taste to discuss sex in mixed groups; even the most modern young couples tend to be reserved here.

The mass culture has promoted an egalitarian code for sex which permits white women and girls more freedom than their mothers and grandmothers enjoyed. During the recent war many local girls went to work in the cities or near army posts; there was a noticeable relaxation of morals. Venereal disease and its prevalence have been made public through the maternity clinics and by a recent compulsory state-wide annual blood test outside the clinics which affects all sections of the population in the proper age groups. This information is also coupled with an increasing use of prophylactics and contraceptives. Illegitimacy has been reduced among whites (where it was never too high) and among Negroes—sex education, rather than continence, has probably been responsible. There are fewer "shotgun marriages" than during the past generation.

One evidence of the general liberal attitude toward sex is the response of the population of Plantation Town and the surrounding country to the showing of a sex education film called "Mother and Dad." There were separate showings for men and for women. The men were somewhat embarrassed when they left the movie to find the women waiting in line to see exactly the same showing, but the women were quite enthusiastic about being able to take their daughters to see such a film. Upper- and upper middle-class white women seemed to react more favorably to this vehicle of sex education than other groups, however. Sex is one of the topics for Sunday school during the year. The high school age group at the white Methodist church which I observed during that lesson seemed to take a scientific interest in learning about normal sex attitudes and wholesome family life. There was little giggling or embarrassment among the children;

however, I had to teach the class because the old man who was the teacher refused to handle the subject. One possible consequence of liberalizing sex information and behavior among young upper- and middle-class white women may be a reduction of frustration as evidenced in their awakening interest in current events and a de-emphasis of the Old South and the plantation tradition.

10

ADULTHOOD AND OLD AGE

YOUNG PEOPLE begin to think about settling down to a job and to family life when they make the decision to remain in Plantation County or to leave. This decision is made during the last few months of public school when the young people begin to consider full-time employment.

All young people in Plantation County feel the lack of opportunity for economic and social advancement. They complain of nothing to do on Saturday nights and during vacation time. White youths go to town to "have a good time." Negro youths gamble and drink at Saturday night frolics and often end up in jail the next day.

These are reasons why such a high proportion of the young people in the county leaves for the cities. Young Negroes who have not been equipped to earn a living at moderately skillful occupations feel starved for the cities and for adventure. They usually end up as common laborers there; if they "get into trouble" in town, the density of population is high enough to conceal them from the law. Many young people return to Plantation County after this fling, however. A love for the soil seems to be in their blood.

White young people whose parents own no property or businesses see little future in remaining behind. Those who stay generally find the intimacy of small town life and its peacefulness pleasant to them. They may have their fling too, but they soon settle down and become family men. High school and college graduates from the upper and middle classes likewise find little reason for remaining behind. Their parents' businesses or plantations do not fill their social needs—those who attend college, especially, find fraternity and campus life an introduction to newer and more liberal social customs than they had known back home. Yet the realities of the economic and social world keep many of them in the county and cause others to return. Having status in Plantation County by virtue of inheriting a business or plantation is an inducement to continue in this enterprise. The competition necessary to achieve status in the outside world is overwhelming to many.

Up until recently the leaders of the community did little to halt the annual out-migration of young people. Now there is a growing feeling that young people should be prepared to make their way in the outside world if they prefer to go—the schools teach clerical practice, mechanical and trades courses. Moreover, the town fathers' plans to bring in more industry may keep young people behind as well as strengthen the economic base of the entire community.

Young people who remain in Plantation County find their niche on the farm or in their parents' businesses; otherwise, they continue to work for the plantation owner or they seek work in sawmills or stores. While military service in the recent war opened new vistas to many young people, it also satiated their need for "adventure," and they are content now to settle down. Moreover, the federal government, through the Veterans Administration program, has opened many new areas of opportunity for young people, so they find it worth their while to stay. We have already discussed the vocational agriculture and the on-the-job training programs. Veterans of the First World War report how much more opportunity the new veterans have than they had in 1920. These older veterans have fostered new enterprises in the community because they realize how little hope for employment there was when they returned from military service thirty years before.

Although a good many of the emigrants represent the "cream of the crop," enough potential leaders remain in the community to supply it with leadership. Many of these people prefer small town intimate life—they like to be called by name when they walk down the street to the post office. The young man who inherits his father's business and status has a strong incentive for staying behind and taking his place as a leader in the community. Then there are new people who come into the community from elsewhere; they are generally from other small towns, but some represent refugees from the anonymity of city life. We have already noted the great contribution of the newcomers to the dynamism of Plantation County life today.

The decision to stay behind is in part motivated by the decision to establish a home in Plantation County. Once a young man is on his own economically, he begins to think about "settling down" with a wife and eventually having a family. His immediate family and the community have motivated him, and in addition to this there are his own physiological drives. During adolescence he has gone to parties and has had dates with girls generally of his own social class and friendship group. There have been contacts with girls from neighboring communities and even distant communities through visits out of town or the coming of new girls into town. The wider the social horizons have been, the greater is the probability that marriage will be exogamous. Marriage generally stays within the confines of one's social class, however.

The approved pattern for sexual outlet is eventual pairing off in courtship, then marriage and the establishment of a home. There are no legal penalties for bachelorhood (except increased income tax payments), but the man with a family has higher status in the eyes of the entire community and its institutions. The unmarried man finds it difficult to participate in adult activities which are of a mixed or family nature. When young men who are friends become married, they eventually part company because each man's activities become related to his wife and the new home; married couples' groups develop after the less stable mixed groups of adolescents. The men's and women's groups which function are subordinated to the business of establishing a home and family. At dances in Plantation Town the husbands agree to cut in on single men who dance with their wives. There is more potent gossip about the sexual activities of unmarried men than about adolescents. Young women who remain celibate have to guard against gossip about their sexual exploits, if they have them. Virginity for unmarried women is still an ideal though gossip is the only powerful means for enforcing it. Among the lowest classes there is less emphasis on continence as a virtue. For men, sexual prowess is a sign of virility; the upper classes insist on secrecy and discretion, however. The double standard prevails, especially in the white community; women have to appear virtuous if unmarried and faithful if married. But Plantation County forgives even women's failings if they eventually marry; a "shotgun wedding" is subject for gossip, but it is no permanent disgrace.

Class and property are important in marriage considerations. Physical attractiveness is the main criterion for marriage or mating among those classes which have fewer problems about inheritance and maintaining status. Manners, education, family background, property, and such complexities enter into upper- and middle-class courtship and marriage patterns above all. It is considered preferable in those groups to marry in one's own class. When a wealthy woman marries a man with less means she is apt to dominate him, or so it is reputed in Plantation County. A young man of the upper or middle class may marry a "good girl" of the middle class, but she must learn upper-class customs to become accepted.

In higher-status groups parents usually arrange for their children to meet congenial young people of the same class at parties in the home or at college fraternities and sororities if they are in school. Church groups also tend to keep young people of the same class together. Although contract marriage is not practiced here, family and community participate in match-making through such channels as recreational activities, gossip, and expressions of approval and disapproval.

While it is considered preferable to marry within one's religious group, and Sunday school social functions aim toward this, property and general status are more significant. In cases of mixed religious marriages, it is usual to have the children take over the faith of the more religious parent. Other considerations, however, favor the church with higher status. In the emotional denominations, where theology is emphasized and there is an ingroup feeling based on rejection and protest, strong effort is made to retain members; however, religious loyalty and status goals operate here as well.

Residence may be patrilocal or matrilocal during the first few months of marriage, but it is usually considered desirable to establish a separate domicile. Even where children are in the same business with parents and siblings, they establish separate residence. In upper-class white families, older parents may live in the same large home with married children, but they arrange to have their own rooms or apartment. As long as parents remain able to care for their own economic needs, the married children live separately. It is considered desirable for these young parents to take the responsibility for rearing their own children; grandparents are said to spoil them. Married children may take in infirm parents or move into the parental home before taking over property. Among Negroes and lower-class people who live in crowded quarters, it is usual to find parents and children living intimately together, especially if the parents are infirm. These old folks care for the young grandchildren while the parents are out working; middle- and upper-class white families can afford nurses.

A consequence of the preference for separate domicile is to make economic considerations for marriage more important than they might otherwise be.

In the upper and the middle white classes it is traditional to make an announcement of an approaching wedding or have a period of engagement. There may be some announcement of intentions to marry in the lower classes also, but this is less formalized. Marriage intentions are usually preceded by a period of courtship, so the engagement is usually no surprise to the community. There are class differences in the emphasis placed on the symbolic importance of engagement and marriage. The importance of property, plus the means to put on display, make upper- and middle-class engagements and weddings ostentatious. A big church wedding, or a garden ceremony at a plantation home, is considered the height of social distinction. This contrasts strongly with the general lack of ceremony among lowest-class persons who may merely take up common residence without benefit of license or ceremony. We have already discussed the influence of education and government agencies on Negro acculturative trends toward formal marriage and the consequence for family stability.

The married couple attains full adult status in the eyes of the community when the young people return from their honeymoon and start housekeeping. The honeymoon period may vary from a trip to the Gulf or the mountains for upper-class people to a night in a hotel in the city for poorer folk. The young couple seeks privacy for the first few days and weeks of marriage, but shortly thereafter they begin to participate in the usual activities of young adults. Wedding gifts help furnish the new household. The wife may continue to work in order to help furnish the home; she leaves work when she is in advanced pregnancy. Many mothers continue working full time after they can entrust the infant to the care of a Negro nurse or another adult in the household. On the farm, of course, woman's work is closely bound with man's, and there is no hiatus in farm work. Farm women are usually well-trained in homemaking, because as girls they were under the supervision of mothers and older sisters.

Husband and wife begin to enter the social world of the young married couples. They discuss housekeeping and preparation for the coming of children. They join the young couples' class in Sunday school and begin to hold responsible positions in church. They become active in social, civic, and economic organizations, depending on their interest, status, and the amount of free time they can or are willing to offer to such activities.

Since children are considered very desirable in Plantation County society, it is not more than a year or two before the family unit is cemented by the birth of a baby. This is true of planned families as well as families that do not use child spacing. The community approves children, and childless married couples are pitied; many of them adopt children if they are unable to bear them. Unplanned families become an economic burden before long; therefore child spacing is preferred and is increasing. No religious injunctions exist in the community against contraceptive practice. (Roman Catholic groups are neither influential nor do their local members have abnormally large families.) Children do not restrict the social activities of young mothers too much—the whites have Negro nurses; older adults or children also care for infants. The intimacy of the community makes child care a relative community responsibility. Negro families, especially, never find their quarters or means too limited to take in a stray child.

Full adult status is thus achieved when marriage leads to the establishment of home and family and when adults participate in institutionalized approved patterns of activity. The family functions as the approved institution for satisfying sexual needs and for the procreation and rearing of children. In this it serves the needs of the society for more members and for socializing them.

The sex patterns of married people in Plantation County give the impression of being relatively satisfactory. While I made no systematic study of adult sex habits in Plantation County, there were certain impressions that came from observation and interview which might throw light on the subject.

Modern married women in Plantation County do not go on crusades as their mothers and grandmothers did. They do not condemn drinking, gambling, and dancing. The most modern young married women spend less time in southern historical reflection than do the older women. Victorianism is no longer a factor in the sexual life of adolescent girls. While rumors about extramarital sex activities among men persist, it is apparently less extensive than in former years. Wives are physiologically and psychologically better sexual partners—there are fewer pregnancies; also their general health is better since childbirth has been reduced both in its hazards to life and in numbers. Women of this generation are not embarrassed at discussing sex, marriage, and family life. The introduction of modern conveniences has opened up mobility and work outside the home for women. The modern wife is a more interesting partner than her ancestors; she is less bound to the cook stove; she is more nearly equal to her husband.

The above applies in the main to the white upper and middle classes; sex life for Negroes and lower-class whites has always been more or less natural. This does not mean that it has been satisfactory, however. The instability of Negro and "poor white" family life and the attendant worries brought on by insecurity feelings, poverty, and low prestige serve to indicate trouble areas in sex relations. The incidence of violence among these groups may be laid partially to insecurities in sexual matters. Negro men resent and fear white men and their attentions to Negro women; they cannot respond in kind. Miscegenation seems to be declining, though, and economic conditions are tending to stabilize Negro family life.

The increase in divorce in Plantation County may be a symptom of unsatisfactory sexual adjustment, but it seems to be as much a result of the incompatibility of personalities, the increasing freedom of women (especially white women), and the conflicts in values introduced by the mass culture. Movies, magazines, and literature that overemphasize the romantic aspects of marriage and the increasing desire for material goods contribute to increasing dissatisfaction with the old ways. White women are no longer tolerant of drunken husbands or nonproviders. Separation has always been informal among Negroes, and it is significant that family life in that area is becoming more stable. This suggests that divorce among whites may be an outlet for incompatibility that was formerly resolved by extramarital sex relations by white men engaged in miscegenation; white women worshipped piety and tradition. Divorced persons generally remarry, and there is no social stigma attached to divorce, per se. Even obvious cases of infidelity are forgiven after the affected persons separate and each goes his way, usually to new marriages.

The ideal white or Negro family is very much like the family promoted by the mass white culture and the movies—the father who earns a fair living, the mother who is interested in making a pleasant home and rearing the children, children who are obedient, yet who express a personality and will of their own to demonstrate that they will "amount to something." Children are expected to pay attention to what their elders tell them, yet they are permitted and variously encouraged to adventure on their own. The patriarchal family of Victorian days among upper- and, to an extent, middle-class whites has practically disappeared. The father may dominate in lower middle- and lower-class white families. The mother often dominates in middle and lower class Negro families. The ideal family in Plantation County follows the American ideal of the egalitarian family—it is a democratic unit, aimed at giving each parent individuality and responsibility for the socialization of the children. The children, likewise, are taken into the confidence of their parents and made to feel they are an important part of the functioning unit.

The ideal family in Plantation County is influenced by the rurality of the area. The mother is generally home and predominates in the early years of the child and in training girls later. Most fathers do not have to commute great distances to work, and they "pal around" with their sons, teaching them the work of the farm from early years. Farm parents, especially, are close to their children, and the farm family operates as a social and an economic unit.

The situation is not so ideal when the parents feel social and economic insecurities. Lower middle-class white families and many middle-class Negro families are rent by the difference in values inculcated upon the young people by the schools. Young people become dissatisfied with home life and leave the area after they are grown. In lower-class families, there is instability in sex relations; parent and child relations are disturbed by poverty and socio-psychological insecurities. The influence of schooling is perhaps not so divisive in lower-class families because children do not remain in school long. If they do, they tend to seek upward mobility and turn from the values of their lower-class parents.

The mass culture introduces divisions in the family. Men, women, and children, each begin to become absorbed in worlds of their own. Young people want the family car to go their way; women become interested in unburdening themselves of household cares; men find it more difficult to earn enough to support these increased desires for material goods. The situation in Plantation County is similar to that elsewhere in the United States, but the influence of rural living tends to slow down the trends toward family divisions. The acceleration of mass culture tends to make formal education for young people much more inclusive than it was for their parents. But adult organizations, the farm and home demonstration clubs and the civic societies bring adults up to date so that they are not too far behind their children. The parents of this generation of white children in Plantation County seem fairly receptive to new ideas (except in race-caste, where even the younger generation of whites is slow to accept "radical" ideas); the exceptions among parents are in the lowest classes, and here the two generations find themselves in greatest opposition to each other. The situation is most noticeable among Negroes, where the younger generation desires to acculturate faster as the school removes them from the values of the home.

Adults engage in the activities of formal and informal associations to a large extent. Upper- and middle-class whites participate in the church, civic clubs, Masonic Lodge and Eastern Star, patriotic clubs, farm organizations, and the women's culture clubs. The ideology of these associations seems far less important to the mass of members than the opportunity to socialize and/or to achieve status and office. Negroes also have church groups, lodges, farm associations, and mutual aid societies (burial and sickness insurance). Many associations are local chapters in national organizations. The formal programs are inspired by visitors from regional or state chapters, and the national publications of these associations try to sustain interest. Actually, the majority of the members are quite passive; the community seems overburdened with organizations, and only the leaders seem to derive maximal benefits. A certain group tends to lead each type of association, so that there is a group in the community that may be classified as leaders. Occasionally, a lower-status person has special interests or qualifications to be chairman of an association. Since leadership is much in demand (especially on committees), such a person finds himself in the limelight and might achieve higher status. In more important associations, such as political, leadership is concentrated, and there is real competition for office; where economic goals are paramount in an association there is also competition for leadership and control of the program. It seems significant that these organizations have to do with securing white supremacy and the general status of the groups already in power. Such organizations include the local Democratic party and political offices, membership on the county school board and, to a lesser extent, leadership in the Exchange Club and the Chamber of Commerce.

The lower classes do not participate in the above organizations to any significant degree. They feel "out of place" in the company of the upper and upper middle classes if the organization is intimate. Since they also desire prestige, they form their own cliques. Some white associations are noted for their members being lower middle class rather than upper or upper middle class. Men's groups tend to be less class oriented than women's groups; hunting and fishing parties, gambling, drinking, and sports activities are more likely to be carried on among a variety of classes than are the culture clubs of the women or their gossip cliques.

The aged in old Plantation County society were a secure group indeed. Old plantation owners or farmers could expect to be taken care of by their many children when they became infirm. They enjoyed status by virtue of their accomplishments. They may have had property and wealth that could be passed on to their descendants when they died. Even old slaves who had nothing were assured of care by the plantation owner. They had worked hard for him, and he was expressing his beneficence, they felt, by caring for them when they could no longer work. The old days were days of paternalism. The old plantation owner had created a small empire for his children; the old "darkey" had contributed to this creation. Each was assured the security of old age by those he had produced for.

But the situation is different today. There are more old people now because people live longer. And there are fewer children today because families have been getting smaller. The old generation either created a plantation, or they knew the lore of farming and other ways of making a living. Today young people do not necessarily want to stay on the farm. Textbooks, schoolteachers, and government workers give better information about agriculture than old farmers. The older generation failed in large measure to conserve natural resources. The younger generation of Negroes scoffs at the illiteracy of the aged and the superstition of their lore. The mass culture has influenced both races in the values of science and materialism. Money has become increasingly important; land, religion, lineage, and tradition are correspondingly less important. The power and prestige of the aged has consequently declined. While there is always a gap in values between generations, the acceleration of change today is phenomenal. Hence we find a decline in the security system of the aged and strain in their relations with the younger generation.

The aged still participate in church activities and, to a lesser extent, in other community activities such as the patriotic societies of upper-class whites (where old ladies are the leaders). The aged are especially active in gossip groups—the gatherings under the pecan tree at the courthouse square or on the curb benches (for Negroes) in front of the stores in Plantation Town. They try to make themselves useful; the men do a little repair work or help look after some of the stock. Women can still cook well, and they are adept at caring for grandchildren. Old Negro men rake leaves and cut hedges for white folks.

The younger generation is still obliged to care for the aged; children represent an economic as well as a social investment. The younger generation still shows deference to the achievements of the aged, especially those who have acquired property or who have established businesses. Old people who have reared families of distinguished children also command respect. It is considered bad manners in Plantation County society to speak rudely to the aged or to desert them. In a way this is an area where traditional race-caste codes are breached; old men and women of both races are treated with deference by the young people of either race. If the words of advice of the aged do not seem modern enough for young folks, at least they permit them to have their say. Old Negroes have special status in the homes of whites they have worked for all their lives; they are given food and clothing and are called "Aunty" or "Uncle." Whites see that they are buried in proper style when they die.

There is mixed response in Plantation County to a new agent which has entered to provide for the security of the aged—the government. Negroes whose children have left the area and who see no security in the present trends on the plantation look upon the public welfare service as successor to paternalistic plantation owners. Although the whites object to this intrusion, they also see the government welfare program as another block removed from converting the plantation from paternalism to an efficient business enterprise. Public old-age assistance is provided by the state with federal and local grants included. The average payment of fifteen dollars a month is not much for a middle-class town dweller, but for the majority of poor old Negro plantation tenants receiving old-age assistance, this is more cash than they have ever seen so regularly. Their housing is very meager and inexpensive; they are able to keep a small garden or borrow vegetables from a neighbor; fuel gathering privileges come with the rental. The old Negroes consider the "welfare lady" a messenger of Almighty Providence, Himself. The plantation owners are not quite so enthusiastic; they think it is another step toward "socialism" and an attack on white supremacy.

Old white people feel less secure about the future of white supremacy as they see the acculturation trends among Negroes and the emphasis of the mass culture on Civil Rights. Many of these old white men complain that the young whites "don't know how to work a nigger." Modern young whites have tended to be reared away from direct contact with many Negroes; they have not had the experience of ordering Negro labor about on the plantation. There are some old Bourbons in Plantation County who fight every move by federal and even local authorities to improve conditions among local Negroes. They consider the liberal southerners "sorry whites" who are selling out their race. This dying Bourbon class is witnessing the factory in the field and the acculturated Negro emerging from the plantation with skepticism and disapproval.

Old Negroes do not dare to believe what they see and hear. They are at best confused about the resentment of the younger Negro generation against race-caste. They cannot understand why the Negro should want to "be like a white man." The old Negroes feel they have always been "good Negroes"; they warn the impulsive young men that they will only get into trouble for their actions. The old world in which the plantation owner was a kindly if stern father is crumbling; when white men were unable to provide for old Negroes during the depression, government social workers or the Farm Security Administration agents saw to it that they received checks which they could cash at the crossroads or plantation commissary for food. Even though the cash does not go very far, the monthly pension gives them a feeling that "somebody way off yonder" is looking out for them. The forces of education, mechanization, and the mass culture confuse them as young people "go down the big road" to hedonism and to opportunity at the same time. The old Negroes prefer to swing on their porch gliders and listen to the whippoorwill; young people are too busy and educated to listen to them anyway.

The aged in Plantation County are on the threshold of a new technological and social era. Their reaction is to withdraw to the memories of the old days. Their security system which depended on the full power of white supremacy and the paternalistic plantation owner is being shattered. In its place, the government is taking over financial support. Young people are busying themselves with mechanical and scientific gadgets and new ideas about efficiency and equality. It is disconcerting or confusing to the aged, depending on their previous station.

A people who live as close to nature as the inhabitants of Plantation County learn to accept the cycle of birth, death, and regeneration without difficulty. The belief system in religion provides a Heaven for the righteous and a Hell for the damned. But though the church is powerful in this country, the folk believe that life on earth is rich and meaningful, and they hate to leave it. People say Heaven and Hell may or may not be what the preachers say they are; at least they know what they have in this world. For those who face death and for those who remain to mourn, however, the concept of a life hereafter is very comforting. It is a reward to look forward to after a life of obeying rules and struggling for material needs.

Old people prepare themselves for death by setting their houses in order. They pay up their life insurance and burial insurance; they go through all the legal procedure to certify wills; and they attend church as often as possible or visit with the minister to be nearer to God. But death is not resignation in Plantation County—the doctor is called in for the slightest illness; every means possible is employed to prolong life.

As the last breath is drawn, kin and friends bow their heads and prepare to mourn. Some of the women cry, but neighbors are at hand to comfort them and to see that funeral arrangements are proper. Relatives are summoned, and a stream of friends and distant kin bear down upon the house with food and condolences to ease the strain of the mourners.

The dead man does not leave the world of the living altogether. Once the deceased is embalmed and laid in state in the house, he becomes the subject for conversation by the mourners—men who sit on the porch and women who sit inside the house. His entire life is reviewed bit by bit both by contemporaries and juniors. The good points and some of the bad features emerge in a type of epic tale which in some instances actually develops into folk legend.

Embalming insures a display of the body which the traditional manner of shrouding does not. The dead man lies lifelike in his casket "listening" to what transpires; his presence seems as corporeal as it is spiritual. During the all night watch, or wake, the men spin great yarns about old times when the deceased was a boy. They speak of the changes since then, and they ponder on the future for the area. The family of the deceased have little occasion to grieve by themselves; loyal neighbors and kin of all classes are on hand to share the sorrow.

The funeral is a public and religious expression of feeling for the deceased. The Negroes previously buried their dead with dispatch and held the funeral later, sometimes months later, when all the distant kin could come to pay homage. Most white funerals and an increasing number of Negro funerals are now "preached" before interment. Friends fill the church with flowers. The pews overflow as faces turn toward the doors that admit the casket and the mourners who file behind. Whether the casket is of pine or of lead, the six pallbearers carry their load with care and feeling. The mourners sit at the front, and the choir sings hymns of comfort for the dead and the "home over there." At a Negro funeral there may be semiprofessional "c'reeners," or wailing women, who emit curdling sounds during the preacher's eulogies and descriptions of Heaven and Hell. The women weep softly or loudly, depending on the status of the church and the group. Upper- and middle-class white funerals are generally stately. Negro funerals permit the deceased's relatives and the congregation to rid themselves of pent-up emotions by giving vent to ecstacy, the like of which results in screaming and twitching and frothing. Brothers and sisters from the lodge run up and down the aisles to control the affected ones if they themselves are not participating.

The whites and Negroes who have not already buried their dead before preaching bear the coffin by ambulance or by mule cart to the cemetery where the body is interred. It is considered desirable to bury the dead in ancestral soil when possible. Thus many old timers return to Plantation County who left it many years before in their youth. The preacher presides over the grave which today is contracted for by a digging company, but traditionally it was dug by friends and servants. The preacher recites some prayers, then throws clumps of sod on the lowered coffin to represent the return of the body to the dust from which it is believed to have risen. In old plantation days, white kin began to fill the grave and a faithful old "darkey" crew

188   *Plantation County*

BASIC ADAPTIVE PATTERN

Basic Component of the Situation	Old Patterns
NATURAL ENVIRONMENT	Agricultural potentialities; extensive agricultural methods. Cotton, cash crop; corn, second. Little crop rotation, fertilization. Small farmers raise cotton and corn on poor land. Trees felled to clear the land and to sell for cash—clean-cut. Land burned over annually.
DEMOGRAPHIC CHARACTERISTICS	No control of conception. Midwives at births; unsanitary conditions, superstition. Unbalanced diets—corn bread, pork fat, greens, syrup (sorghum). Few gardens. No control of insects, no water purification. High morbidity—malaria, typhoid fever, malnutrition (lower-status persons). High infant mortality. Venereal disease (no prophylaxis). Miscegenation between white men and Negro women—many mulattoes. High emigration of young people because economic opportunities lacking. White men insecure, anxious, drinking, miscegenation, violence toward Negroes. White women piety crusades. Negro women miscegenation, infidelity. Negro men unstable in family life, intra-group violence.
SOCIAL POTENTIALITIES	White supremacy values. Upper-status whites dominate the social structure. Lower-status whites support white supremacy. Race-caste views projected through fundamentalist interpretation of Scriptures. Negroes a subordinate race-caste; segregated; lack economic, political, social, cultural opportunities; insecure. Negro middle class, "good Negroes." Lower status Negroes and whites have few inhibitions.
FOREIGN OR CULTURE CONTACT	See above for the influence of the mass culture—science an provement of transportation, belief in the importance of ed

Adulthood and Old Age

F PLANTATION AREA CULTURE

Changing Components of the Situation Necessitating or Fostering Readjustment	New Patterns
Soil erosion; loss of soil fertility. Boll weevil destroys cotton acreage. New Deal and Fair Deal scientific agricultural agencies promote education, economic incentives for improving the soil, production, conservation. Unstable cotton market.	Soil conservation practices increasing—terracing, crop rotation, cover crops, forestry conservation (selective cutting), cropping trees. Diversification on small farms—cotton, corn, hogs, legumes, gardens, "live at home" policy. Plantations introduce cattle, grass feeding; extend pastures; utilize woods.
Improvement with introduction of scientific medical practices; public health and welfare agencies. Improved communications, transportation. American national brands foods, goods, advertising. War and postwar prosperity. Scientific agriculture education through schools, New Deal and Fair Deal agencies. Increased Negro education, acculturation to middle-class white values; race pride. White women given social freedoms, also economic. Hygiene, sanitation, sex education; state government blood test for venereal disease; maternity clinics. Industry introduced. Cattle introduced to replace cotton as market unstable, boll weevil, federal government crop restrictions.	Improvement of sanitary facilities; midwives trained and registered; increasing use of physicians and hospitals at birth; public maternity clinics. Teach balanced diets in clinics, schools. Increasing variety of foods in stores; increasing financial ability to make purchases; travel broadens tastes. Scientific agriculture education promotes gardening, canning, self-sufficiency on small farms. Public health department sprays D.D.T. Child spacing. Increased health among women. Decrease in miscegenation with contraception, Negro race pride, white women's emancipation; fewer mulatto births. Reduction or control of venereal disease. White and Negro families more stable, smaller. Negro men work. Negro acculturation to middle-class white values. Attempt by upper-status whites in business and industry to retain productive white youth, also Negroes. Negro emigration from converted plantations.
Growth and spread of American democratic value-ideals. New Deal and Fair Deal legislation, welfare measures. Education and acculturation of the Negroes. Denominationalism, formalism, liberalism, secularism in the church. Plantations to cattle farms; newcomer group in business, industry. Federal government agriculture policy.	White insecurity over Negro advance and pressure from outside for Civil Rights; Dixiecrats. White liberal southerners confused. Lower-status whites form sects when churches no longer serve them; Negro denominationalism also increasing. Negro upper class, youth race pride, emigration. Plantation owners accept business and industrial developments; accelerate conversion of plantations to cattle farms. Seek smaller, more solvent Negro population.

chnology, urbanization, industrialization, secularism, materialism, mass communications, im-
tion to achieve democratic opportunities.

completed the job. Today the contracting company does both digging and filling. A canopy and carpeting of green mark the new grave in a cemetery full of ornate or simple headstones which indicate the families and clans whose descendants make up the living members of the society.

After a few days, the tangible effects of the dead are dispersed according to the will among the heirs. Land, money, houses, and large or valuable pieces of property are usually settled equally among the children. If the wife is still living, she may retain all of this until her death. Personal effects are given to kin and to friends according to the last expression of the deceased. Disputes among families sometimes result when unprobated wills turn up—controversies and feuds mar the solemnity and unity of the bereaved. Greed and occupation with the mundane eventually take the place of mourning and reverence for the dead.

The period of bereavement for most mourners ends shortly after the funeral and the burial. It lasts much longer if it is a young person or if the circumstances surrounding the death have been especially terrifying and tragic. For those who have been closest to the deceased, his spirit is ever present and the absence of the body is difficult to bear. But with the passage of time, new activities begin to make up for the loss. The community enters into the breach by visitations and by the decoration of the cemetery. There is a local memorial day once a year when the entire neighborhood decorates the cemetery and honors the dead. Old friends and relatives come from long and short distances to give public recognition to the world of the dead. But the world of the living is not neglected either—hymns, prayers, and dinner-on-the-ground unite the spirit of the dead with the world this side of the beyond. The entire society recognizes that from birth to death and regeneration the individual belongs to the society and the group.

11

PLANTATION AREA CULTURE

WE HAVE approached Plantation County from the points of view of structure, institution, status and role, culture and personality. It is time for us to draw our operational concepts together and analyze the configuration of the whole.[1]

The natural environment of Plantation County in the plantation area has favored the pursuit of an agricultural way of life. The simple Indians who lived here before the invasion of the white man in the early nineteenth century practised a hunting and gathering and primitive agricultural economy. The European settlers brought the tools and the knowledge of westernized agriculture and established cotton plantations in the Black Belt and alluvial soil areas; they penetrated the less fertile clay hill regions and farmed the land in cotton and corn. The pine woods and the hardwood reserves near the bottoms were either destroyed to clear land or they were cropped without reference to conserving and building up this natural resource.

Poor soil practices and the ravages of the climate caused the soil to erode severely and to lose its fertility. The boll weevil invaded this area from the Southwest about the second decade of the twentieth century. The farmers have recently begun to combat soil erosion with such techniques as terracing, superior crop rotation, and the introduction of cover crops; conservation measures are also being put into practice in the woods. Beef cattle raising has replaced cotton to a large extent in the Black Belt. A diversified cotton, corn, vegetable, hog, cattle, and timber program is advancing in the small-farm sections in the hills.

The plantation system and the lack of conservation in small-farm production have not been compatible with the natural environmental component of the situation. The farmers have been able to compensate for the resultant impoverishment of the soil by adhering to the

---
[1] Much of the theoretical framework for this chapter will be based on John Gillin, *The Ways of Men* (New York: D. Appleton-Century, 1948).

scientific agriculture programs of the federal and state governments. Cattle raising has proved more profitable, in the long run, than cotton. Timber production is an increasingly important aspect of agriculture. Diversified small farming seems to be the best adjustment this segment of the farmer group is making. The trend seems to be toward a more efficient management of the natural resources for the benefit both of nature and man.

There is too large a population in Plantation County considering the emphasis on agriculture and the present techniques of production. However, there has been a steady emigration rate and an attempt to adapt technology to increasing the level of living of the inhabitants.

The potentialities of the Negro element in the population have been restricted by the race-caste character of social stratification in this area. A consequence of the race-caste system has been high birth and death rates, disease from malnutrition and from the natural elements, low standards of hygiene and sanitation, and a low degree of mechanical and intellectual output. The poorer whites, to an extent, may be compared with the Negroes in describing the incompatibility of the stratificational aspects of the culture with the demographic component of the situation.

Still another consequence of the stratification system is the high degree of anxiety and insecurity that characterizes each sector of the population. Neither those believing in white supremacy nor their Negro subordinates derive any ultimate psychological satisfaction from the relations between the races and classes.

Such recent trends as the introduction of light industry may enable an increasing segment of the population to gain a living from the area. At present, civic leaders are attempting to retain the white small-farm population. There has been little effort as yet to retain Negroes, aside from selling them small farms under the Farmers Home Administration or the Veterans Administration programs. Small farming, however, is proving less than fully rewarding because the American mass culture is raising levels of aspiration among all groups in the population so that they desire additional material goods. The emigration rate among Negroes is likely to be increased as the plantations are further mechanized and as beef cattle production replaces cotton cultivation. Outside factors are accelerating this trend.

The health and welfare of the population is aided by public health and welfare services which have replaced paternalism in this area to a large degree. Information concerning child spacing is increasing and is permeating the lower strata of the population. The state is combatting venereal disease by annual compulsory blood tests and by examinations and treatment at public maternity clinics. The schools, scientific agriculture services, and the maternity clinics are spreading information about nutrition, infant and child care, and other health measures. The war and postwar economic prosperity has enabled lower income groups to put these programs into practice. Many endemic diseases, like malaria and typhoid, have been reduced through public health department D.D.T. spray programs.

Anxiety and tension in the population are evident among Negroes who fear being closed out of plantations converted to cattle raising. Likewise, the civil rights program of the federal government and American mass culture are producing tension among the whites; they are reaffirming white supremacy as a defense mechanism. Negroes are becoming increasingly dissatisfied with the race-caste situation; they have been influenced by the schools and the mass culture.

Upper- and upper middle-class whites have benefited from white supremacy. Lower middle- and lower-class whites and the Negro population have been deprived of exercising their social and psychological potentials. The upper- and upper middle-class whites have manipulated the power structure by rallying the lower- and lower middle-class whites to white supremacy as a common cause; this has more or less united all whites against the powerless Negro group.

The Negro upper class is acculturated to white values and is frustrated because it is segregated and suffers other socio-economic disabilities. The group has reacted by developing race pride, by working for the betterment of the position of the race, and also by verbal aggression against those Negroes who are less acculturated than themselves. The middle class of Negroes has adjusted by being "good Negroes" to the whites. They have also developed Negro community life as fully as possible considering the potentialities inherent in the situation. The lower class of Negroes has retained a lack of inhibition in sex, drink, violence, and other patterns unapproved by the higher-status groups.

While the plantation owner group has dominated the power structure until recently, a merchant and industrial group, sparked by white middle-class newcomers, is beginning to challenge their authority. The white upper class is threatened by the growing economic potential of the newcomer group and must, itself, enhance its economic position in order not to be displaced in the power structure.

The merchant-industrial group needs the capital resources of the plantation owners, however; so an alliance and *modus vivendi* is being worked out. The plantation system has been extended into the area of business and industry, especially paternalism and race-caste features. Economic considerations, moreover, are causing many members of the young adult white group to desire a smaller but economically substantial Negro group as consumers. Emigration and small-farmer trends among Negroes have already been discussed.

The social potentialities in the plantation area tend to be limited by the almost forced emigration of diligent members of the population, especially Negroes. While industrial-business elements are increasing among the white population, educated local Negroes continue to be siphoned off for lack of opportunity at home.

Plantation County is merely a political unit within a larger cultural region. It is therefore quite natural that certain cultural elements found in Plantation County should be shared in various degrees with the region. Plantation County also lies within the great area of Western Civilization and shares various patterns of culture with it. (No trace of the indigenous American Indian population remains except occasional evidence of Indian blood in the local Negro population or the use of Indian names for some towns and other sites.)

Throughout this discussion we have noted the most important foreign component in the situation to be the mass culture.[2] The mass culture is American national culture and also Western technological civilization. It is characterized by science and technology; urbanization; industrialization; an emphasis on secular and materialistic values; mass communications through mass advertising, newspapers, magazines, movies; increasing federal government control and interest in the institutionalized areas of the society; belief in the ideals of equality of opportunity and in democracy; and belief in the importance of education to achieve democracy and opportunity.

We have already examined the effects of science and technology toward improving the health and welfare of the people. The scientific agriculture, public health and social welfare, and educational agencies

---

[2] Cf. John W. Bennett and Melvin M. Tumin, *Social Life* (New York: Knopf, 1948) and Howard W. Odum, *Understanding Society* (New York: Macmillan, 1947).

of federal, state, and local governments have effected these changes.

Science and technology have likewise influenced the traditional economy of the area. The scientific agriculture program has made the culture more compatible with the natural environment and its resources than it was previously. On the other hand, the conversion of cotton plantations to cattle farms threatens to displace a large segment of the demographic component. Industrial expansion in the plantation area will improve the lot of white merchants and small-farmer part-time factory workers to a degree, but this is not extensive enough to retard the displacement of Negro tenants. Race-caste and class aspects of the social structure and culture enable the upper- and upper middle-class whites to derive more from science and technology than other groups in the population since they control the power structure.

Urbanization and industrialization in the South, especially, have drawn young people continuously from the rural areas in the plantation country. Some of the most ambitious and potentially valuable human material has left for the cities because there is a lack of social and economic opportunity at home. The emigration trend will be accelerated by the conversion of cotton plantations to cattle farms, but even Plantation County is experiencing a concentration of population in the towns which with new industry may retain certain elements of the population. Though the upper-class whites wish to prevent the growth of a mill village around Plantation Town by hiring female labor from small farms, additional industry would require labor from great distances, and it would facilitate concentration in the town itself. This has happened in towns neighboring Plantation Town.

While the predominant Protestant churches in Plantation County are still fundamentalist in outlook, there is a definite trend toward formalization, secularism within the churches, and other features of denominationalism. Rejected white groups have formed protest sect churches which are emotional and extremely fundamentalist. The white Presbyterian, Methodist, and Baptist churches are in the majority and are denominational; the new sects include the Church of Christ, the Church of God Holiness, Russellites (Jehovah's Witnesses), and to a lesser degree, the Church of Jesus Christ of Latter Day Saints (Mormons). Additional sects are represented in neighboring counties among the same low-status element of the population.

Negro churches are less formal in outlook and organization than white churches because the Negroes are less acculturated in the American mass culture. One sign of a trend toward denominationalism in Negro religion, however, is the introduction of Presbyterian, Lutheran, and Roman Catholic missionary churches which are associated with parochial schools established in the area by northern philanthropic and missionary societies. Negro Methodist and Baptist churches still predominate, but they are becoming more like the white denominations. While there are no protest sects as yet among Negroes in Plantation County, such sects have developed in near-by cities where the larger churches have become so formalized that they fail to serve the needs of the poorer classes.

The growth of communications has spread the mass culture to all sections of the United States. In Plantation County everyone is influenced by radio, newspapers, magazines, and movies. Local diets and food habits have been affected by national brand foods; clothing, housing, and other aspects of material culture have been influenced likewise. Great dissatisfaction exists among the poorer classes because their level of aspiration for material goods has been increased without a corresponding increase in income. Young people, especially, seek economic opportunity elsewhere when they cannot find it at home.

Discussion of democracy, civil rights, and other ideologies opposed to traditional white supremacy has caused great consternation among all elements in the plantation area. Upper- and upper middle-class whites have drawn lower-class whites to them in a last battle to uphold white supremacy. The Dixiecrat party is the last great hope of these people. Negroes have been influenced through communications, and they have been acculturated through education. They do not have the leadership or the economic strength to enter into local aspects of the controversy, but they are vigilant, nevertheless.

The federal government has been active in promoting many aspects of the mass culture. Its activities, through its agencies and agents, have had profound effects on the society and culture of the plantation area. Agricultural technology has been made compatible with the natural environment; education has helped communicate new ideas to the people; public health and social welfare have benefited all sections of the population. On the other hand, the federal government has disrupted the race-caste system in the plantation area. Its agencies have created small-farm owners from Negro tenants; they have administered public welfare, once the prerogative of the plantation owners; Civil Rights legislation threatens the entire social structure. The federal government's activities have likewise disrupted such local values as individual initiative and private enterprise—farmers have accepted financial and educational programs which have bettered their economic lot though they still criticise certain measures of the New Deal and the Fair Deal as "socialistic." The power groups resent such federal administrative measures as those which would limit cotton acreage or upset the socio-economic structure which benefits them.

We are interested in the dominant and basic controlling patterns that distinguish Plantation County and the plantation area from other regions and subregions in the United States and Western Civilization. For this, the concept of themes or major orientations is useful for analyzing these aspects of the cultural configuration.[3] Three themes appear to manifest themselves in the culture we have been investigating. These particular themes have been selected because they appear to dominate all other aspects of the culture, and at the same time they are distinctive in the plantation area. These themes are related to other subcultural features in Western Civilization, to be sure, but they are none the less derived from the peculiar conditions in the plantation area as much as from Western Civilization.

The theme, *Mastery of the Land,* is somewhat akin to the First Estate under feudalism, but it is also related to capitalism. The theme, *Conformity with the Word of God,* is derived from the Judaeo-Christian and Protestant ethics. The theme, *"Ideal" Stratification of Mankind,* is only remotely related to the Hindu caste system, slavery, feudalism or Nazi-fascism.

Mastery of the Land is the traditional basis for property and power in this culture. Exploitation of the land, itself, is the physical basis for the plantation and other agricultural patterns in the plantation area. The plantation owner has controlled caste and class in the structure. The belief system of plantation area culture supports agriculture as a desirable way of life and private property in land as a

---

[3] Cf. Gillin, *op. cit.,* p. 496; Morris E. Opler, "Some Recently Developed Concepts Relating to Culture," *Southwestern Journal of Anthropology,* 4 (1948), pp. 107-22.

MAJOR ORIENTATIONS OF THEME

Theme	Old Patterns (functions)
MASTERY OF THE LAND	Power rests in control of the land. Plantation system in agriculture. Race-caste created and supported. Plantation owner class in power. All capital put in land. Laissez faire for power groups. Lower classes seek land.
CONFORMITY WITH THE WORD OF GOD	Fundamentalist Protestantism. "Confusion of tongues" (Babel) and "curse of children of Ham" used to justify race-caste. Upper status white groups interpret Calvinism to prove God's favor is symbolized by material possessions. Industry, thrift, honesty, etc., made virtues; used to encourage whites and Negroes to work and to serve. Lower status groups grasp delayed rewards aspect and otherworldliness. Religious opposition to worldly "pleasures," e.g., drinking, gambling, dancing. Status of white women restricted and symbolizes purity of the race.
"IDEAL" STRATIFICATION OF MANKIND	Race-caste with white supremacy. White plantation owners dominate; unite lower status whites to keep white supremacy. Negroes learn to "keep their place." Negroes subordinate to whites. White women symbol of purity of the white race.

PLANTATION AREA CULTURE

Changing Components of the Situation Necessitating Reinterpretation or Compromise	New Patterns
Crises in cotton market. Economic depression. Scientific agriculture education. War and postwar prosperity. Newcomer merchants and industrialists. Federal government aid to small farmers.	Introduction of industry. Plantations convert from cotton to cattle. Plantation owners consider investing in industry to maintain economic power. Industrialists and merchants bid for upper-class status. New emphasis on capitalism—Mastery of the means of production. Plantation system in industry—Negro and poor white employees subordinate. No unions. Paternalism prevails.
Science, secularism, humanism, materialism. Churches become formalized, denominational, secularized, liberal. American democratic values emphasized in American mass culture.	Liberal interpretation of Scriptures emphasizes broad Judaeo-Christian ethics. Churches of upper-status groups become formalized denominations; lower-status groups react by forming protest sects. Negro denominationalism and formation of sects retarded because of slower rate of acculturation to middle-class American values compared with whites. Liberal churches begin to oppose unrestricted race-caste and capitalism.
American mass culture and democratic ideals spread, especially since Second World War. Negroes acculturating to American middle-class values. Merchant and industrial white group assumes power in Southeast, plantation area. Plantations converted to cattle farms.	White liberals a small group opposed to traditional race-caste patterns. Most whites enrolled in Dixiecrat political party. Upper-class Negroes race-conscious and influence Negro youth through the schools. Dissatisfied Negro youth leave (also white). Negro lower class lacks inhibitions. White newcomers seek more stable Negro consumer group and small farmers. Negroes lack leadership but watch trends. Negro emigration from converted plantations in the offing.

major goal for all groups and classes in the society. Mastery of the Land spells security for the individual and the group, according to the belief system.

Conformity with the Word of God is expressed largely through the church. Church buildings and equipment, social organization, and symbols and ritual are all supposed to aid in spreading the Word of God and the value of conforming to it. Individuals and groups who identify themselves with this goal by participation in church activities are rewarded with status and a feeling of security and righteousness. The fundamentalist Protestant character of the religion allows a variety of interpretations by different classes and religious groups so that each group may feel its spiritual needs met by Conformity with the Word of God. Whites cite the "confusion of the tongues" (at Babel) and the curse on the children of Ham as justification for white supremacy and segregation. A Calvinistic interpretation of Scripture sanctions industry, frugality, private property and free enterprise, and the acquisition of material goods as a sign of God's beneficence. This serves to justify the behavior of the upper- and middle-class whites and fills their needs. Emphasis on delayed rewards in Scripture, particularly in the Book of Job, and otherworldly emphases by the religion of lower status groups often help to soften the hardships of the present world and give hope for a life after death. Conformity with the Word of God serves as rationale for much of the belief system.

The "Ideal" Stratification of Mankind is a concept that describes the particular race-caste nature of the stratification system in the plantation area. Race-caste had its social origins in the plantation system of the nineteenth century and before (Mastery of the Land). The rationale for slavery could be found in a literal interpretation of Scriptures by the dominant classes (Conformity with the Word of God). Until quite recently, belief in Scriptures has served to pacify the Negroes. Lower-class whites have benefited psychologically from white supremacy and its privileges. The "Ideal" Stratification system has been maintained, moreover, through a belief in the purity and sanctity of white womanhood which had always to be defended.

Until quite recently, the three major orientations of the plantation area have been consistent with each other and mutually reinforcing. The plantation owners have maintained their power by rallying lower-class whites to the cause of white supremacy, thus preventing an alliance between lower-class whites and Negroes. They have fostered Protestant religion in the area, first converting Negro slaves to Christianity to pacify them, then justifying their gains through a Calvinistic interpretation of Scripture. Lower-class groups have still believed in the ideal of private ownership of property and the possibility of achieving status and power through property, but where this has been impossible, the delayed rewards aspect of the religion has given some hope for a better life in an afterworld.

Today the major orientations are no longer mutually reinforcing or consistent with each other. The American mass culture, in particular, has forced great changes throughout the plantation area. There have had to be compromises and reinterpretations.

The economic depression and the development of industry have challenged the position of the plantation owners. A newcomer merchant class has introduced small industry to help create a better consumer market. Agencies of the federal government have helped to develop a small-farmer class. The plantation owners have found it to their advantage to support the new industry in order to retain their economic, and thus their social, position. While Mastery of the Land continues to be a dominant theme in the plantation area, it has been extended to include industry and other capitalistic ideals and goals— Mastery of the Means of Production.

Science, secularism, humanism, and the growth of materialistic values have intruded on the power of fundamentalism in religion. Conformity with the Word of God has been reinterpreted by liberal and denominational churches and churchmen to emphasize broad Judaeo-Christian ethics rather than narrow and strict interpretations of Scriptural passages. This has weakened the value of otherworldliness as a balm for the dispossessed and rejected. Democratic values have contested such interpretations of Scripture as would justify white supremacy and extreme forms of capitalism. Conformity with the Word of God is becoming increasingly opposed to the "Ideal" Stratification of Mankind and Mastery of the Land (or Mastery of the Means of Production) as ends or means for the acquisition of power. The old religion fails to satisfy acculturated groups; some unacculturated lower-status groups have reacted against liberalism and denominationalism and have returned to strict fundamentalism by forming new protest sects.

The mass culture has had its greatest effect on the "Ideal" Stratification of Mankind. Acculturation has made the Negro group rebel against race-caste; the white group has become increasingly uneasy and has sought to defend its position through the Dixiecrat political party. But the mass culture has introduced doubts among educated and younger white age groups. The southern liberals seem almost as bewildered as the Bourbons. The plantation system in industry is an attempt to retain the social structure; but industry, itself, needs workers with some degree of skill and an adequate consumer market.

Inconsistencies among the major orientations in plantation area culture are matched by inconsistencies in what people think and feel, what they say, and what they do. A few examples will illustrate.

White supremacy and the principle of segregation have been flouted continuously by miscegenation. A double standard is permitted for men; white men have extended this prerogative by cohabiting with Negro women. On the other hand, Negro men have been forbidden, by the strongest taboo in the culture, from exercising similar privileges with white women. Legal marriages between the races are forbidden. The culture recognizes mulattoes as illegitimate and Negro. White supremacists defend the "purity" of the race by rallying to white womanhood as a symbol; this is a justification, in their eyes, for segregation and white supremacy.

The Temperance Movement in the Black Belt and the Bible Belt is in reality a total abstinence movement fostered by Protestant fundamentalist groups to forbid worldly "pleasures." There is some relationship among drink, card playing, gambling, dancing, theatergoing, and other "pleasures" which have been banned in tradition. Today, only drink remains the chief target of all church groups. Still, all the above "sins" are practised by all groups; the difference is in the mode of practice. The lowest-status groups drink openly; middle- and upper-class whites drink while riding in automobiles and behind locked doors, drinking to finish a bottle and to "get a buzz," or euphoria. Such city ways as mixed cocktail parties are beginning to come to Plantation County also, especially among young married couples of the upper- and upper middle-class white group.

White supremacy is inconsistent with such teachings of the church and schools that stress the brotherhood of man and the essence of American democracy. We have already noted the trends among whites and Negroes—liberalism, the Dixiecrats, and acculturation. Such lack of integration among the levels of the culture in the plantation area as we have noted has had repercussions in the rest of the United States and in our international relations.

The traditional patterns of infant care in Plantation County may be summarized as follows: (1) birth at home with midwife or physician attending; trend toward hospital births, beginning with upper-status whites; (2) breast feeding for about one year; trend toward the bottle-feeding complex among upper-status whites; (3) weaning accomplished by gradual, but sometimes sudden, withdrawal from the breast; infant sometimes weaned by separating it from mother physically or coating breast with bad-tasting substances; shaming used for children; (4) toilet training initiated by placing infant in position to evacuate or micturate to train according to a schedule; infant punished by loss of favor or shaming, physical punishment when older; (5) soiled areas of the body cleaned fairly regularly and clothing changed; less regularity among lower-status groups; (6) body surface and uro-genital areas bathed, massaged, powdered, and clothed in light-weight clothing; no intentional masturbation of infant; (7) infants pacified by holding in the cradle of the arm or against the chest, patting back or buttocks, feeding, consoling, kissing cheek or forehead; (8) encouragement of first walking steps and word forms; (9) mother is chief surrogate among all groups; Negro nurse in upper-status white families becoming part-time surrogate; grandmother or older siblings surrogates in families where mothers work out; fathers assist mothers to varying degrees; (10) rewards for conformity include approval, feeding, petting; punishment for nonconformity includes withdrawing approval, shaming, spanking (after child understands speech).

The basic personality of individuals in the plantation area is undoubtedly influenced by the general status of their families. In ideal upper- and middle-status families there is some consistency in the moderately severe care and training of infants by modern mothers. Negro nurses or other surrogates may exercise over-indulgence or, at the other extreme, laxness. In lower-status homes, where the mother works out and the father may be absent, infant care and training are liable to be erratic. Older women surrogates, siblings, or hard-working mothers do not satisfy the infants' needs consistently or adequately.

These differential ways of rearing infants suggest that the security system of the middle-status modern home environment is possibly most adequate for the development of personality in this culture. The moderate severity of training may possibly lead to a compulsive and conforming behavior which later encourages the drive for prestige and recognition. Overprotection of children, on the other hand, may not prepare them for competition in later life. In lower-status groups, alternating patterns of severe and mild training may create insecurity feelings on the one hand and a lack of inhibition on the other. The above materials are not adequate, to be sure, but they are stated as possible hypotheses for further investigation.[4]

Public personality is as much influenced by the status of the family as is basic personality. The child is ascribed the status of his parents; this ascribed status creates a potential for achieving status later on. Lower-class status limits the possibilities of individuals achieving status. Race-caste, economic, educational, sex, and age factors influence the achievement and ascription of status. Herein lies the explanation of public personality in the plantation area. Cultural lack of integration creates inconsistencies and confusion in institutionalized roles; the result is frustration, anxiety, tension, and aggression. Expectations, rewards, and punishment are conditioned by both the ascribed and the achieved statuses of individuals. We have already noted the consequences of confused goals and expectations for the educated Negro youth who emigrates, for the plantation owner who supports the Dixiecrats, for the liberal upper middle-class white woman who supports educational advances for Negroes yet who hates to see her domestic help quit, and for the lower-status white who joins a fundamentalist emotional religious sect because churches uptown cater to the well-to-do.

The plantation system and the race-caste doctrines are the chief conservative forces in the plantation area. White supremacy survives in industry and politics, seeking to maintain the old order in the face of American mass cultural efforts to foster change. Although competitive capitalism and private enterprise are the ideals of these groups in power, they hold a virtual monopoly on economic, social, and political status and power and prestige.

The effect of the mass culture in promoting cultural and social

---

[4] Cf. Abram Kardiner, and others, *The Psychological Frontiers of Society* (New York: Columbia University Press, 1945), especially chapters 1, 2, and 10-14, analysis of the basic personality characteristics in *Plainville, U.S.A.* and Western civilization.

change in the plantation area has been to create forces which are causing the new patterns to be dysfunctional and inconsistent with the old ones. The traditional patterns, moreover, are no longer compatible with the changing components of the situation looked upon as a whole. Old ways are being redefined, but compromise is slow. The young people of the plantation area will have to examine the old ways and the new ways with clear and analytic minds in order to discover that goal of a good life they want and deserve.

APPENDIX

THEORETICAL FRAME OF REFERENCE

The following questions provide a summary of what the author hoped to discover during his year's stay in Plantation County. They are basic to the organization and procedure of the study:

1. What is distinctive about the way of life in the plantation area as compared with the rest of the United States and the world?

2. What is a plantation area person? What is characteristic of the typical public personality? Can inferences be drawn about basic personality type?[1] If persons in the plantation area are thus and so, how do they get this way?

3. What are the dynamic forces in plantation area life? What are the explicit factors making for change at the present time? What trends are observable? How have historical circumstances influenced present and future trends? What are the consequences of these trends?

4. What is characteristic about the changing social structure in the plantation area? Which individuals, in what status groups, acting what institutionally patterned roles are involved? What are the consequences of the changing social structure for the individual and for the social system?

5. What is the influence of mass culture[2] and technology on the plantation area? What are the consequences for different aspects of the social system, including individuals and status groups?

These foci of interest constituted the basic questions which the investigation attempted to answer. The next step was to formulate a theoretical frame of reference which would lead to the most satisfactory answers in the light of social science research.

---

[1] See Abram Kardiner, *The Individual and His Society* (New York: Columbia University Press, 1939) and Abram Kardiner, and others, *The Psychological Frontiers of Society* (New York: Columbia University Press, 1945), for an explanation of the concept "basic personality." The concept refers to certain supposedly common ways of raising children which in turn result in typical basic emotional patterns within a cultural group.

[2] See J. W. Bennett and M. M. Tumin, *Social Life* (New York: Knopf, 1948) for a definition of the term "mass culture" and its implications. Mass culture refers to that common culture of a heterogeneous nation-society which functions to preserve and reinforce its unity in a modern nationalistic world.

Appendix

The reader may now ask, "What is there to justify spending so much energy and money on just another study in the plantation area? Haven't other social scientists covered this part of the country many times already?"

This present study does have a host of predecessors in the annals of social science writing and research. Among social scientists, the rural sociologists and the social anthropologists have been in the forefront.[3]

The present study cannot ignore the factors of natural environment, agriculture, standard of living, community and social organization, race relations, or the other aspects of plantation area life that have been treated by so many researchers. The particular approach of this study, however, is a modified culture-structure-function approach. It is believed that this approach will throw the greatest light on the questions asked in the foci of interest. The modified culture-structure-function approach provides a more or less integrated overall picture of the way of life, viewed both in its static and its dynamic aspects.

The "grand old men" of the culture-structure-function school are Vilfredo Pareto, Emile Durkheim, and Max Weber.[4] Pareto

---

[3] Studies of the South with an ecological and human geographical approach include: Rupert B. Vance, *Human Factors in Cotton Culture* (Chapel Hill: University of North Carolina Press, 1929) and *Human Geography of the South* (Chapel Hill: University of North Carolina Press, 1935). Rural sociological studies of the South employing quantitative and qualitative methods to describe standards of living, methods of agriculture, institutions, community and social organization include among others: T. J. Woofter, Jr., and others, *Landlord and Tenant on the Cotton Plantation* (Washington, D. C.: U. S. Government Printing Office, 1936); Arthur Raper, *Preface to Peasantry* (Chapel Hill: University of North Carolina Press, 1936) and *Tenants of the Almighty* (New York: Macmillan, 1943); Arthur Raper and Ira de A. Reid, *Sharecroppers All* (Chapel Hill: University of North Carolina Press, 1941); H. C. Nixon, *Forty Acres and Steel Mules* (Chapel Hill: University of North Carolina Press, 1938); and selected chapters in W. T. Couch (ed), *Culture in the South* (Chapel Hill: University of North Carolina Press, 1935). Some of the studies oriented toward race relations and problems in the South include: A. Davis and J. Dollard, *Children of Bondage* (Washington, D. C.: American Council on Education, 1940); A. Davis, B. B. and M. R. Gardner, *Deep South* (Chicago: University of Chicago Press, 1941); John Dollard, *Caste and Class in a Southern Town* (New Haven: Yale University Press, 1937); Charles S. Johnson, *Growing Up in the Black Belt* (Washington, D. C.: American Council on Education, 1941) and *Shadow of the Plantation* (Chicago: University of Chicago Press,

[4] See Talcott Parsons, *The Structure of Social Action* (Glencoe, Ill.: The Free Press, 1949). The main works of these men include: Pareto's *Mind and Society;*

analyzed non-logical action and social heterogeneity. He demonstrated the manner in which society was differentiated and the way human behavior was motivated by subjective non-logical considerations as well as logical objective views of the situation. Durkheim's sociologism emphasized the importance of society and the functions of the society in meeting the needs of its members for survival. Max Weber considered the importance of the actor's definition of the situation in studying human behavior. His institutional analyses, especially of religious and economic behavior, laid the foundations for the study of human behavior within an institutionally patterned framework of social action. His work on the "action" level led to a study of the structure of social relationships in ideal situations. This approach fostered research in the possibilities of variational behavior within structures and their classification.

Durkheim's sociologism influenced the anthropologists, Bronislaw Malinowski and A. R. Radcliffe-Brown, to study the structural and functional aspects of culture.[5] Malinowski considered functionalism as the satisfaction of a need by an activity. He regarded institutions as the bridgehead between the structure of a culture and its functioning. The function of a recurrent activity, for Radcliffe-Brown, is the part the activity plays in the social life as a whole and therefore its contribution to the maintenance of structural continuity. The structure, as he sees it, consists of a set of relationships among unit entities. The continuity of the structure is maintained by a life process made up of the activities of the constituent units. These culture-structure-function theorists, like other social scientists, have drawn heavily on biological materials for their conceptual schema.

Ralph Linton's significant contribution to culture-structure-function theory is his development of the concepts, status and role, and his recognition of the importance of the individual and personality development in cultural analysis.[6]

Durkheim's *The Division of Labor, The Elementary Forms of the Religious Life, Suicide;* Weber's *The Protestant Ethic and the Spirit of Capitalism, The Theory of Social and Economic Organization.*

[5] See especially, Bronislaw Malinowski, *A Scientific Theory of Culture* (Chapel Hill: University of North Carolina Press, 1944), A. R. Radcliffe-Brown, "On the Concept of Function in Social Science," *American Anthropologist,* N. S. 37 (1935), 394-402; "On Social Structure," *Journal of the Royal Anthropological Institute,* 70 (1940), pp. 1-12.

[6] See Ralph Linton, *The Study of Man* (New York: D. Appleton-Century, 1936)

John Gillin has described customs as habits which are socially learned, shared, and transmitted. Culture, for Gillin, is composed of patterned and functionally interrelated customs common to specifiable individual beings composing specifiable social groups and categories. Gillin describes culture in behavioral terms, as patterned activity which is goal-directed to satisfy the needs of individuals and groups to adjust to the changing conditions. Compatibility is a measure of the adaptive aspects of a culture (a custom or a cultural system) to its situation. Consistency is a measure of the integration of various elements of a culture.[7]

Among American sociologists, Talcott Parsons and his colleagues have contributed to the development of culture-structure-function theory, first by drawing together the works of the European theorists, then by refining operational concepts and testing hypotheses in the light of empirical research.[8] Among recent attempts to unite the approaches of sociologists, social anthropologists, and certain psychologists, John W. Bennett and Melvin M. Tumin's *Social Life* represents an ambitious undertaking. The authors, anthropologist and sociologist, list certain functional prerequisites for societal survival, then relate the basic institutions as ways of meeting these conditions for social life. Culture, for Bennett and Tumin, is the actual patterning of solutions to the prerequisite problems.

Among the empirical studies involving a modified culture-structure-function approach, the community researches of the Lynds, the Warner school, the southern community studies of Dollard and Powdermaker, and James West's *Plainville, U.S.A.*, occupy positions more or less similar to that attempted in this study in the planta-

---

and *The Cultural Background of Personality* (New York: D. Appleton-Century, 1945). Status or position in society is a collection of rights and duties ascribed to individuals or achieved by them. Role is the dynamic aspect of status. Linton's classification of cultural patterns as universals, specialties, and alternatives is useful.

[7] See John Gillin, *The Ways of Men* (New York: Appleton-Century-Crofts, 1948).

[8] See especially Parsons, *op. cit.* and Talcott Parsons, *Essays in Sociological Theory* (Glencoe, Ill.: The Free Press, 1949). An excellent collection of articles and excerpts from publications is to be found in Logan Wilson and William L. Kolb, *Sociological Analysis* (New York: Harcourt, Brace, 1949). The contribution of W. I. Thomas and Florian Znaniecki, *The Polish Peasant in Europe and America* (New York: Knopf, 1927), especially in developing the concept, definition of the situation, is not to be minimized. Likewise, topological psychologists like Kurt Lewin and neo-Freudians like Fromm and Kardiner have also made contributions to the development of culture-structure-function theory.

Appendix 213

tion area.[9] There are differences in time, place, and emphasis, however, among these studies from that which is presented in this book. The Lynds' study of Middletown takes place before and after the economic depression of the 1930's. The emphasis is on the institutional framework with a secondary emphasis on change. The Warner studies in Yankee City emphasize stratification in all its aspects. Their southern study, Davis and the Gardners' *Deep South,* shows a similar emphasis on class and caste. There is a further attempt to relate the stratification system and the economic institution. Dollard utilizes the life history in order to study the stratification system in the South; he is especially interested in race relations. Powdermaker studies Negro life, and to a lesser extent the southern whites, by means of institutional analysis. The influence of Ralph Linton is noted in West's emphasis on social structure, status, role, and personality in Plainville. West is also interested in social and cultural change. Kardiner's further analysis of the Plainville materials leads to a preliminary consideration of a basic personality type for Western civilization.

This study of Plantation County draws on the theories, empirical approaches, and findings of the above persons. But the particular interests of this investigator and the exigencies of the situation in the field make this study unlike previous socio-cultural studies of modern communities and the South.

The following assumptions are listed as the frame of reference by which the materials gathered in answer to the foci of interest have been interpreted in the text:

1. Culture consists of the patterned and functionally interrelated customs common to specifiable individual human beings composing specifiable social groups and categories. Three aspects of culture which can be studied include—artifactual or cultural equipment, social or structural,

---

[9] See R. S. and H. M. Lynd, *Middletown* (New York: Harcourt, Brace, 1929) and *Middletown in Transition* (New York: Harcourt, Brace, 1937); W. L. Warner and Paul S. Lunt, *The Social Life of a Modern Community* (New Haven: Yale University Press, 1941) and *The Status System of a Modern Community* (New Haven: Yale University Press, 1942); W. L. Warner and Leo Srole, *The Social Systems of American Ethnic Groups* (New Haven: Yale University Press, 1945); Davis and the Gardners, *op. cit.;* Dollard, *op. cit.;* Powdermaker, *op. cit.;* James West, *Plainville, U. S. A.* (New York: Columbia University Press, 1945); and Abram Kardiner, and others, *The Psychological Frontiers of Society* (New York: Columbia University Press, 1945).

and psychological or belief system aspects. Culture may be conceived of as patterned on three levels of behavior—actional or overt, representational or symbolic, and mental or covert. The patterned activity characterizing culture may range from the unit custom, to the trait-complex, to institutions and major orientations.

2. Situational analysis studies culture in its relation to a situation. Culture is the means whereby men adjust to the components of their situation. These components include the natural environment, the demographic component, the social potentialities in a situation, and the culture-contact or foreign component of a situation. Culture may be measured by the compatibility of practices with the components of the situation. Culture must respond to changes in the components of the situation which necessitate differential adjustments on the part of men.

3. The psychodynamics of culture shows that people behave the way they do because the patterns of cultural activity set up patterns of expected behavior which yield rewards for the performer. Cultural patterns are no longer practiced or else they are changed when the old practice does not yield rewards and/or new practices yield greater rewards. New cultural practices may in turn produce new acquired drives. This necessitates further adjustment and cultural change to attain the new goals. (Reward implies the satisfaction of primary and secondary needs.)

4. General status or public personality is a constellation of the statuses of individuals and groups in a society. The institutionalized roles associated with status may or may not be consistent with each other and complementary. Status and personality are derived from the system of rights, duties, and expectations in the institutional framework. Members of the society are socialized or enculturated to occupy and/or to desire certain valued statuses. Persons may be ascribed status or they may be motivated to achieve it. Status and personality are rated according to the value-objectives of the society and its subgroups.

5. It is possible to measure the integration of culture by analyzing the consistency among major orientations of a society and also among the value-objectives of its subgroups. There are certain aspects of culture that are common to all groups, yet certain outstanding cultural practices distinguish one cultural group from other groups. There are also subgroups within certain societies which practice subcultures to a greater or lesser degree than other societies. The whole may be classified in a scheme of universal, specialty, and alternative cultural patterns.

6. Cultural change may be studied historically as changes in practice brought about by the changing components of the situation which necessitate men's finding more compatible means of adjustment to meet the needs of the group. These needs may be primary or derived. Social change may be studied as the consequence of changing cultural practices

Appendix

for the social structure. Individuals and groups, occupying statuses and playing institutionalized roles, participate in cultural change and are affected by it.

Keeping the above assumptions of culture-structure-function theory in mind, it is important to see what methods and techniques were used to gather materials in the plantation area study. The limitations, interests, and aspects of the situation also help us to understand the reason for the present organization and presentation of the materials.

BIBLIOGRAPHY

BIBLIOGRAPHY

SECTION I

THE SOUTH

Botkin, B. A. *A Treasury of Southern Folklore*. New York: Crown, 1949.
Brogan, D. W. *The American Character*. New York: Knopf, 1944.
Cash, W. J. *The Mind of the South*. New York: Knopf, 1941.
Cason, Clarence. *Ninety Degrees in the Shade*. Chapel Hill: University of North Carolina Press, 1935.
Cohn, David L. "Lament for the South That Is No More." *New York Times Magazine* (Jan. 22, 1950), pp. 14, 41.
Couch, W. T. (ed.). *Culture in the South*. Chapel Hill: University of North Carolina Press, 1935.
Davis, Allison and John Dollard. *Children of Bondage*. Washington, D. C.: American Council on Education, 1940.
Davis, Allison, Burleigh B. Gardner and Mary R. Gardner. *Deep South*. Chicago: University of Chicago Press, 1941.
Dollard, John. *Class and Caste in a Southern Town*. New Haven: Yale University Press, 1937.
Gunther, John. *Inside U. S. A.* New York: Harper, 1947.
Hagood, Margaret J. *Mothers of the South*. Chapel Hill: University of North Carolina Press, 1939.
Heberle, Rudolf. "A Sociological Interpretation of Social Change in the South," *Social Forces*, 25 (Oct., 1946), pp. 9-15.
Johnson, Charles S. *Growing Up in the Black Belt*. Washington, D. C.: American Council on Education, 1941.
———. *Statistical Atlas of Southern Counties*. Chapel Hill: University of North Carolina Press, 1941.
———. *Shadow of the Plantation*. Chicago: University of Chicago Press, 1934.
Mangus, A. R. *Rural Regions of the United States*. Washington, D. C.: U. S. Government Printing Office, 1940.
Myrdal, Gunnar and others. *An American Dilemma*. New York: Harper, 1944. 2 vols.
National Resources Planning Board. *Regional Planning: Part XI—The Southeast*. Washington, D. C.: U. S. Government Printing Office, 1942.
New Industry Comes to the South. Report No. I. Washington, D. C.: National Planning Association, 1949.

Nixon, Herman C. *Forty Acres and Steel Mules*. Chapel Hill: University of North Carolina Press, 1938.

Odum, Howard W. *The Way of the South*. New York: Macmillan, 1947.

———. *Southern Regions of the United States*. Chapel Hill: University of North Carolina Press, 1936.

Pope, Liston. *Millhands and Preachers*. New Haven: Yale University Press, 1942.

Powdermaker, Hortense. "The Channeling of Negro Aggression by the Cultural Process," *American Journal of Sociology*, 48 (1943), pp. 750-58.

———. *After Freedom*. New York: Viking Press, 1939.

Puckett, Newbell N. *Folk Beliefs of the Southern Negro*. Chapel Hill: University of North Carolina Press, 1926.

Raper, Arthur F. *Machines in the Cotton Fields*. Atlanta: Southern Regional Council, Pamphlet No. 7, 1947.

———. *Preface to Peasantry*. Chapel Hill: University of North Carolina Press, 1936.

———. *Tenants of the Almighty*. New York: Macmillan, 1943.

——— and Ira de A. Reid. *Sharecroppers All*. Chapel Hill: University of North Carolina Press, 1941.

Sheppard, Muriel E. *Cabins in the Laurel*. Chapel Hill: University of North Carolina Press, 1935.

Simkins, Francis B. *The South Old and New*. New York: Knopf, 1947.

Study of Agricultural and Economic Problems of the Cotton Belt. Washington, D. C.: U. S. Government Printing Office, 1947.

Vance, Rupert B. *All These People*. Chapel Hill: University of North Carolina Press, 1945.

———. *Human Geography of the South*. Chapel Hill: University of North Carolina Press, 1935.

———. *Human Factors in Cotton Culture*. Chapel Hill: University of North Carolina Press, 1929.

Walker, Harry J. "Changes in the Structure of Race Relations in the South," *American Sociological Review*, 14 (June, 1949), pp. 377-83.

Woofter, T. J., Jr. and others. *Landlord and Tenant on the Cotton Plantation*. Washington, D. C.: U. S. Government Printing Office, 1936.

SECTION II

CULTURE-STRUCTURE-FUNCTION THEORY

Becker, Howard. "Four Types of Religious Organization," in Logan Wilson and W. L. Kolb, *Sociological Analysis*. New York: Harcourt, Brace, 1949, pp. 655-58.

Benedict, Ruth. "Continuities and Discontinuities in Cultural Conditioning," *Psychiatry*, 1 (1938), pp. 161-67.

Bennett, John W. and Melvin M. Tumin. *Social Life*. New York: Knopf, 1948.

Blackwell, Gordon W. Theoretical Framework for Sociological Research in Community Organization. Unpublished manuscript read before the annual meeting of the Southern Sociological Society. Knoxville, Tenn., 1949.

Bibliography

Clark, Elmer T. *The Small Sects in America,* rev. ed. Nashville, Tenn.: Abingdon-Cokesbury, 1949.

Cohen, Albert K. "On the Place of 'Themes' and Kindred Concepts in Social Theory," *American Anthropologist,* 50 (July-Sept., 1948), pp. 436-43.

Cox, Oliver C. *Race, Caste, and Class.* New York: Doubleday, 1948.

Dai, Bingham. "Some Problems of Personality Development Among Negro Children," *Sociological Foundations of the Psychiatric Disorders of Childhood.* Langhorne, Pa.: Child Research Clinic, The Woods Schools (May, 1946), pp. 67-100.

Davis, Allison. "Caste, Economy, and Violence," *American Journal of Sociology,* 51 (July, 1945), pp. 7-16.

———. "American Status Systems and the Socialization of the Child," *American Sociological Review,* 6 (1941), pp. 345-54.

——— and Robert J. Havighurst. "Social Class and Color Differences in Childrearing," *American Sociological Review,* 11 (1946), pp. 698-710.

Frazier, E. Franklin. "Race Contacts and the Social Structure," *American Sociological Review,* 14 (Feb., 1949), pp. 1-11.

Gerth, H. H. and C. Wright Mills. *From Max Weber: Essays in Sociology.* New York: Oxford University Press, 1946.

Gillin, John. "Methodological Problems in the Anthropological Study of Modern Cultures," *American Anthropologist,* 51 (1949), pp. 392-99.

———. *The Ways of Men.* New York: Appleton-Century-Crofts, 1948.

———. "Personality Formation from the Comparative Cultural Point of View," *Sociological Foundations of the Psychiatric Disorders of Childhood.* Langhorne, Pa.: Child Research Clinic, The Woods Schools (May, 1946), pp. 13-27.

Goldhamer, H. and E. H. Shils. "Types of Power and Status," *American Journal of Sociology,* 45 (1939), pp. 171-82.

Goldschmidt, Walter R. *As You Sow.* New York: Harcourt, Brace, 1947.

Gregg, Dorothy and Elgin Williams. "The Dismal Science of Functionalism," *American Anthropologist,* 50 (Oct.-Dec., 1948), pp. 594-611.

Havighurst, Robert J., Hilda Taba, and others. *Adolescent Character and Personality.* New York: Wiley, 1949.

Herskovits, Melville J. *Man and His Works.* New York: Knopf, 1948.

Hollingshead, A. B. *Elmtown's Youth.* New York: Wiley, 1949.

———. "Community Research: Development and Present Condition," *American Sociological Review,* 13 (Apr., 1948), pp. 136-46.

Kang, Chang Pei. *Agriculture and Industrialization.* Cambridge, Mass.: Harvard University Press, 1949.

Kardiner, Abram. *The Individual and His Society.* New York: Columbia University Press, 1939.

——— and others. *The Psychological Frontiers of Society.* New York: Columbia University Press, 1945.

Kluckhohn, Clyde and Dorothea Leighton. *The Navaho.* Cambridge, Mass.: Harvard University Press, 1946.

——— and Henry A. Murray. *Personality in Nature, Society, and Culture.* New York: Knopf, 1949.

Lewin, Kurt. *Resolving Social Conflicts.* New York: Harpers, 1948.

Linton, Ralph. *The Cultural Background of Personality.* New York: D. Appleton-Century, 1945.

———. *The Study of Man.* New York: D. Appleton-Century, 1936.
——— (ed.). *The Science of Man in the World Crisis.* New York: Columbia University Press, 1945.
Lynd, Robert S. and Helen M. *Middletown.* New York: Harcourt, Brace, 1929.
———. *Middletown in Transition.* New York: Harcourt, Brace, 1937.
Malinowski, Bronislaw. *A Scientific Theory of Culture.* Chapel Hill: University of North Carolina Press, 1944.
———. "The Group and the Individual in Functional Analysis," *American Journal of Sociology,* 44 (1939), pp. 938-64.
Mead, Margaret. *And Keep Your Powder Dry.* New York: Morrow, 1942.
———. "Social Change and Cultural Surrogates," *Journal of Educational Sociology,* 14 (1940), pp. 92-110.
———. *Coming of Age in Samoa.* New York: Morrow, 1928.
Merton, Robert K. "The Sociology of Knowledge," in Georges Gurvitch and W. E. Moore, *Twentieth Century Sociology.* New York: The Philosophical Library, 1945, pp. 366-405.
Miller, Neal E. and John Dollard. *Social Learning and Imitation.* New Haven: Yale University Press, 1941.
Murdock, George P. and others. *Outline of Cultural Materials,* rev. ed. New Haven: Yale University Press, 1945.
Odum, Howard W. *Understanding Society.* New York: Macmillan, 1947.
Ogburn, William F. *Social Change.* New York: Viking Press, 1922.
Opler, Morris E. "The Context of Themes," *American Anthropologist,* 51 (Apr.-June, 1949), pp. 323-25.
———. "Some Recently Developed Concepts Relating to Culture," *Southwestern Journal of Anthropology,* 4 (1948), pp. 107-22.
———. "Themes as Dynamic Forces in Culture," *American Journal of Sociology,* 51 (1945), pp. 198-206.
Parsons, Talcott. *The Structure of Social Action.* Glencoe, Ill.: The Free Press, 1949.
———. *Essays in Sociological Theory.* Glencoe, Ill.: The Free Press, 1949.
——— and A. M. Henderson. *Max Weber: The Theory of Social and Economic Organization.* New York: Oxford University Press, 1947.
Radcliffe-Brown, A. R. "Functionalism: A Protest," *American Anthropologist,* 51 (Apr.-June, 1949), pp. 320-23.
———. "On Social Structure," *Journal of the Royal Anthropological Institute,* 70 (1940), pp. 1-12.
———. "On the Concept of Function in Social Science," *American Anthropologist,* 37 (1935), pp. 394-402.
Tawney, R. H. *Religion and the Rise of Capitalism.* London: J. Murray, 1926. Reprint New York: Mentor Books, 1947.
Taylor, Carl C. "Techniques of Community Study and Analysis as Applied to Modern Civilized Societies," in Ralph Linton (ed.), *The Science of Man in the World Crisis.* New York: Columbia University Press, 1945, pp. 416-441.
Tumin, Melvin M. "Reciprocity and Stability of Caste in Guatemala," *American Sociological Review,* 14 (Feb., 1949), pp. 17-25.
Warner, W. Lloyd. "Social Anthropology and the Modern Community," *American Journal of Sociology,* 46 (1942), pp. 785-96.

──. "American Caste and Class," *American Journal of Sociology*, 42 (1937), pp. 234-37.

────── and Paul S. Lunt. *The Status System of a Modern Community*. New Haven: Yale University Press, 1942.

────── and Paul S. Lunt. *The Social Life of a Modern Community*. New Haven: Yale University Press, 1941.

──, Marchia Meeker, and Kenneth Eells. *Social Class in America*. Chicago: Science Research Associates, 1949.

────── and Leo Srole. *The Social Systems of American Ethnic Groups*. New Haven: Yale University Press, 1945.

Weber, Max. *The Protestant Ethic and the Spirit of Capitalism*. Translated by Talcott Parsons. London: G. Allen & Unwin, Ltd., 1930.

West, James (pseud.). *Plainville, U. S. A.* New York: Columbia University Press, 1945.

Wiese, Leopold von and Howard Becker. *Systematic Sociology*. New York: J. Wiley and Sons, 1932.

Wilson, Logan and William L. Kolb. *Sociological Analysis*. New York: Harcourt, Brace, 1949.

INDEX

INDEX

Absenteeism, in sawmills, 77
Absentee ownership, 34, 81, 82
Acculturation of Negroes, 102-3, 123, 141-42, 147, 185, 193; in religion, 136; and race-caste, 202
Activities, community, 182
Adolescents, assume adult role, 168-69; social activities of, 170; sexual education of, 168, 171, 172, 173
Adulthood, 174-83
After Freedom, Hortense Powdermaker, 109 n., 213 n.
Aggression, of Negro toward whites, 106
Agricultural Adjustment Administration, 57
Agricultural Extension Service, 9, 153
Agricultural program, 195, 196
Agricultural training, in schools, 167
Ancestor worship, of plantation women, 45, 51, 52, 112, 116
Anders Family, upper middle class, 118
Antagonism, toward plantation tradition, 83
Arnold Family, small farmer, 60
Arnold, Bill, and Veterans Administration vocational training program, 60
Associate Reformed Presbyterian church. *See* Presbyterian church

Baptist church, function in community, 134, 135, 136, 195; beliefs of, 138-39, 140; membership of, 139-40; Negro, 141
Behavior patterns, old, 188; new, 189
Belief system, 186. *See also* Churches
Bennett, John W., *Social Life,* 194 n., 209 n., 212
Blakely Plantation, bought for experimental station, 81-82
Book of the Month Club, 116

Boys, traditions of, 161
Branchley Family, lower middle class, 120
Breast feeding, 154
Business, and industry, xxiii; owned by Negroes, 74
Boll weevil, 9, 35, 50, 57

Cabins, of Negro tenants, 12, 14-16
Carroll Plantation, dividing of, 40 ff.
Cash tenants, Negro, 30
Catholic. *See* Roman Catholic
Cattle raising, conversion to, 9, 24, 36, 38, 41, 42, 191; causing anxiety among Negroes, 193
Chamber of Commerce, organized to sponsor industry, 84, 85, 86
Childbearing, 154
Children, desire for, 154, 179; training of white, 155; definition of, 159-60; training of, 160; playmates of, 160; tasks of, 160; sex differentiation in, 160-61; race-caste in, 162; outside the home, 162-63; and the school, 163; who leave school early, 168-69; assume adult role, 169
Children of Bondage, Allison Davis and John Dollard, 210 n.
Churches, and relation to stratification system, 133; Episcopal, 134, 135, 136, 137; Presbyterian, 134, 136, 138, 139, 195, 196; Methodist, 134, 135, 136, 138, 139, 141, 142-44, 195; Lutheran, 136, 196; Baptist, 134, 135, 136, 138-40, 141, 195; Roman Catholic, 135, 136, 146, 196; Church of Christ, 136, 144, 195; Russellites, 136, 144, 145, 195; Church of God Holiness, 145, 149, 195; Mormon, 145-46, 195; union services of, 138

Church of Christ, as sect, 136, 195; beliefs of, 144
Church of Jesus Christ of Latter Day Saints. *See* Mormon church
Church of God Holiness, beliefs of, 145; membership of, 149; as sect, 195
Clark, Elmer T., *The Small Sects in America*, 135 n.
Class and Caste in a Southern Town, John Dollard, 109 n., 210 n., 213 n.
Clay hill region, 52 ff.
"Climber," 94
Clubs, of upper-class women, 116
Commissary, on Sampson Plantation, 17-20, 31; in Lumberton, 78
Communications, improvement of, 73, 74; growth of, 196
"Concept of Function in Social Science, On the," A. R. Radcliffe-Brown, 211 n.
Conformity with the Word of God, 197, 200-1
Contraceptives, 153, 179
Conversion of slaves, 134
Cooperatives, gin and gristmill, 68
Corn crop, 24
Cornwall, small farmers in, 53 ff.; frontier element in, 55
Cotton crop, conversion from, 9, 20-21, 35, 191
Cotton gin, 23-24
Couch, W. T., *Culture in the South*, 210 n.
County agent, white, 58, 61, 70-71; Negro, 64-66
Cox, Oliver C., *Race, Caste, and Class*, 89 n.
Creek Indians, 9
Creosote plant, 25
Cultural Background of Personality, The, Ralph Linton, 212 n.
Culture in the South, W. T. Couch, 210 n.
Culture, adaptive patterns of, 188-89; of Plantation area, 191 ff.
Culture-structure-function theory, 32, 210-13
Curio Catalogue, 149-50

Davis, Allison, *Deep South*, 109 n., 117 n., 210 n., 213 n., *Children of Bondage*, 210 n.; mentioned, 213

Dean, Brady, 63-64, 126-27
Deep South, Allison Davis, Burleigh B. and Mary R. Gardner, 109 n., 117 n., 210 n., 213 n.
Demographic characteristics, 188
Denominations, as sociological construct, 135; beginning as sect, 135; union services of, 138. *See also* Churches
Depression years, small farmer in, 58; effect on Negro tenants, 67
Despotism, beneficent, 27-28
Dinner-on-the-ground, 144
Diversified crops, of small farmers, 52 ff., 191. *See also* Jackson-Dolphin Plantation, Sampson Plantation
Division of Labor, The, Emile Durkheim, 211 n.
Divorce, increase of, 180
Dollard, John, *Class and Caste in a Southern Town*, 109 n., 210 n., 213 n., *Children of Bondage*, 210 n.; mentioned, 212, 213
Dress, typical Negro, 12
Durkheim, Emile, contribution to culture-structure-function school, 210-11; *The Division of Labor*, 211 n.; *The Elementary Forms of Religious Life*, 211 n.; *Suicide*, 211 n.

Ebony, 93
Education, of small-farm children, 55; of Negroes, 99
Elementary Forms of Religious Life, Emile Durkheim, 211 n.
Emigration, of Negroes, 102; of young people, 174-75, 195
Employees, on plantation, 29
Episcopal church, introduction to frontier, 134; began as sect, 135; membership of, 137; decline of, 136, 137
Erskine, Miss Erma, 4-5
Essays in Sociological Theory, Talcott Parsons, 212 n.
Experimental station, 80-82

Factories, introduction of, 73 ff., 83-87
Family, the ideal, 180-81
Farm Bureau Federation, 58
Farm Credit Corporation, 58
Farmers Home Administration, 39, 58, 66, 70, 78, 80, 99, 154, 192

Farm Security Administration, 35, 60, 68, 185
Fear of Negro advance, 39-40
Federal agencies, help small farmer, 58
Fellers, Mr., small farmer, 56
Folk Beliefs of the Southern Negro, N. N. Puckett, 149 n.
Forty Acres and Steel Mules, H. C. Nixon, 210 n.
4-H Club, 167
Frontier aspect, of plantation owners, 42, 45, 51; of small farmers, 55
Frye, Norma, upper-class Negro, 127
Funeral customs, 186-87
Furnishings, of Negro cabin, 14, 16; of plantation house, 17; of small farmer, 53
Future Farmers of America, 167
Future Homemakers of America, 167

Gardner, Burleigh B. and Mary R., *Deep South,* 109 n., 117 n., 210 n., 213 n.; mentioned, 213
Gillin, John, *The Ways of Men,* 191 n., 197 n., 212 n.; definition of culture, 211
Girls, traditions of, 161
Good Housekeeping, 116
"Good Negro," 90
Government control of plantation, 67-70
Gristmill, 24
Growing Up in the Black Belt, Charles S. Johnson, 210 n.

Hartley Plantation, poor for cotton, 45; cattle raising on, 46; seed business on, 46; hourly rate for tenants, 47-48; improvement of tenant housing, 48; an industry, 49
Health, improvement of, 153 ff.; information on, 193
Hersey, Tom, lower middle class, 120
"High-type white," and relations with Negro, 91-92; status of, 117
House and Garden, 116
House Beautiful, 116
Housing, of Negro tenants, 12, 14-16; of plantation owner, 17; of small farmer, 53 ff. *passim;* in lumbering village, 78
Hughes Plantation, keeping up house, 41; lumbering on, 41; cattle raising on, 41
Human Factors in Cotton Culture, Rupert B. Vance, 210 n.
Human Geography of the South, Rupert B. Vance, 210 n.

"Ideal" Stratification of Mankind, 197, 200-2
Individual and His Society, The, Abram Kardiner, 209 n.
Infants, breast feeding of, 154, 156; sanitation in care of, 154-55; family milieu surrounding, 155; training of, 155; feeding of, 156; weaning of, 156; toilet training of, 157; bathing of, 157; clothing of, 157; sleeping habits of, 157-58; fondling of, 158; speech of, 158; punishment of, 158; status of, 159; naming of, 159; care of, 203-4; training of Negro, 156; clothing of Negro, 157; naming of Negro, 159
Industry, need for, 83; as aid to small farmer, 83-87; introduction of, 192; gains power, 193-94; challenge to plantation owners, 201
In-group aggression, of Negroes, 104-6
Intermarriage, 96

Jackson-Dolphin Plantation, formation of, 33-34; traditional house on, 34; lumbering on, 35; cattle raising on, 35, 38; cotton growing on, 35, 38; as family affair, 36; owner as operator, 37
Jehovah's Witnesses. *See* Russellites
Johnson, Charles S., *Growing Up in the Black Belt,* 210 n.; *Shadow of the Plantation,* 210 n.

Kardiner, Abram, *The Psychological Frontiers of Society,* 204 n., 213 n.; *The Individual and His Society,* 209 n.; mentioned, 213
Kolb, William L., *Sociological Analysis,* 212 n.

Landlord and Tenant on the Cotton Plantation, T. J. Woofter, Jr., 210 n.
Levin sport shirt factory, 83-87

"Liberals," relations with Negroes, 92
Life, 116
Linton, Ralph, contribution to culture-structure-function school, 211; *The Study of Man,* 211 n.; *The Cultural Background of Personality,* 212 n.; mentioned, 213
Literary Guild, 116
"Live-at-home" program, 57, 59
Lower-class Negroes, economics of, 125; family of, 125; residence of, 125; religion of, 125; community of, 125; education of, 125; morality of, 125; mobility of, 125; occupations of, 130; and white protection, 130; in-group aggression, 130; instability of, 131-32
Lower-class whites, as tenants, 28; economic conditions of, 111; family of, 111; residence of, 111; religion of, 111; community of, 111; education of, 111; morality of, 111; mobility of, 111; social stratification of, 113; competition with Negro labor, 121, 122; occupations of, 122; mobility of, 122; emigration of, 122; instability of, 131-32; living arrangements of, 177, wedding customs of, 178; sexual patterns of married, 179-80
Lower middle-class whites, as tenants, 28; economic conditions of, 111; family of, 111; residence of, 111; religion of, 111; community of, 111; education of, 111, 120; morality of, 111; mobility of, 111, 121; social status of, 120; occupations of, 120; occupations of women of, 121
Lumbering, growth of, 9, 25, 35, 41, 52, 57, 192; as major industry, 75 ff.
Lumberton, mill village, 77-78; commissary in, 78; housing in, 78
Lunt, Paul S., *The Social Life in a Modern Community,* 109 n., 213 n.; *The Status System of a Modern Community,* 213 n.
Lutheran school, 136, 147, 165, 196
Lynd, Robert S. and Helen M., *Middletown,* 213 n.; *Middletown in Transition,* 213 n.; mentioned, 212, 213

Magic, 148-51
Malinowski, Bronislaw, contribution to culture-structure-function school, 211; *A Scientific Theory of Culture,* 211 n.
Marriage, considerations in, 176-77; customs in, 178
Mass culture, and small farmers, 55; divides family, 181-82; influence of, 194, 196; effects of, 204-5
Mastery of the Land, 197, 200-1
Masturbation, 171-72
Maternity clinic, 152-53
"Mean nigger," 92-93
Medical program, cooperative, 69-70
Mercer Family, upper middle class, 119
Merchant group, gains power, 193-94, 201
Methodist church, frontier, 134; becomes denomination, 135; membership, 136, 139; beliefs of, 138; Negro, 141, 142-44; as majority group, 195
Middle-class Negroes, economic conditions of, 125; family of, 125, residence of, 125; religion of, 125; community of, 125; education of, 125, 128-29; morality of, 125, 128; mobility of, 125; occupations of, 128, 129; social activities of, 128; social status of, 131
Middle-class whites. *See* Upper middle-class whites, Lower middle-class whites
Middletown, Robert S. and Helen M. Lynd, 212, 213, 213 n.
Middletown in Transition, Robert S. and Helen M. Lynd, 213 n.
Millhands and Preachers, Liston Pope, 135 n.
Mill village, commissary in, 78, housing in, 78
Mind and Society, Vilfredo Pareto, 210 n.
Miscegenation, decrease of, 96, 98, 202
Mormon church, beliefs of, 145-46; as a sect, 195
Morrell Family, small farmers, 52-53; as lower-class whites, 124
Mourning, 186-87
Murdock, George, *Outline of Cultural Materials,* 5 n.

Natural features, of Plantation County, 7-9, 188, 191
Negroes, typical dress of, 12; means of transportation, 12; tenant housing of, 12, 14, 16, 48; furnishings of cabin, 14, 16; attitude of whites toward, 20, 29, 30, 39, 40, 62, 65; as overseers, 28-29; as straw boss, 29; as specialist, 29-30; as cash tenant, 30, 47-48; as share tenant, 30; as pacemakers, 39; whites fear advance of, 39-40; improvement of tenant housing, 48; displacement of as tenants, 50; as owner-operators, 61 ff.; as small farmers, 61; subsidization of, 62, as plantation owner, 63-64; as county agent, 64-66; as tenant purchasers, 68; employed in sawmills, 76-77; housing in mill village, 78; ratio to whites in 1850, 88; ratio to whites in 1900, 88; ratio to whites in 1947, 96; relations to whites, 89 ff.; "passing," 89-90; cultural differences of, 89; the intellectual, 93-94, 105; white definition of, 95-96; development of race consciousness, 94-95; development of race pride, 97; and money, 98-99; education of, 99, 126, 127; and politics, 99; and the law, 100-1; emigration of, 102; acculturation of, 102-3, 125, 136, 141-42, 147, 185, 193, 202; occupations of women, 104; family, 104; in-group aggression of, 104-6; aggression toward whites, 106; occupations of, 123, 126; morality of, 126-27; and religion, 136, 140-44; and magic, 148-51; and superstition, 148-51; and maternity clinic, 152-53; schools for, 165-66; and truancy, 169; as teacher, 166-67; living arrangements of, 177; sexual patterns of married, 179-80; community activities of, 182; funeral customs of, 187; treatment of aged, 184. *See also* Upper-class Negroes, Middle-class Negroes, Lower-class Negroes
Negro Activities Center, 153
Newcomer group, status of, 83, 84; in business, 75 ff.
New Republic, 116

New Yorker, 116
Newsweek, 116
Nixon, H. C., *Forty Acres and Steel Mules,* 210 n.
Northern business, attracted to South, 85

Oberlin Sisters' Plantation, abandonment of, 43-44
Odum, Howard W., *Understanding Society,* 194 n.
Old age, decline in security of, 183; participation in community activities, 184; treatment of, 184; and government welfare program, 184-85; preparation for death, 186; funeral customs, 186-87
Old-age assistance, 184-85
Old Neville, 62-63
"On Social Structure," A. R. Radcliffe-Brown, 211 n.
Opler, Morris E., "Some Recently Developed Concepts Relating to Culture," 197 n.
Outline of Cultural Materials, George Murdock, 5
Overseer, white, 28; Negro, 28-29

Pacemaker, 29
Parent-Teachers Association, 166
Pareto, Vilfredo, *Mind and Society,* 210 n.; contribution to culture-structure-function school, 210-11
Parochial schools, 136, 147, 165, 196
Parsons, Talcott, *The Structure of Social Action,* 210 n., 212 n.; contribution to the culture-structure-function school, 211; *Essays in Sociological Theory,* 212 n.
"Passing," 89-90
Paternalism, toward tenants, 32, 34-35, 38-39, 44; in industry, 77, 78; as part of plantation culture, 91; and Negro nurse, 155; and old age, 183
Plainville, U. S. A., James West, 204 n., 213 n.
Plantation, Sampson, 9 ff.; as a business enterprise, 10 ff.; as mechanized farm, 20; Jackson-Dolphin, 33 ff.; as organized business, 35; Carroll, 40 ff.; Hughes, 41; Oberlin, 43-44; Hartley, 45-49; as family enterprise,

48; Blakely, 81-82; Starlings, 113-15; Warner, 42-43
Plantation house, traditional style, 16, 34; preservation of, 41-42
Plantation owner, social and economic influence of, 10 ff.; paternalistic attitude of, 32, 34-35, 38-39, 44, 91, 155; Negro as, 63-64; loses power, 193
Plantation system, carried over to sawmills, 77, 78
Plantation Town, first impressions of, 4; in 1820's, 9; as trade center, 73-74
Plantation tradition, antagonism toward, 83; in industry, 87
Polish Peasant in Europe and America, The, W. I. Thomas and Florian Znaniecki, 212 n.
"Poor white," and relations with Negroes, 93
Pope, Liston, *Millhands and Preachers,* 135 n.
Powdermaker, Hortense, *After Freedom,* 109 n., 213 n.; mentioned, 212, 213
Preface to Peasantry, Arthur Raper, 210 n.
Preparation for field work, xxi
Presbyterian church, and the frontier, 134; membership, 136, 138, 139; Southern, 138; Associate Reformed, 138, 139; beliefs of, 139; as majority group, 195
Presbyterian school, 136, 147, 165, 196
Professional people, status of, 118-19
Protestant churches, in Plantation County, 133-34, 195; and sin, 202
Protestant Ethic and the Spirit of Capitalism, The, Max Weber, 134 n., 211 n.
Psychological Frontiers of Society, The, Abram Kardiner and others, 204 n., 213 n.
Puckett, N. N., *Folk Beliefs of the Southern Negro,* 149 n.

Race-caste, behavior and beliefs, 31, 50, 63, 69, 71, 77, 86, 88, 89, 90, 91, 93, 106-7, 113, 182; defines group, 89; contradictions of, 95; and white women, 97-98; breaches of, 98, 101; in the school system, 99, 166; in politics, 99, 101; Negro response to, 102-6; and churches, 133; recognition of in children, 162; basis of school segregation, 166; and the aged, 185; and social stratification, 192; and the government, 196-97; and acculturation, 202
Race, Caste, and Class, Oliver C. Cox, 89 n.
Race consciousness, development of, 94-95, 97
Race pride, 97
Radcliffe-Brown, A. R., "On the Concept of Function in Social Science," 211 n.; "On Social Structure," 211 n.; contribution to culture-structure-function school, 211
"Radicals," 92
Ramsey Brothers, 83, 84
Raper, Arthur, *Preface to Peasantry,* 210 n.; *Tenants of the Almighty,* 210 n.; *Sharecroppers All,* 210 n.
Readers' Digest, 116
Reading habits, of upper-class whites, 116
Reconstruction Finance Corporation, 76, 80
"Reformers," and relations with Negroes, 92
Reid, Ira de A., *Sharecroppers All,* 210 n.
Religion, attitude toward, 139 ff. *See also* Churches, Denominations, Sects
Religion and the Rise of Capitalism, R. H. Tawney, 134 n.
Revival time, 141, 144
Role of investigator, xx-xxii, 4-7
Roman Catholic church, as sect, 135; membership of, 146
Roman Catholic school, 136, 147, 196
Rosenwald school, 165
Russellites, as sect, 136, 195; beliefs of, 144; membership of, 145

Sampson Plantation, tenant houses on, 12, 14, 16; commissary of, 17-20, 31; owner as operator, 18 ff.; warehouses of, 21-22; gins of, 21-23; cattle raising on, 24; gristmill on, 24; sheep raising on, 24; creosote plant, 25; lumbering on, 25
Sawmills, combined with plantation work, 37; selective cutting of, 75;

employees of, 76-77; Negro workers in, 129
Schools, in development of child, 163 ff.; inculcates folkways and mores, 163-64; consolidation of, 164; curriculum of, 164-65; for Negroes, 165-66; and scientific agriculture, 167, 169; develops leadership, 167-68
Science, effects of, 194-95
Scientific agricultural experiments, 80-82
Scientific Theory of Culture, A, Bronislaw Malinowski, 211 n.
Sects, as sociological construct, 135; Church of Christ, 136, 144, 195; Russellites, 136, 144, 145, 195; Church of God Holiness, 136, 145, 149, 195; become denominations, 139; growth of, 144 ff.; membership of, 145
Seed business, 46
Selection of site, xix
"Settlement time," 23, 24
Sex, differentiation, 160; experimentation in, 168; education of adolescents, 171-73; proof of virility, 172; liberal attitude toward, 172; patterns of unmarried, 176; taboos, 176; patterns of married, 179-80
Sharecroppers All, Arthur Raper and Ira de A. Reid, 210 n.
Share tenants, 30, 31
Shadow of the Plantation, Charles S. Johnson, 210 n.
Sheep raising, 24
Sheriff, duties of, 101-2
Sims, Art, and Veterans Administration vocational training program, 59
Slater, Jim, Negro small farmer, 66-67
Slave population in 1850, 88
Small business, growth of, 73
Small farmer, transition of, xxiii; diversified crops of, 9, 52 ff.; social and economic influence of, 52; housing of, 53 ff. *passim;* furnishings of, 53; education of, 55; mass culture of, 55; Negro as, 61 ff.; sells to lumbering industry, 77
Small Sects in America, The, Elmer T. Clark, 135 n.
Social Life, John W. Bennett and Melvin M. Tumin, 194 n., 209 n., 212

Social Life in a Modern Community, W. Lloyd Warner and Paul S. Lunt, 109 n. 213 n.
Social potentialities, 188, 194
Social status, of women, 45; of small farmer, 52; of upper middle-class whites, 110, 118-19; lower-class whites, 111; upper class whites, 112; lower middle-class whites, 120; lower-class Negroes, 123; upper-class Negroes, 130-31; middle-class Negroes, 131
Social Systems of American Ethnic Groups, W. L. Warner and Leo Srole, 213 n.
Sociological Analysis, Logan Wilson and William L. Kolb, 212 n.
Soil Conservation Service, 58, 61
Soil, types of, 9; erosion combatted, 191
"Some Recently Developed Concepts Relating to Culture," Morris E. Opler, 197 n.
Southern Presbyterian church. *See* Presbyterian church
Specialists, Negro as, 29-30
Sponsors, xix
Sport shirt factory, 83-87
Srole, Leo, *The Social Systems of American Ethnic Groups,* 213 n.
Starlings, Joe, upper-class family, 113-15
State Agricultural Extension Service, 58
Status, of whites in society, 109; correlation between denominationalism and, 135 ff.
Status System of a Modern Community, W. L. Warner and Paul S. Lunt, 213 n.
Stratification system, and race-caste, xxiii; in white society, 109 ff.; in Negro society, 125 ff.; and relation to church, 133 ff.
Straw boss, Negro as, 29
Structure of Social Action, The, Talcott Parsons, 210 n.
Study of Man, The, Ralph Linton, 211 n.
Subgroups within race-caste, 108 ff.
Suicide, Emile Surkheim, 211 n.
Supernatural beliefs, xxiii

234   Index

Superstition, 148-51, 157
Systematic Sociology, Leopold von Wiese, 135 n.

Tawney, R. H., *Religion and the Rise of Capitalism,* 134 n.
Tenant-purchasers, program for, 68-72; education of, 71
Tenants of the Almighty, Arthur Raper, 210 n.
Technology, effects of, 194-95, 196
Theoretical frame of reference, 209 ff.
Thomas, W. I., *The Polish Peasant in Europe and America,* 212 n.
Theory of Social and Economic Organization, The, Max Weber, 211 n.
Timber production. *See* Lumbering
Time, 116
Trade and vocational schools, 82-83
Trade center, Plantation Town as, 73-74
Training of infants and children, 155 ff.
Transportation, Negro means of, 12; plantation owner means of, 18
Tumin, Melvin M., *Social Life,* 194 n., 209 n., 211

Understanding Society, Howard W. Odum, 194 n.
Unions, fear of by sawmill owners, 77; organizers handled in neighboring community, 85-86
Unmarried men, 176
Unmarried women, 176
Upper-class Negroes, economic conditions of, 124; family of, 124; residence of, 124; religion of, 124; community of, 124; education of, 124, 126, 127; morality of, 124, 126-27; mobility of, 124; acculturation of, 123; occupations of, 123, 126; status of, 130-31
Upper-class whites, economic conditions of, 110; family of, 110; residence of, 110; religion of, 110; community of, 110; education of, 110; morality of, 110; mobility of, 110, 117-18, 118-20; status of, 112; typical family of, 113-18; clubs of, 116; reading habits of, 116; marriage in, 116-17; social life of, 117; occupations of its women, 117; values of, 130; infants of, 154; playmates of children of, 160; sex education of, 171, 172-73; emigration of, 174-75; living arrangements of, 177; wedding customs of, 178; sexual patterns of married, 179-80; community activity of, 182; and white supremacy, 193
Upper middle-class whites, economic conditions of, 110; family of, 110; residence of, 110; religion of, 110; community of, 110; education of, 110; morality of, 110; mobility of, 110; values of culture, 112; occupations of, 118, 119; community activity of, 118, 119, 182; professional people in, 118-19; infants of, 154; playmates of children of, 160; sex education of, 171, 172-73; emigration of, 174-75; wedding customs of, 178; sexual patterns of married, 179-80; and white supremacy, 193

Vance, Rupert B., *Human Factors in Cotton Culture,* 210 n.; *Human Geography in the South,* 210 n.
Veneer mill, 75-76
Veterans Administration, vocational training program of, 58-61, 66, 76, 175, 192
Vocational training, program of Veterans Administration, 58-61, 66, 76, 175, 192; and trade schools, 82-83

Wage hands, 30
Waller, Labe, and Veterans Administration vocational training program, 59-60
War of 1812, 7, 9, 88, 109
Warner Plantation, cattle raising on, 42; modernization of, 42
Warner, W. Lloyd, *The Social Life of a Modern Community,* 109 n., 213 n.; *The Status System of a Modern Community,* 213 n.; *The Social Systems of American Ethnic Groups,* 213 n.; mentioned, 213
Waters, Frank, Negro county agent, 64-66, 90
Ways of Men, The, John Gillin, 191 n., 197 n., 212 n.
Weaning of infants, 156
Weber, Max, *The Protestant Ethic*

and the Spirit of Capitalism, 134 n., 211 n.; contribution to culture-structure-function school, 210-11; *The Theory of Social and Economic Organization,* 211 n.
Wedding customs, 178
West, James, *Plainville, U. S. A.,* 204 n., 212, 213 n.; mentioned, 212, 213
"White man's nigger," 29, 65, 90-91
Whites. *See* Upper-class whites, Upper middle-class whites, Lower middle-class whites, Lower-class whites
White supremacy, definition of, 96; opposition to, 196; flouting of, 202; survival in industry, 204; economic motives of, 98-99
Wiese, Leopold von, *Systematic Sociology,* 135 n.

Wilson, Logan, *Sociological Analysis,* 212 n.
Window-frame plant, 76
Women, position of in community, 18, 42, 46; outside employment of, 42, 45, 51, 83, 84, 85, 117, 178; and ancestor worship, 42, 45, 51, 52, 112, 116; social status of upper-class, 45; social status of small-farm, 59; social status of Negro, 64; outside employment of Negro, 104
Woofter, T. J., Jr., *Landlord and Tenant on the Cotton Plantation,* 210 n.

Znaniecki, Florian, *The Polish Peasant in Europe and America,* 212 n.